100 THINGS
RAVENS FANS
SHOULD KNOW & DO
BEFORE THEY DIE

Jason Butt

TRIUMPH
BOOKS

Library of Congress Cataloging-in-Publication Data
Butt, Jason, 1985–
    100 things Ravens fans should know & do before they die / Jason Butt.
        pages cm
    Summary: "With 100 essential Ravens facts, trivia tidbits, and even activities, this book is perfect for any fan looking to relive the moments of the team's past while looking forward to the future of the franchise. Recalling the organization's important moments, milestones, and achievements, it describes the historic 1996 and 2008 drafts, the 2012 championship season, and the conclusion of Ray Lewis' career. It identifies the highs and lows that naturally come with being a Ravens fan, from two Super Bowl titles to the 2007 regular season that ultimately led to former coach Brian Billick's dismissal. Detailing the Ravens' short but memorable history, this treasury of information invites longtime Ravens fans to reminisce about their beloved team and allows new fans to catch up on what they have missed" —Provided by publisher.
    ISBN 978-1-60078-903-8 (pbk.)
1. Baltimore Ravens (Football team)—History. 2. Baltimore Ravens (Football team)—Miscellanea. I. Title. II. Title: One hundred things Ravens fans should know and do before they die.
    GV956.B3B88 2013
    796.332'640975271—dc23
                                                                    2013027115

This book is available in quantity at special discounts for your group or organization. For further information, contact:

Triumph Books LLC
814 North Franklin Street
Chicago, IL 60610
(312) 337-0747
www.triumphbooks.com

Printed in the United States of America

ISBN: 978-1-60078-903-8
Design by Patricia Frey
Editorial production by Alex Lubertozzi
Photos courtesy of AP Images

*To the late, great Conrad Fink,
whose lessons resonated with me far
more than he ever realized*

Contents

Foreword

Having covered the Ravens since the 2001 season, first for the *Carroll County Times* and now for the *Baltimore Sun*, I've witnessed a lot of great moments in franchise history.

Obviously, the top moment was them capping an up-and-down season with a dramatic Super Bowl XLVII victory over the San Francisco 49ers in New Orleans.

I covered the majority of middle linebacker Ray Lewis' career prior to his retirement, watching one of the most dynamic leaders and defensive players in NFL history. And I observed the maturation of quarterback Joe Flacco, the Super Bowl Most Valuable Player who delivered three touchdown passes against the 49ers.

Under the leadership of coach John Harbaugh, the Ravens have made the playoffs every season after some inconsistent times during the Brian Billick era following the AFC North club's first Super Bowl win.

Now, the challenge is on the Ravens to try to repeat, which will be a difficult task considering the roster has taken some hits with Lewis retiring, Ed Reed signing with the Houston Texans, and wide receiver Anquan Boldin traded to the San Francisco 49ers.

Given their tradition, though, the Ravens figure to be a contender again after signing Flacco to a landmark $120.6 million contract and returning Pro Bowl running back Ray Rice.

The Ravens are rarely dull, and rarely unsuccessful.

—Aaron Wilson
Baltimore Sun

1 Super Bowl XXXV

It was a unique situation for the Baltimore Ravens to be in, having had this team in Charm City for only five seasons. Yet there they were, poised for a Super Bowl title with a dominating defense, one led by an emerging star at middle linebacker named Ray Lewis. The Ravens were rolling through the 2000 postseason, demolishing each team in their path, even though they possessed one of the most pedestrian offenses in the modern era.

But that's the beauty of defense in football. There's a saying in the sport—offense wins games, defense wins championships. Lewis set the tone. Rod Woodson was the veteran presence at free safety. Chris McAlister and Duane Starks were lockdown cornerbacks, making it difficult on receivers.

Tony Siragusa and Sam Adams were behemoths up front, eating space and creating lanes for negative plays to be made. It was one of those defenses that will go down in history as one of the best to ever line up.

Outside of Week 2's game against Jacksonville, which saw Baltimore surrender 36 points (a 39–36 Ravens win), only two teams put up 20 or more points against the Ravens (Tennessee and the New York Jets) all season.

The city of Baltimore hadn't fielded an NFL championship football team since 1971, when kicker Jim O'Brien knocked in a 32-yard field goal to give the Baltimore Colts a Super Bowl V championship over Dallas.

With the Colts moving to Indianapolis in 1984, Baltimore football fans were hungry for the sport to return. There was a brief stint

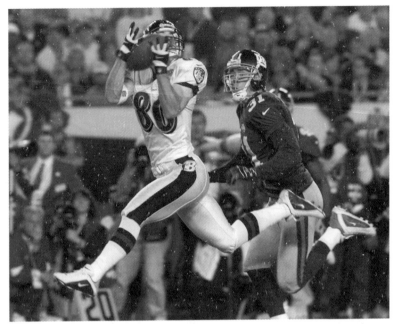

Ravens wide receiver Brandon Stokley hauls in a 38-yard touchdown pass from Trent Dilfer against the Giants in the first quarter of Super Bowl XXXV, the first score in a 34–7 Baltimore win over New York.

with the USFL's Baltimore Stars and a short-lived run with the CFL's Baltimore Stallions. The Stallions, which were embraced by the city, did win the 1995 Grey Cup championship. Even so, it wasn't the same kind of glory an NFL title brings.

With the Ravens one game away from bringing Baltimore another championship, the city was buzzing, excited, and optimistic for what was in store.

In the postseason, the Ravens only surrendered one touchdown—to rival Tennessee in a 24–10 victory in the divisional round. Baltimore first dispatched Denver 21–3 in the wild-card round and later took care of business against Oakland in a 16–3 win in the AFC Championship Game.

And then it was on to the Super Bowl, to face the New York Giants, champions of the NFC. The Giants weren't exactly offensive slouches, either. Running back Tiki Barber, in his fourth NFL season at the time, had just run for 1,006 yards and eight touchdowns during the regular season. Quarterback Kerry Collins had one of his better NFL seasons, throwing for 3,610 yards and 22 touchdowns, posting an 83.1 quarterback ranking for the year. Ike Hilliard and Amani Toomer were reliable receivers for Collins in what was a fairly balanced attack for the Giants.

But they hadn't seen a defense quite like this. Prior to Super Bowl XXXV, only the Washington Redskins had been able to contain the Giants to single digits in scoring. Otherwise, the Giants' balance had been fairly effective, not to mention they were riding a seven-game winning streak heading into the championship game.

That would all change early in Super Bowl XXXV.

Even with a Sam Adams offside penalty before the first play of the game, the Ravens forced a three-and-out from the Giants without giving up a yard from scrimmage. The Giants punted, though it would take a couple of possessions for the Ravens offense to get started.

The Ravens went three-and-out the first two times it held the ball, but the offense would begin its third possession in good field position, thanks to a 43-yard punt return from Jermaine Lewis that set the ball at the New York 41. After a three-yard run from rookie running back Jamal Lewis, quarterback Trent Dilfer found receiver Brandon Stokley for a 38-yard touchdown and the game's first score. The Ravens would add to the lead with a field goal from Matt Stover with just under two minutes remaining in the first half, giving Baltimore a 10–0 advantage after two quarters.

The Giants were only able to pick up four first downs in the first half and looked shell-shocked offensively. More was to come in the second half.

Late in the third quarter, Collins dropped back to pass and tried to force the ball into Toomer. But Starks stepped in front of the pass, picked it off, and raced 49 yards in the opposite direction for a touchdown. However, on the ensuing kickoff, Giants receiver Ron Dixon went 97 yards for New York's score, cutting the lead to 17–7. Was there a game all of a sudden?

Not quite. Because when the Giants kicked off to Baltimore, Jermaine Lewis fielded the ball at Baltimore's 16-yard line before running 84 yards to the end zone. Just like that, Baltimore had a 24–7 lead over the Giants, with the game wrapped up.

From that point, the Giants would only manage one first down the remainder of the game. Jamal Lewis added a rushing touchdown, and Stover kicked a 34-yard field goal, giving the Ravens a 34–7 victory in the Super Bowl. The Lombardi Trophy would come home to Baltimore.

The Ravens picked off Collins four times, with Jamie Sharper, Chris McAlister, and Kim Herring joining Starks with an interception each. The Giants were only able to manage 152 total yards, which ranks as the third lowest in Super Bowl history. Ray Lewis was named Super Bowl MVP for his performance, which included five tackles and four pass deflections.

"It was amazing the way we came out," Lewis said. "I mean, it was incredible to see the way we came out and played as a team. This defense has been doing this all year and never, never got the credit. This win is something they can't take away from us. We are the best ever, the best ever right now."

2 Cleveland Browns Move to Baltimore

Baltimore fans were devastated when the Colts packed their bags in the middle of the night on March 29, 1984. Fast forward 12 years later, and Baltimore was about to receive a team the way Indianapolis did. Plenty of fans were naturally ecstatic to get a football team back.

Business is business in their minds. But there was still a faction that felt odd about welcoming a team that left its city in circumstances similar to those that led the Colts out of Baltimore.

Both situations played out in like fashion. A little bit of ego, a little bit of politics, and a lot of fans wondering why enough measures weren't done to ensure each team stayed in its respective city. The Colts wanted a new stadium in Baltimore, but the city and state governments could never get on the same page. The majority of the citizens, at the time, didn't want a tax increase for a new stadium, which Robert Irsay wanted since Memorial Stadium was becoming increasingly outdated. For a decade Irsay waited on Baltimore to bring him a new stadium, but it never happened. And on March 27, 1984, the city tried to institute eminent domain on Irsay's Colts to force him to stay. Irsay got on the phone with the Indianapolis city government and accepted a loan of $12.5 million, a training facility, and use of the new Hoosier Dome (later renamed the RCA Dome). He called up his buddy, John B. Smith, the owner of Mayflower Transit, and moved the team on March 29. Die-hard Colts fans will never understand how someone could have moved a storied team overnight. But business is business, much as what transpired in Cleveland.

Art Modell had long been the operator of Cleveland Stadium, which housed both the Browns and Major League Baseball's Cleveland Indians. However, the Indians didn't receive any stadium revenue from Modell's business, Stadium Corporation, which was running the day-to-day operation. Eventually, the Indians wanted a share of the money and lobbied the city government for their own stadium. This spawned the Gateway Project, which was designed to build new facilities for the Indians and the National Basketball Association's Cleveland Cavaliers. Though asked to be a part of it, Modell declined, opting to stick with his current situation. Modell didn't realize it at the time, but this turned out to be a mistake. Revenues began to decline now that he didn't have the Indians playing at Cleveland Stadium anymore. Factor in NFL salaries rising each year in the 1990s, and almost overnight, Modell was in financial turmoil.

In 1995 Modell announced the Browns had lost $21 million over the past two years and requested a bill that would bring in $175 million in tax revenue to help cover the recent losses. Learning from its old mistakes, the Maryland General Assembly passed a bill in 1986 that created the Maryland Stadium Authority, with the purpose of bringing the NFL back to Baltimore. With Modell needing a revenue generator, Baltimore came calling, letting Modell know he'd have funding secured for a stadium if he chose to move the Browns to Baltimore. It was a tough decision for Modell. For 35 years he was the Cleveland Browns' owner. Perhaps he was prideful, because selling the franchise to keep it in Cleveland wasn't an option. He wanted to keep the franchise in his name to possibly hand it over to his son, David. It was also the family business, Modell's livelihood.

The Cleveland voters would pass the proposed $175 million tax bill, but it wouldn't matter. On November 6, 1995, Modell told the world, from Baltimore's Camden Yards, that the Browns would relocate. Modell would wind up paying the city $11.5 million, to break his lease with Cleveland Stadium, and hand over the Browns' history to the city while taking the current players, coaches, and staffers to Baltimore.

After various focus groups, citywide polling, and a fan vote, the new team in Baltimore became known as the Ravens, named after the famous Edgar Allan Poe poem "The Raven." The city of Cleveland would never forgive Modell for the move, much like the city of Baltimore never forgave Irsay.

The Ravens played in Memorial Stadium in 1996, while Ravens Stadium at Camden Yards was being built. The Ravens played their first game in the new stadium in 1998.

Unfortunately for Modell, the financial problems didn't end. In 2000, Modell sold Steve Bisciotti a 49 percent minority stake in the franchise, with the option to pick up the remaining 51 percent in

2004. Both sales went through, and Modell was never able to hand down the franchise to his son.

Longtime Baltimore fans from the 1980s understand what Cleveland fans went through. It was an odd situation for Baltimore to be in. But one it welcomed once football was finally played. Business is business, after all. Football was back in Baltimore, and the city had the NFL to look forward to again after a 12-year absence.

3 1996 and the NFL Draft

The best NFL teams draft well. Considering the Ravens were in their infancy in 1996 (sort of), they needed a class that could become the foundation for the future. A lot of the draft is scouting skill. Each team must employ those devoutly dedicated to discovering talent across the country. But the majority of the draft is luck. Evaluating the best college athletes is easy when each player has to attend college for a minimum of three years. But predicting which players will pan out for a franchise in the NFL is easier said than done, and requires a lot of intangible measurables that don't show up on a draft board.

Take for instance the Baltimore Ravens' 1996 draft class. Was there any chance Baltimore peered into a crystal ball to discover it would be taking two future Hall of Famers with its first two picks? Not a chance. Front offices put the work in and do their due diligence. Sometimes it works, sometimes it doesn't. In 1996 it worked. Baltimore put in the necessary work and received the reward.

Baltimore, which had just moved from Cleveland, was coming off a 5–11 season and needed help in the worst way. There was some speculation that Baltimore would take Nebraska running back

First-round Picks

The Ravens rarely miss when it comes to the draft, especially in the first round. The organization has made it a focal point to build its roster through the draft, realizing the long-term value is better than in free agency. Here's a look at Baltimore's first-round picks and how they've fared within the organization:

1996 Jonathan Ogden (fourth overall) and Ray Lewis (26th overall)—Ogden is already in the Pro Football Hall of Fame, and Lewis will be in when he's eligible. This was the best draft tandem in team history.

1997 Peter Boulware (fourth overall)—Boulware sacked quarterbacks 70 times during his career and earned a spot in the franchise's Ring of Honor.

1998 Duane Starks (10th overall).

1999 Chris McAlister (10th overall)—McAlister was Baltimore's first shutdown cornerback in the back end. He received a Pro Bowl invite three times and played 10 seasons in Baltimore.

2000 Jamal Lewis (fifth overall) and Travis Taylor (10th overall)—Lewis became the fifth running back in NFL history to enter the 2,000-yard club in 2003, finishing 16 games with 2,066 rushing yards. Taylor played five seasons with the Ravens but never posted a 1,000-yard receiving season.

2001 Todd Heap (31st overall)—Heap was a reliable option for the slew of quarterbacks Baltimore trotted out there during his 10 years with the Ravens. Heap caught 41 touchdowns in a Ravens uniform.

2002 Ed Reed (24th overall)—Reed is arguably the greatest safety to play the game. He won the AP Defensive Player of the Year award in 2004.

2003 Terrell Suggs (10th overall) and Kyle Boller (19th overall)—As of 2013 Suggs is still considered to be in the prime of his career and is the franchise's all-time leader in sacks ($84^1/_2$). Boller was Baltimore's biggest first-round bust, only throwing for over 2,000 yards once as a Raven.

2004 No pick.

2005 Mark Clayton (22nd overall)—Clayton had moderate success in Baltimore with his best season coming in 2006 (939 yards, five touchdowns). The Ravens traded Clayton to St. Louis in 2010.

2006 Haloti Ngata (12th overall)—Ngata's become one of the premier defensive linemen in football, with the ability to play defensive end or inside at nose guard. From 2010 to 2012, Ngata recorded $15^1/_2$ sacks.

2007 Ben Grubbs (29th overall)—Grubbs was arguably Baltimore's best offensive lineman by the time his rookie contract was up in 2012. He chose to sign with New Orleans via free agency.

2008 Joe Flacco (18th overall)—Flacco's led the Ravens to five trips to the playoffs, three AFC Championship Games, and one Super Bowl championship (while being named Super Bowl MVP). Despite the inconsistencies early in his career, Flacco has become one of the NFL's better quarterbacks.

2009 Michael Oher (23rd overall)—Oher was drafted to play left tackle down the road but has fared better at right tackle. Oher has started every game since his rookie season.

2010 No pick.

2011 Jimmy Smith (27th overall)—The jury's still out on Smith, though he did keep the 49ers' Michael Crabtree from catching a game-winning touchdown in Super Bowl XLVII.

2012 No pick.

Lawrence Phillips, based on the combination of speed and power he possessed. Phillips was regarded as one of the top prospects in the draft, and Baltimore certainly needed a running back. But at what cost?

After a superb sophomore season at Nebraska that saw Phillips run for 1,722 yards and 16 touchdowns, he became a Heisman frontrunner for the 1995 football season and was spectacular early in the season. But Phillips was arrested midseason for assaulting his then girlfriend, Kate McEwen, who was on the women's basketball team at Nebraska. Though Phillips was suspended for a large portion of the season, he returned to the field near the end and was able to start against Florida in the Fiesta Bowl. As a football player, Phillips was one of the best to ever tote the pigskin in college. As a citizen, Phillips had some serious issues, and that's putting it lightly.

Though Phillips was on the radar, the Ravens passed on him and selected UCLA left tackle Jonathan Ogden with the fourth overall pick. It wasn't a sexy selection, but one that did fit a need at the time. Phillips would go to the St. Louis Rams two picks later. Baltimore likely had no idea how much it gained that day by taking Ogden instead of Phillips.

Ogden would go on to start in 176 of the 177 games that he played in. He was named to 11 Pro Bowl rosters and was placed on the All-Pro team four times. He was regarded as one of the league's top left tackles from early in his career until the end.

Conversely, Phillips became one of the biggest busts in draft history. Phillips didn't make it two seasons in St. Louis and bounced around the NFL, the CFL, the Arena Football League, and NFL Europe. He had flashes of brilliance but could never control himself when he wasn't playing football. Phillips was sentenced to 31 years in prison for assaulting another girlfriend and then driving his car into three teenagers following the incident.

But that wasn't the end of the first round for Baltimore in that 1996 draft. After Ogden, the Ravens had to monitor the draft board for its next selection at No. 26. This pick came courtesy the San Francisco 49ers in a trade during the 1995 draft. The Ravens were looking to draft a linebacker, with one falling seemingly into their lap.

His name: Ray Lewis.

Lewis was a star at the University of Miami, earning All-America honors in both his sophomore and junior seasons. He decided to forego his final year of eligibility for a shot at the NFL. Ultimately, he was the fourth linebacker selected during that draft.

Again, there was a lot of luck involved in getting Lewis. The No. 1 linebacker on Baltimore's board was Reggie Brown out of Texas A&M. But the Detroit Lions jumped on Brown with the 17th pick of that draft, meaning the Ravens checked down to their next option, which was Lewis. On top of that, if Baltimore hadn't selected Lewis, he might've become a member of the Green Bay Packers, which were looking to take Lewis at pick No. 27.

Brown's NFL career lasted just two seasons and ended in tragedy. While attempting a tackle against the Jets in 1997, Brown suffered a severe spinal cord contusion and nearly died on the football field. Emergency surgery saved Brown's life and kept him from being confined to a wheelchair, but his football career was over.

Ogden became a member of the Hall of Fame in 2013, the first year he was eligible for it. Lewis won't be eligible until the 2018 class, though he's a lock to enter the Hall as a first-ballot entry. In 17 seasons, Lewis accounted for 2,643 total tackles, $41^{1}/_{2}$ sacks, 31 interceptions, and 67 pass deflections. He's arguably the greatest middle linebacker to ever play the game.

4 Ray Lewis, Baltimore's Hero

Ray Lewis was synonymous with Baltimore's defense for the 17 seasons he spent as a part of it. Coming out of the University of Miami, it was certainly not expected for Lewis to experience the kind of career he went on to have. When comparing Lewis to the other greats, he'll likely go down as the best middle linebacker to ever play the game.

He didn't just get there over night, now. Lewis enjoyed training his body until it couldn't push any further. He considered it a test of will power, to fight through the natural response of the human body wanting to shut down during a strenuous workout. Late in his career, he rode countless miles on his bicycle so he could keep up with the younger, faster, more agile players of the new generation.

Lewis didn't necessarily set out to become the beloved figure of Baltimore. Drafted 26th overall in the first round, Lewis figured to play an integral role on a rebuilding defense looking to scale younger.

But beyond the physical attributes that made Lewis the athletic specimen he was during his prime, Lewis had—and still has—the ability to inspire anyone in a room. It could be about football. It could be about being a better man. It could be about fighting a terminal illness. Lewis has a captivating presence that forces your ears to listen, even if you wouldn't otherwise want to.

"He was the undisputed leader of the Ravens, their spiritual heart and soul," wrote Kevin Cowherd, a columnist for the *Baltimore Sun*. "He was a master motivator, a true gridiron preacher who made believers of his teammates. [Former Ravens linebacker] Paul Kruger was just one of several Ravens who told me that after listening to one of Lewis' amped-up pregame sermons, you'd go out and fight a pack of timberwolves for the man."

His teammates, from his rookie years to his last days, marveled at Lewis' charisma. People gravitate to him. When Lewis announced that the 2012 postseason would be his "last ride," his team bought in, wanting to win for him.

"The main thing that Ray Lewis has done for my career was he taught me how to be a pro," said Ravens running back Ray Rice. "Being a pro has everything to do with how you act, not only on the field, but off the field as well. He was a leader by example, but his words get across to not only us, but everywhere in America. It feels good to know that he's my guy not only on the field, but for life."

"When he started in 1996, I was seven years old," said Ravens receiver Torrey Smith. "I had known about him, and I played with his brother [Keon Lattimore] in college. I was starstruck when he came to Maryland to see him. Now…I look at him like a brother you can talk to about anything."

Lewis has his critics, who claim he's not genuine, who criticize him for the moment in Atlanta when he was initially charged and arrested in connection with a double homicide (charges were later dropped after reaching a plea agreement to obstruction of justice).

In his later years, Lewis learned to be himself and not worry about what others thought of him, for better or for worse.

Lewis made play after play on Baltimore's defense. He was named Super Bowl XXXV MVP. He was invited to the Pro Bowl 13 times.

During Ray Lewis' 17-year, Hall of Fame career with the Ravens, he was named to the Pro Bowl 13 times, earned two NFL Defensive Player of the Year awards, and helped his team claim two Super Bowl titles.

Twice he was named the NFL Defensive Player of the Year. He's been a part of two Super Bowl championships. There isn't an accolade he doesn't have.

"I've done it. I've done it," Lewis said. "I used to sit back, and I used to marvel, rest in peace, at Junior Seau's legacy, and how he had his run, how he ran at it, Pro Bowl after Pro Bowl after Pro

Bowl. I'm like, 'Wow. Who does that? How can you be at that level?' And then I started making my own mark, and then I realized that I can do a lot of things to be great individually, but I wanted to be known differently. I wanted to make men better. I wanted to figure out ways to challenge men to not let the game dictate your emotions and not let the game dictate if you are mad, you're glad, you're sad—no. Be who you are as a man. Walk with who you are as a man and be okay with being a man. So, my whole focus changed, kind of almost in the middle of my career, and I was blessed."

5 Jonathan Ogden, the First Raven

He wasn't the trendiest pick heading into the 1996 draft. Baltimore had a pressing need at running back, considering it was inheriting a team with Earnest Byner as the team's starter in the backfield. But the Baltimore front office knew it needed to go with value over making a splash, and it did just that. The Ravens took UCLA offensive tackle Jonathan Ogden with the fourth overall pick of the 1996 draft.

Ogden had a spectacular collegiate career that saw him become a consensus All-American, win the Outland and Morris Trophies, and earn the UPI Lineman of the Year award as a senior. Ogden was a can't-miss prospect on the offensive line, with a bright future at left tackle.

As a rookie, he played at left guard and only surrendered one sack. He was named to *USA Today*'s All-Rookie team and was a consensus All-Rookie selection. *Sports Illustrated* and the *Dallas Morning News* deemed Ogden an All-Pro selection.

In 1997 the Ravens traded Tony Jones, which allowed Ogden to move back to his natural position at left tackle and show why he was picked as high as he was in the 1996 NFL Draft. In Baltimore's 11th game of the season, against Philadelphia, receiver Michael Jackson caught a pass and was looking for room to run. Ogden took on two defenders on the same play, making room for Jackson to complete a 29-yard gain. Not many linemen could match Ogden's toughness and mental acumen during his era.

By 2000 the Ravens made Ogden the highest paid lineman in the history of the game at that time. Ogden signed a deal worth $44 million, with a signing bonus worth $12 million.

"We consider Jonathan Ogden the best tackle in football today, and I think his future is extremely bright," Ravens owner Art Modell said at the time. "Right now he is the best there is, and he may be the best ever to play."

The 2003 season might have been the most fun for Ogden, as he got to block for running back Jamal Lewis, who ended up running for 2,066 yards. At halftime of Baltimore's Week 2 game against Cleveland, Ogden went up to Lewis, who looked like he was on his way to a career afternoon, and told him to shoot for the single-game rushing record. The Ravens kept pounding the ball with Lewis, and he ended up with 295 yards and set what was then the single-game record.

In 12 NFL seasons, Ogden made it to 11 Pro Bowls, all in consecutive years beginning with his second season. There's a chance Ogden could have played longer, but he hyperextended his toe during the 2006 season. The injury was nagging, but Ogden fought through the pain. After hinting at retirement, Ogden came back for the 2007 season but reinjured the toe. He missed five games during the year, which was an abysmal 5–11 season that resulted in coach Brian Billick getting fired. With the injury, and the successful years Ogden had put in, including the Super Bowl XXXV championship, Ogden decided to call it quits.

Ogden left quite a legacy in Baltimore as the first player selected by the organization. On top of that, he's done a lot of community work in the city. With the Jonathan Ogden Foundation, he's worked with inner-city students to help guide them to positive paths that involve attending college, whether athletics are involved or not.

Ogden remains beloved in Baltimore and still visits the Ravens' training facility frequently. He was inducted into the Pro Football Hall of Fame as a part of the class of 2013. Ogden will be remembered as one of the top left tackles to ever play this game, something Ravens fans will be proud of for many years to come.

6 Super Bowl XLVII

Baltimore entered the 2012 playoffs having lost four out of its past five games. Not much was expected in a postseason run. In those last five games, Baltimore only looked stellar in one—against the New York Giants in a 33–14 blowout win. However, the Giants, winners of Super Bowl XLVI, had been faltering down the stretch of the regular season, which led many to believe the Ravens' win wasn't much of anything.

Baltimore was only expected to beat Indianapolis in the wild-card round, and it did, 24–9. After the Ravens defeated the Broncos 38–35 in double overtime in the divisional round, experts around the league assumed the Ravens lucked out and wouldn't get past the New England Patriots in the AFC Championship Game.

So, when the Ravens held the Patriots scoreless in the second half in a 28–13 win, it was seen as a surprise that the organization would be playing for a second Super Bowl title.

More motivating than the wins was when Ray Lewis, Baltimore's leader since being drafted in 1996, announced he would retire after the postseason. It seemed to spark this club, knowing it would be the last time Lewis would have a chance to add more hardware to his résumé.

Ravens quarterback and Super Bowl MVP Joe Flacco holds up the Vince Lombardi Trophy after Baltimore's 34–31 victory over the San Francisco 49ers in Super Bowl XLVII in New Orleans.

"We all focused ourselves, and you know, the reality set in that we're not all going to play forever," linebacker Terrell Suggs said. "We always say about [how] the window of opportunity is closing. That kind of got everybody's mind right to go on a run."

With Lewis knowing he had one more game in his career, and a group of 52 others wanting the same as Lewis, it was going to be tough to bring down this surging group.

Enter the San Francisco 49ers, coached by John Harbaugh's brother, Jim. The 49ers were looking strong with second-year quarterback Colin Kaepernick at the helm. Kaepernick became the starter mid-season after Alex Smith sustained a concussion, and the organization never looked back, despite the success Smith had been able to have. But Kaepernick added an option element that had been tough to defend throughout the second half of the NFL season.

When game time approached, Kaepernick was seen as an X-factor for San Francisco's offense. If he could play sound football and limit mistakes, the 49ers would have a good shot.

After forcing a three-and-out on San Francisco's opening drive, Baltimore's offense drove down the field with ease, capping the drive off with a 13-yard pass from Joe Flacco to Anquan Boldin to go up 7–0. After a lengthy 49ers drive, Baltimore was able to hold San Francisco to a David Akers field goal, which cut Baltimore's lead to 7–3.

But Baltimore's offense exploded in the second quarter. Flacco found Dennis Pitta for a touchdown and followed it with a bomb that Jacoby Jones finished off for a 56-yard touchdown. Jones actually fell down after his catch, but video evidence never determined if a San Francisco defender touched him. Jones stood back up and ran into the end zone for six points.

After halftime ended, Jones once again made a big play for his team. He took the opening kickoff 108 yards for a touchdown to put the Ravens up 28–6. It looked like a blowout in the making, a time to turn out the lights.

And then the lights actually did go out. With 13:22 remaining, half of the power to the Superdome in New Orleans got turned off, which included the scoreboard and press box. San Francisco was about to run a third-down play before referees signaled to stop the game.

As the Superdome crew worked to restore power, 34 minutes passed. Baltimore was up 28–6 and had all the momentum. Now the Ravens were in danger of losing it. At one point, John Harbaugh was seen verbally lashing out at a stadium official, which he later apologized for.

When play picked back up, San Francisco began gathering steam. San Francisco picked up a first down with an 18-yard completion from Kaepernick to Vernon Davis. On the next play, Kaepernick hit Michael Crabtree for a 31-yard touchdown to cut the lead to 28–13.

After the 49ers forced Baltimore into a three-and-out, San Francisco was back in scoring position after Ted Ginn Jr. ran a punt back to the Ravens' 20-yard line. Two plays later, running back Frank Gore cut Baltimore's lead to 28–20. Suddenly, it was a game.

Two offensive plays later, San Francisco was back in business. After a quick dump-off to Rice, the diminutive running back fumbled with the 49ers' Tarell Brown there to recover. Baltimore's defense limited the Niners to a field goal, which cut the lead to 28–23.

Early in the fourth quarter, Baltimore got down to the San Francisco 1-yard line with three downs remaining. On second down, Ray Rice was stopped for no gain. On third down, Flacco's pass fell incomplete. Rather than risk coming away with nothing, Harbaugh sent in Justin Tucker and the field goal unit to add three points. The Ravens now led 31–23.

Here came the 49ers once again, though, led by Kaepernick. On second-and-5 from the 49ers' 29, Kaepernick completed a 32-yard pass to Randy Moss. Gore then rushed for a 21-yard gain. Two plays later, Kaepernick ran in a 15-yard touchdown to make the game Baltimore 31, San Francisco 29. The 49ers elected for a two-point conversion but were unable to convert.

Baltimore began its next possession at the 9:51 mark in the fourth quarter and wanted to run some clock. Three completions

Matt Jeffers Visits Ravens

The Ravens were in the midst of a rough patch near the end of the 2012 regular season, having lost three in a row before beating the New York Giants 33–14 in Week 16. Baltimore wasn't playing well, and it had fired offensive coordinator Cam Cameron after a loss to the Redskins. They received a surprisingly emotional lift from Matt Jeffers, a Towson University student and Ravens fan. Jeffers emailed the organization with hopes his message would reach the team. The email was ultimately forwarded to John Harbaugh, who passed it along to his players.

Jeffers told his story, that he's a short-statured person who stands 4'2". He's undergone 20 surgeries, some of them major. His last surgery was in 2003, and just when he thought he could finally live his life, his mother was diagnosed with a Stage IV brain tumor. His message, as posted on the Ravens' team website:

> We live in a painful world, no doubt about it. But let me tell you this: The ONLY disability in life is a bad attitude. The ONLY disability in life......is a bad attitude. A positive attitude is the most powerful combatant to life's misfortune. The will to fight, to survive, to win. It is the secret weapon I use, and I think I'm turning out OK. When you play on Sunday, let it not be to win a division or to silence the critics or prove somebody wrong or end a losing skid. Let it be a dedication to that simple yet powerful notion that life can be conquered with the right outlook. And I promise you, I promise you that everything else will take care of itself. Go get 'em on Sunday. I wish you all the best on your journey to The Lombardi.

The Ravens invited Jeffers to attend a practice as a thank you for the letter. Jeffers' motivation possibly worked too. Baltimore came back from its journey with the Lombardi in hand.

from Flacco and five runs later, the Ravens were facing a third-and-2 situation at San Francisco's 20. Flacco looked for Dennis Pitta but couldn't connect, forcing a field-goal opportunity. Tucker, a rookie, made a clutch 38-yard field goal to force San Francisco to play for the win with a touchdown.

With 4:19 remaining, the 49ers went to work and did so fast. Gore and Kaepernick ran for eight-yard gains on consecutive carries. Kaepernick then found Crabtree for 24 yards to move the football into Baltimore territory. On first-and-10 from the Ravens' 40, Gore took a handoff and rumbled for 33 yards down to the 7-yard line.

Could it be that the 49ers would finally move ahead?

On first down, backup running back LaMichael James mustered two yards, with Ravens defenders Dannell Ellerbe and DeAngelo Tyson bringing him down. On second down, Kaepernick threw a pass intended for Michael Crabtree but broken up by cornerback Corey Graham. On third down, Kaepernick went Crabtree's way again, with corner Jimmy Smith in position to make a play on the ball.

That left one last play for the 49ers on this series. Kaepernick dropped back and looked for the fade to Crabtree in the right corner of the end zone. Crabtree and Smith were engaged on the play, with contact made from both players. The ball fell incomplete and out of bounds, yet possibly catchable. However, no flag was thrown. Baltimore had stopped the 49ers with 1:46 remaining.

Rice, Bernard Pierce, and Vonta Leach each took carries without picking up a first down. Up five, the Ravens elected to sacrifice a safety with little time remaining on the clock. The strategy was to run time off the clock and avoid a special teams meltdown. The plan worked, with punter Sam Koch running down the back line of the end zone, burning eight seconds off the clock.

Four seconds remained from immortality. Koch punted from the 20, and Ginn took off running. The clock hit triple zeroes, and Ginn was corralled at midfield. The Ravens had just won their second Super Bowl championship.

"It's always the goal to win the Super Bowl, and by me being able to come home and play, that was like icing on the cake," Jones said. "You can drop the cherry on it, the strawberry, and the sprinkles."

Joe Flacco was named Super Bowl MVP with his performance, which included 287 yards passing and three touchdowns. A lot of people doubted the 2012 Baltimore Ravens. But only the Ravens were left standing when the NFL season ended. Terrell Suggs summed up the postseason best after the game:

"We beat the future in [Colts quarterback] Andrew Luck. We beat the past in [Broncos quarterback] Peyton Manning. We beat the present in [Patriots quarterback] Tom Brady. Then we beat the best show on offense in the NFL in the 49ers in Colin Kaepernick. The toughest road in these playoffs, we did it. We did it together."

7 Art Modell: Forever Loved in Baltimore

It's quite the circumstance for one human being, such as Art Modell, to be loathed in one city and revered in another. Cleveland residents hated him so much that once he relocated the Browns to Baltimore, he could never set foot in his old city ever again. When he announced he was moving the team, he received death threats. What's believed to be the reason Modell has been refused entry to the Pro Football Hall of Fame is that the Cleveland contingency of the voters refuse to allow him in.

The reasons are obvious as to why Cleveland hates Modell and his legacy. And can Baltimoreans blame them? After all, the city of Baltimore resented Robert Irsay for moving the Colts to Indianapolis. No one wants to feel left behind the way both of these cities felt at one point in time. In fact, when LeBron James ditched Cleveland for the Miami Heat, a subsequent poll showed Modell was still hated more.

But Modell would wind up having a lasting, positive impact in Baltimore. Those who stayed close with him through the franchise's relocation describe him as kind, generous, and thoughtful. If any of his former players were in need, he would do his best to look out for them, including loaning money to them.

Modell passed away on September 6, 2012, at the age of 87. He received a tremendous amount of support from those in Baltimore, with talk radio lines flooded with fans expressing thanks to Modell for bringing football back to Charm City.

Tight end Shannon Sharpe, who played with the Ravens in 2000 and 2001, said Modell was one of the reasons he decided to play for Baltimore when he was a free agent.

"One of my favorite moments in the NFL was when he spoke to us in the locker room after the Super Bowl victory," Sharpe said. "He said, 'This is the proudest day of my life; you guys make me proud.' And then he started to break down. That touched me. You could not only see the emotion from him and from all of us in that room, you could feel it. Knowing how long he had been in the NFL and how many great players he had been around, it was such a great feeling to give him something that he wanted for so long. We all wanted it for him."

Former Baltimore Colts defensive back Bruce Laird was also fond of Modell, understanding he made the move to keep the football team in his family, which had to be a tough situation to grapple with.

"He ran a family football business, and it was family first," Laird said. "For Art, it was also the family of football—not the business of football. And obviously, he entered the league when it needed him most, at the right time, in 1961."

If it wasn't for what happened in Cleveland, Modell would be an easy inclusion into the Hall of Fame. Modell was the innovative mind behind putting the NFL on television, including coming up with the concept for *Monday Night Football,* along with Pete Rozelle and Roone Arledge. Modell was also part of the committee that helped merge the AFL and NFL.

Art Modell's Funeral

When Art Modell passed away at the age of 87, plenty of old friends and NFL colleagues made the trip to the Baltimore Hebrew Congregation. NFL commissioner Roger Goodell and Dallas Cowboys owner Jerry Jones attended the service, along with plenty of present and former Ravens players. Ray Lewis gave an inspiring eulogy, and closed it with, "Rest in peace, Pop Art." Former players who attended Modell's funeral included Michael McCrary, Peter Boulware, and Rob Burnett. Present players included Ray Rice, Joe Flacco, Haloti Ngata, and Torrey Smith.

Any ill feelings of receiving a team the way Baltimore lost one in 1984 were put aside in early 2001, when Modell's Ravens won Super Bowl XXXV. The Lombardi Trophy had long eluded him, and it was finally his. Even though Steve Bisciotti took the majority ownership in 2004, a giant portrait of Modell is still on display in the lobby of the team's facility in Owings Mills, Maryland.

During his scheduled media availability the day Modell passed away, Ray Lewis started to tear up when recalling memories of Modell, the man who brought him to Baltimore.

"You're talking about coming into a situation where everything was brand new," Lewis said. "Everything was. But the way he treated you was never new. He respected you as a man. But me, he grabbed me as a son from day one and never let me go. It didn't matter what it was, whenever he saw me, he would always tell me how much he loved me and always tell me how much I meant to him."

Added Lewis, "He would always make you smile. And no matter how bad things were going, he could reverse it. That's why I keep bringing up that word, *father*. I never looked at him any different than a father."

Picking a Team Name

The original Cleveland Browns had just moved to Baltimore but were assuming a new identity. Cleveland would keep the rights to its football history with Baltimore receiving a new team of its own. It was like an expansion team in a way, but not in totality since a team already in place packed its bags and moved to the East Coast.

And as Baltimore began operations as an NFL football club, it was without an identity. Who was this team in Baltimore? What would it be called?

At some point during the NFL Draft process, the organization was in talks with Ray Lewis, who recalled receiving a call from Ozzie Newsome, who was the vice president of player personnel at the time. With Baltimore's football team nameless, Lewis had some questions for Newsome, including one that sounds fairly basic, looking back on it.

"Ozzie, what's our team name going to be? Who are we?" Lewis remembers asking Newsome.

The Ravens were in transition at the time and still didn't have uniforms of their own. Former Browns and Ravens kicker Matt Stover remembers the situation vividly.

"We didn't even have a name, we didn't have colors. We didn't have anything," Stover said during his Ravens Ring of Honor induction.

Owner Art Modell had already begun the process of trying to come up with a team name. Though it was never likely to happen, Modell approached the Indianapolis Colts about taking their team name back, considering the Colts name was in Baltimore first. Indianapolis rejected that idea.

The Baltimore organization then organized panel discussions and multiple meetings to figure out what name would work best. Staffers began conducting surveys around the city to figure out what name would work best. One name kept popping up on each list: Ravens.

One of the reasons had to do with one of America's greatest poets being from Baltimore, the legendary Edgar Allan Poe. His historic poem "The Raven" is one of the most well-known American works of literature and has long held a special place in the heart of Baltimore.

The Baltimore football club wanted fans to decide the nickname. It came up with a list of finalists to choose from and partnered with the *Baltimore Sun* to get residents to vote. The finalists were Ravens, Americans, Marauders, Mustangs, and Railers.

Using a phone service in conjunction with the *Sun* called Sundial, Baltimore residents voted for their favorite nickname. An overwhelming 22,463 out of 33,748 voters chose the Ravens nickname, which was announced on March 29, 1996. The name stuck and has been popular with Baltimore fans ever since.

On Wednesday, June 5, at noon, the organization revealed the team's colors, which were black, purple, and gold. Ravens quarterback Vinny Testaverde, defensive end Rob Burnett, and wide receiver Michael Jackson modeled the uniforms for fans at the Inner Harbor Gallery Mall.

In reference to Poe's poem, the name *Ravens* couldn't have been a more perfect fit. The predominant theme of "The Raven" is undying devotion, which is something the city of Baltimore has long had for the sport of football. Baltimore adored its Colts before they up and moved to Indianapolis in 1984. To prove the city deserved another NFL franchise, fans came out in droves to support the CFL's Stallions when they were briefly in Charm City.

Symbolically, Ravens fans have proven their devotion. Home games at M&T Bank Stadium are regarded as one of the toughest places for visiting teams to play in.

Baltimore football was back, and it was the new home of the Ravens.

9 The Inaugural Season

The Ravens weren't an expansion team, yet they were treated like one. When owner Art Modell moved the franchise to Baltimore, he made a deal so Cleveland could keep the history and incorporate it back into the new Browns franchise it would receive in 1999. In strange fashion, the Ravens were brand new without any team records or history, yet fielded many players from the 1995 Cleveland Browns.

Oddly enough, the Ravens had a talented offensive team capable of putting up plenty of points any given week. It was the one time in franchise history, at least up until the Joe Flacco years or even the 2006 season with Steve McNair, that the Ravens possessed an offensive pulse. Testaverde put in one of the best seasons of his career, throwing for 4,177 yards and 33 touchdowns, earning a Pro Bowl berth in the process. Receivers Michael Jackson and Derrick Alexander both topped the 1,000-yard mark. Running backs Bam Morris (737 yards, four touchdowns) and Earnest Byner (634 yards, four touchdowns) were threats as well, combining for 1,371 yards and eight touchdowns.

Baltimore won its season opener and first-ever game against Oakland 19–14, with a strong defensive showing. That was one of the rare times the Ravens' defense looked impressive during the 1996 campaign.

The Ravens earned their second win of the year in Week 5 against New Orleans. It was another defensive struggle, with Baltimore prevailing 17–10 to improve to 2–2 for the season. From there, it was tough sledding for the defense. The Patriots came to town and scored 46 points in a win the next week. The Indianapolis Colts then defeated the Ravens 26–21 in a Week 7 road game. The following game against Denver saw another shootout ensue, with the Broncos winning 45–34. Testaverde matched John Elway's numbers (25-for-29, 326 yards, three TDs, one INT) with a solid outing of his own, throwing for 338 yards, four touchdowns, and one interception. The Ravens were leading after three quarters, 34–31, but Denver was able to score the game's final 14 points to snag the win.

The next week, Baltimore finally got itself back in the win column with an overtime thriller against St. Louis. Testaverde set a Ravens franchise record that still stands as of 2013, throwing for 429 yards in a 37–31 victory. Testaverde was able to find Jackson for a 22-yard game-winner in overtime.

After defeating the Rams, the Ravens then lost four games in a row. However, if you take away San Francisco's 38–20 win, the Ravens lost the remaining three games by a total of just nine points. Baltimore would tally one more win in Week 14 when it defeated Pittsburgh 31–17. Offensive lineman Jonathan Ogden, Baltimore's first-ever selection, actually caught a one-yard touchdown in the first quarter against the Steelers. (Ogden would later catch another one-yard touchdown in 2003. He finished his career with two catches for two yards and two touchdowns.)

Baltimore closed the 1996 season with three consecutive losses. The Ravens finished third in the NFL in total offense with 357.7 yards per game. The defense finished dead last, giving up 368.1 yards each outing. By 2000 this trend was reversing itself. And while the offense wasn't as exciting as the 1996 team's, they won a lot more games, including a Super Bowl championship.

Ravens Pro Bowlers

In franchise history, the Ravens have received 83 Pro Bowl invitations, which averages out to almost five players per season. Here's a year-by-year look at who was invited to the Pro Bowl:

1996 QB Vinny Testaverde, S Eric Turner

1997 LB Ray Lewis, OT Jonathan Ogden

1998 LB Peter Boulware, WR/KR Jermaine Lewis, LB Ray Lewis, DE Michael McCrary, OT Jonathan Ogden, S Bennie Thompson

1999 LB Peter Boulware, LB Ray Lewis, DE Michael McCrary, OT Jonathan Ogden, S Rod Woodson

2000 DT Sam Adams, LB Ray Lewis, OT Jonathan Ogden, K Matt Stover, S Rod Woodson

2001 DT Sam Adams, WR/KR Jermaine Lewis, LB Ray Lewis, OT Jonathan Ogden, TE Shannon Sharpe, S Rod Woodson

2002 LB Peter Boulware, TE Todd Heap, OT Jonathan Ogden

2003 LB Peter Boulware, TE Todd Heap, RB Jamal Lewis, LB Ray Lewis, CB Chris McAlister, OT Jonathan Ogden, S Ed Reed, LB Adalius Thomas

2004 LB Ray Lewis, CB Chris McAlister, OT Jonathan Ogden, S Ed Reed, LB Terrell Suggs

2005 OT Jonathan Ogden

2006 CB Chris McAlister, OT Jonathan Ogden, S Ed Reed, LB Terrell Suggs, LB Adalius Thomas, QB Steve McNair, LB Bart Scott, LB Ray Lewis

2007 RB Willis McGahee, OT Jonathan Ogden, LB Ray Lewis, S Ed Reed

2008 LB Ray Lewis, LB Terrell Suggs, S Ed Reed, FB Le'Ron McClain, LB Brendan Ayanbadejo

2009 DT Haloti Ngata, FB Le'Ron McClain, RB Ray Rice, LB Ray Lewis

2010 K Billy Cundiff, LB Ray Lewis, DT Haloti Ngata, S Ed Reed, LB Terrell Suggs

2011 OG Ben Grubbs, FB Vonta Leach, LB Ray Lewis, DT Haloti Ngata, S Ed Reed, RB Ray Rice, LB Terrell Suggs, OG Marshal Yanda

2012 WR/KR Jacoby Jones, FB Vonta Leach, DT Haloti Ngata, S Ed Reed, RB Ray Rice, OG Marshal Yanda

10 Go to Training Camp

It was a way for Ravens fans to connect with the team they loved. It was also a way for the Ravens' organization to embrace the tradition set by the first NFL franchise to establish itself in Baltimore.

Beginning in 1996, the Ravens held their training camps at McDaniel College, formerly known as Western Maryland College. The public was invited to attend, which gave fans an up-close look at who the Ravens were and what the Ravens could possibly become.

For many fans in this part of the state, it was the only time they would be able to see their state's NFL team. It was even steeped in tradition, as the Baltimore Colts held their training camps in the city of Westminster from 1953 through 1971.

"Some of my best memories as a kid are my family's visits to the Colts' training camp in Westminster," Ravens owner Steve Bisciotti said. "Part of my devotion to the game and the players who made it great and are heroes to many of us, started on those visits."

Here are a few facts about Westminster: Located in the center of Carroll County, Westminster was incorporated as a city in Maryland in 1818, though it was originally founded by William Winchester in 1764. It's a small town, though steadily growing. In 2010, the census stated that Westminster has more than 18,000 residents, which is an increase of more than 11,000 people since the 1970s.

Westminster is your typical small town nestled away from the busy nature of Baltimore (32 miles), or even Annapolis (50 miles), for that matter. It served as the Ravens' home away from home.

In 2001 the Ravens were featured on the first season of the HBO series *Hard Knocks*, which followed each move of an NFL team through training camp. The city of Westminster got some noted publicity with its being featured on what would become a popular show for NFL fans.

The memories for football fans were evident in Westminster. It was a true intimate setting for fans, as they were able to get as close to the players as possible. It was also an economic boon for the city during late July and August.

But as it happens all too often, good things come to an end. During the 2011 off-season, when the NFL owners locked out the players during collective bargaining negotiations, the Ravens were unable to commit to holding training camp in Westminster. When the lockout ended, just a couple of days before the Ravens were to open practice, the organization had made a decision to hold training camp at its team facility in Owings Mills, Maryland.

For some, it was determined to be a one-time affair. But then the rumors began circulating. Would the Ravens return to Westminster? Would there be open training camp practices in front of the fans on a daily basis?

On December 2, 2011, the Ravens announced their days in Westminster were over. Fans denounced the move. The Ravens said it was needed for the team to be able to use all the technological advances the team's facility had to offer. The team had outgrown the Best Western it stayed at in Westminster. It needed to be able to continue practice indoors if inclement weather interfered. It made practices move more seamlessly, they said. And it made more sense in the modern NFL climate to stay close to home during the preseason.

"In 1996 Westminster was the best place for us to have training camp," general manager Ozzie Newsome explained at the time. "How teams conduct training camp today is vastly different. Our football needs and requirements are different. The absence of two-a-days, how much space we need for the players and the meetings, the limited number of practices allowed by the new CBA

Training at Towson During Lockout

During the 2011 off-season, NFL players were locked out out of their respective facilities across the league, and it was no different in Baltimore. Being that they couldn't get in any off-season workouts with the coaching staff, receiver Derrick Mason organized a get-together of their own at Towson University. Twenty-six players attended the workout, including Joe Flacco, Ray Rice, Dennis Pitta, Anquan Boldin, Torrey Smith, Cory Redding, Arthur Jones, Jameel McClain, and Jarret Johnson.

"We just want to let the fans know that we're working and we're working hard," Mason told reporters. "It's not our choice to be somewhere else working out, we would rather be at [the team facility], but obviously we can't."

[collective bargaining agreement], the importance of having an indoor field when the summer storms come—all of that and more football-influenced factors, had me recommend to Steve [Bisciotti] and [team president] Dick [Cass] that we hold camp [in Owings Mills]."

In a December 26, 2011, column, the *Baltimore Sun*'s Mike Preston wrote, "To put training camp back in Westminster might be the biggest tribute the Ravens could pay the fans," stating his opinion that the Ravens took away a Baltimore tradition. During the 2012 preseason, the Ravens held three public training camp practices at M&T Bank Stadium, Navy-Marine Corps Memorial Stadium in Annapolis, and at Stevenson University in Owings Mills.

Aaron Wilson, one of the Ravens beat writers for the *Baltimore Sun*, didn't think the Ravens were in the wrong for the decision, stating the Ravens were making a move that best suited the organization.

"The primary reason why the Ravens did this wasn't for money or because they felt like the fan attention was a distraction," Wilson said. "It came back to facilities, an outdated hotel they resided in for years, and having built enough loyalty with fans that they didn't need to concern themselves much with the initial backlash from those disappointed with the loss of access to their favorite NFL team. It was a football decision more so than anything having to do with the business operations, but it was expensive to hold camp off-site for years."

11 Peter Boulware, the Sack Master

Baltimore has had no shortage of terrors on the defensive side of the ball. One of the best they ever snagged was outside linebacker Peter Boulware, Baltimore's first pick and the fourth overall selection in the 1997 NFL Draft. Boulware was one of the premier defenders in all of college football in 1996, sacking quarterbacks 19 times and being named a consensus All-American.

The Ravens needed more youth on its defense in 1997, and the plan from the start was to insert Boulware into the starting lineup. Aging linebackers, such as Jerrol Williams, Mike Croel, and Keith Goganious, were phased out and released. It was time for Boulware to team up with Ray Lewis and Jamie Sharper to lead one of the best linebacking units of the era.

The 1997 defense needed some youthful energy on the field after a dismal 1996 group that finished the season ranked dead last in total defense.

The defense only improved to 25th overall in one year, but Boulware was everything the organization hoped for as a rookie. He led the Ravens in sacks with 11$^{1}/_{2}$. The Associated Press took notice and honored him with the Defensive Rookie of the Year award.

Throughout Boulware's career, the sacks continued to pile up. Over the next three seasons, Boulware would add 25$^{1}/_{2}$ more sacks to his career totals before his 2001 campaign, which still stands as the best season statistically for any Baltimore pass rusher ever.

Ravens linebacker Peter Boulware lines up during a 13–7 win over the Arizona Cardinals on December 17, 2000.

Heading into the 2001 regular season finale against Minnesota, Boulware had 11 sacks. Boulware picked up one sack early in the first quarter to give him 12 for the year. But, late in the fourth quarter, with Baltimore up 12–3, Minnesota quarterback Spergon Wynn continued to drop back to throw the ball in an attempt to get back in the game. But Boulware prevented any kind of comeback, sacking him three times in the game's final period. His fourth and final sack of the day resulted in a fumble that Sharper recovered and returned for a touchdown. It also gave Boulware a total of 15 sacks for the season.

Boulware tallied 15½ sacks over the next two seasons before injuries began creeping into the end of his career. Baltimore released Boulware in 2005 and brought him back at a cheaper price. But two knee surgeries toward the end of his career forced him to give the sport up and retire.

In eight seasons with the Ravens, Boulware amassed 70 sacks, which was the franchise record until Terrell Suggs broke it in Week 1 of the 2011 season against Pittsburgh. Former Jacksonville Jaguars quarterback Mark Brunell caught the brunt of most of Boulware's production, as Boulware sacked him 15 of those times.

Boulware was named to the Ring of Honor in 2006 in a ceremony during a game against Cincinnati at M&T Bank Stadium.

"I don't like to get too emotional up there, but I was fighting back tears, I was fighting back the emotions," Boulware said that day. "I tell you, it was one of the most special moments of my life, and I'll never forget it."

12 Ray Lewis' Crossroads

Ray Lewis' life changed forever on January 31, 2000. Depending on what you believe, Lewis was either in the wrong place at the wrong time, or he got away with more than he's led on for all these years.

Public opinions have historically varied on what transpired the night Jacinth Baker and Richard Lollar died outside of an Atlanta nightclub, despite the fact Lewis, originally charged with murder, would see charges dropped against him in exchange for testimony against his friends as well as pleading guilty to obstruction of justice. The prosecution's strategy backfired, as the two men with Lewis that night, Reginald Oakley and Joseph Sweeting, were acquitted.

Since the incident, Lewis has opened up his life on a lot of issues. He revealed the struggles he endured as a child without a father present. He's open about his faith. When it comes to reaching out to teammates or members of the Baltimore community in need, Lewis will lend them a hand.

When it comes to what happened that night in Atlanta, Lewis has been mum for the most part. He's maintained his innocence always and wasn't convicted of any felony charges. As far as the details of that night, the public knows what former Fulton County District Attorney Paul Howard laid out in trial. Lewis, Oakley, and Sweeting were getting into a limousine when a fight broke out outside the club. Lewis' version of events was that he initially tried to break up the fight but stopped and hopped in the limousine because he didn't want to jeopardize his career. When his friends got in the limo, he told them not to say a word to police. Lewis himself lied to police when questioned, which is why he later pleaded guilty to obstruction of justice.

A knife that stabbed the two deceased victims was found at the crime scene, but there was no blood or DNA that could connect the knife to either Oakley or Sweeting. However, traces of Baker's blood were found in the limousine after police searched it. Even so, the prosecution's case unraveled rather quickly. Realizing he didn't have much of a case against Lewis, Howard offered to drop the murder chargers in exchange for obstruction of justice for lying during the initial investigation. With Lewis as a witness for the prosecution, he painted a story where the victims were the aggressors, and that even though Sweeting and Oakley had purchased knives at a Sports Authority store earlier in the week, he didn't see them stab anyone. To this day, the crime has been unsolved. Members of the victims' families have been skeptical of Lewis' story since day one.

It's unknown what Lewis knows because since the trial, he's never publicly talked about the specifics of that night at length. In 2004 Lewis reached a settlement with Lollar's family to provide compensation for his daughter, India Lollar. In a 2010 interview with the *Baltimore Sun*, Lewis said he thinks about that night every day.

"I'm telling you, no day leaves this Earth without me asking God to ease the pain of anybody who was affected by that whole ordeal." Lewis told the newspaper. "He's a God who tests people—not that he put me in that situation, because he didn't make me go nowhere. I put myself in that situation."

Following the trial, Lewis was at a crossroads. In a *Sports Illustrated* interview, Lewis said that, while walking down the courthouse steps in June 2000, he told his mother he was a changed man.

Lewis has since become a devout Christian and philanthropist. He spends a ton of time and effort in the Baltimore community, helping underprivileged youths receive chances many in the neighborhood he grew up in didn't get.

Lewis will continue to have detractors, pointing to that night in Atlanta where two men lost their lives. To Lewis' credit, he did change his life for the better following the events that transpired on January 31, 2000.

"The question was what direction was he going to take?" general manager Ozzie Newsome told *Sports Illustrated* in 2006. "Some athletes, if they get out of a situation like he did, say, 'You know what? I got a free pass to just do it again.' Others learn from the lesson, and it makes them a better person. He jumped on the [right] track in a hurry."

13 Ravens-Steelers Rivalry

Of all the major rivalries in the NFL, Ravens vs. Steelers is the youngest. By the mid- to late 2000s, though, this game became one of the best and most watched rivalries in the NFL. It's an easy sell for folks who aren't fans of either team. Both teams field stout defenses. Both teams love to hate each other, evidenced by the trash talk that goes back and forth each year.

While the Ravens and Steelers were both in the AFC Central before realignment, this game wasn't of the magnitude it later became. In fact, the Ravens and the Titans were just beginning to get going before the NFL added a division in each conference in 2002. The Ravens went to the AFC North with Pittsburgh, Cincinnati, and Cleveland, while Tennessee was ushered into the AFC South. For most Baltimore fans, the rivalry took off a year prior to realignment in 2001, because it was the first time both teams met in the playoffs.

After splitting the regular season games, Baltimore and Pittsburgh met for a rubber match in the divisional round of the playoffs. The Steelers' forced Ravens quarterback Elvis Grbac into three interceptions and were able to roll to a 27–10 win.

This wasn't the first time the city of Pittsburgh got the best of Baltimore in the postseason. In 1975 and 1976, the Steelers knocked the old Baltimore Colts out of the playoffs, so there was some resentment that lingered. For Pittsburgh fans, this game replaced the old Steelers-Browns rivalry due to the fact that their team couldn't play Cleveland for two years. When the new Browns entered the NFL, they had to deal with the growing pains of being an expansion team. Therefore, a lot of attention was diverted from the Browns to the Ravens, who won a Super Bowl championship in 2000 while Cleveland was struggling to build its franchise from the bottom up.

Each year, the rivalry seemed to intensify. But it became arguably the NFL's best in 2008. In the first meeting that season, Baltimore trailed 23–20 midway through the fourth quarter. Joe Flacco then hit Derrick Mason for a 35-yard completion to move the Ravens to the 5-yard line. Le'Ron McClain then punched a two-yard run into the end zone two plays later to tie the game up, and ultimately send the contest to overtime. The Ravens were forced into a three-and-out and punted the ball to Pittsburgh. A short pass from Ben Roethlisberger to Mewelde Moore turned into a 24-yard gain, which helped set up a 46-yard field goal from Jeff Reed to win the game.

A couple of weeks later, Terrell Suggs was on the *2 Live Stews* radio show and was asked if the Ravens put a bounty on Steelers running back Rashard Mendenhall.

"The bounty was out on him and the bounty was out on [Hines Ward]—we just didn't get him between the whistles." Suggs also called Ward a "cheap-shot artist" and a "dirty player."

That drew plenty of yellow flags and appeared to surprise Ward a bit. Suggs said he was joking, which he had a tendency to do at times. The NFL investigated the incident and cleared Suggs. (Suggs won the local media's Good Guy Award that year for being cooperative with the press. As a gag gift, the media presented Suggs with a roll of Bounty paper towels.)

The two teams met again on December 14, 2008, with Pittsburgh winning another close game. The Ravens had a 9–6 lead late into the fourth quarter, but Roethlisberger was able to lead his team down to score a game-winning touchdown with 50 seconds left. Roethlisberger capped the drive with a four-yard score to receiver Santonio Holmes.

Both teams would meet again in the AFC Championship Game, with the rivalry capturing the entire country's attention by this

Injuring Tommy Maddox

In a sense, you can credit the Baltimore Ravens' defense for kickstarting Ben Roethlisberger's career in Pittsburgh. In an early-season meeting in 2004, Ravens cornerback Gary Baxter crashed into Maddox and injured his arm. Maddox was unable to return and ruled out for the next six weeks. Roethlisberger, a rookie out of Miami (Ohio), was called upon to step in and lead.

Roethlisberger would succeed from the start and throw for 2,621 yards and 17 touchdowns as a rookie. Maddox was relegated to second-string status, even after he was available to come back to the lineup. When Roethlisberger and the Steelers had another crack at Baltimore in Week 16, the Steelers capitalized, defeating the Ravens 20–7. Roethlisberger threw for 221 yards and two touchdowns. As a starter, Roethlisberger didn't lose a regular season game. Pittsburgh's only loss in 2004 was to Baltimore in Week 2.

point. The Steelers jumped out to a 13–0 lead and later made it 16–7 in the third quarter. After a poor punt from Pittsburgh's Mitch Berger early in the fourth quarter, Baltimore set up a drive at its own 42. Two passes to receiver Derrick Mason went for 14 and 11 yards, respectively, to help move the ball near the red zone. After a defensive pass interference call put the football on the 1-yard line, running back Willis McGahee scored a short touchdown to cut Pittsburgh's lead to 16–14.

Baltimore's defense forced a three-and-out, giving the Ravens' offense a chance to win the game. But on third-and-13, Flacco's pass to Mason was intercepted by Troy Polamalu, who ran the ball back 40 yards for a touchdown. The play put the game away and earned Pittsburgh a spot in the Super Bowl.

In 2009 the two teams would split the series, both winning their games by a three-point margin. Baltimore won the first game with Billy Cundiff making a game-winning field goal in overtime. In the second game, with Pittsburgh up three at 2:34 left in regulation, and with Baltimore at the Pittsburgh 38, LaMarr Woodley sacked Joe Flacco to close out the game.

Since December 30, 2007, when Baltimore beat Pittsburgh 27–21 in a season finale, single digits have decided each game except one. The lone exception was the 2011 season opener, when Baltimore won 35–7.

The Ravens and Steelers have been two of the most consistent teams over the past decade. As long as that trend continues, we can expect more thrilling meetings between the two teams, and plenty of hate between both sidelines.

14 Fourth-and-29

Joe Flacco was on the turf, with the Ravens now 29 yards away from a first down. San Diego Chargers linebacker Antwan Barnes sacked him off the edge, backing the Ravens up with little hope to pull out a win against an underachieving Chargers team during the 2012 regular season. It was now fourth-and-29, with Baltimore needing a miracle.

But before we delve into the play itself—one John Harbaugh called "the greatest play I've ever seen or been a part of"—let's look at how the Ravens got to this point, down three points with 1:37 to go against a seemingly inferior opponent. San Diego had some top talent on its roster, including quarterback Philip Rivers, tight end Antonio Gates, and safety Eric Weddle. But Chargers coach Norv Turner's group had vastly failed to live up to expectations, which put him on the hot seat prior to the season's beginning. The Chargers were 4–6 at the time, down but not out. A win over the Ravens would surely give them some momentum and more than a chance to climb back into the AFC playoff race in a weak AFC West division.

Neither team could generate any offense in the first quarter, with the first 15 minutes ending with a 0–0 deadlock. The Chargers, after years of being teased with an explosive offense and suspect defense, saw its offense dwindling with no protection for Rivers. Their running game was also nonexistent, with no back totaling 100 yards in a single game through the 2012 regular season.

But it was the San Diego passing game that was able to get on the scoreboard first, with Rivers finding tall receiver Malcom Floyd in the end zone from 21 yards out at the 9:43 mark of the second quarter. The Chargers then added a Nick Novak field goal to extend their lead to 10–0 by halftime.

Flacco finished the first half with just 59 yards on 8-of-16 passing. Running back Ray Rice had 45 yards on nine carries, leaving fans scratching their heads as to why Rice wasn't receiving the ball more.

After notching a field goal on their first drive of the third quarter, the Ravens were back in the mix, cutting San Diego's lead to 10–3. Two possessions later, the Ravens appeared to be poised to score again until an offensive stall set them back. Facing a fourth-and-1 at the Chargers' 14, rookie running back Bernard Pierce was stopped for a loss of two. San Diego's Corey Liuget came unblocked through the offensive line before bringing Pierce down. The Chargers took the defensive play and turned it into three more points, giving San Diego a 13–3 lead with 7:51 left in the game.

Up to this point, Flacco had only improved his halftime yardage total to 133, with 54 of those yards coming on one play to receiver Torrey Smith. It was on Flacco to get the offense moving if the Ravens were to come back.

Flacco completed two passes to Jacoby Jones for a total of 30 yards on the ensuing drive. Flacco then found Smith for two passes, good for 22 yards and 14 yards. From the San Diego 4-yard line, Flacco hit tight end Dennis Pitta for a touchdown with over four minutes remaining. The Ravens now needed a stop and a field goal to tie, or a touchdown to win.

Baltimore got its stop after forcing the Chargers into a three-and-out. So there they were, 3:09 remaining in the game, down

Ravens running back Ray Rice (27) runs a dump-off pass from Joe Flacco for 29 yards on fourth-and-29 against the San Diego Chargers on November 25, 2012. The play set up a game-tying field goal and a 16–13 Baltimore win in OT.

three with a chance to tie or win. Helped with a 16-yard pass to Pitta, Baltimore set itself up in San Diego territory at the Chargers 44. But a holding penalty on a guard Marshal Yanda backed the Ravens up 10 yards, which was followed by two Flacco incompletions. The Ravens then faced third-and-20, and Barnes, who came untouched on Flacco's blind side, sacked the fifth-year quarterback.

There aren't many plays—if any—designed to pick up 29 yards on fourth down. Baltimore needed something out of its control to bounce its way, to prove destiny was on its side.

"I was thinking we needed a miracle," said Terrell Suggs.

That they received.

Flacco took the snap out of the shotgun and immediately looked downfield. His receivers were running vertically down the field, given the distance of the play to complete. Flacco wanted to find Smith, but neither he, nor any other downfield target, was open. Flacco felt he had only one choice, and that was to dump the ball down to Rice and hope the diminutive back could make a defender miss and pick up the needed yardage.

Rice caught the ball just one yard past the line of scrimmage and turned up the field. Initially, Rice ran right. As San Diego defenders converged, Rice cut back to his left swiftly. Immediately, three Chargers players were out of position and Rice suddenly had plenty of room to run. With Rice racing toward the first-down marker, only Weddle, arguably San Diego's best defender, had an angle to make a play before Rice could pick up the first down. But suddenly, Ravens receiver Anquan Boldin stepped in and leveled Weddle to the turf, blocking him and keeping Rice's hopes of picking up a first down alive.

"Anquan Boldin came back and had as good of a football block— a legal, football block, as physical of a football block—that you'll ever see in football," Harbaugh said. "That's Anquan Boldin. That's who he is. That made the play happen."

Rice was almost there, but he still needed to get to the Chargers' 34-yard line. At the 36, Chargers defensive backs Quentin Jammer and Antoine Cason had closed in with hopes of ending Baltimore's comeback hopes. With Rice out of room, he lunged forward. With the play blown dead, all eyes were on the officials to spot the ball.

He was ruled to have reached the 34. First down.

Baltimore's sideline was stunned. Qualcomm Stadium was stunned. The Chargers were in disbelief. That didn't just happen, did it?

"He did not get the first down," Rivers said. "They just did not have a view to overturn it. He did not get it. You can't help it. When you don't have a view to overturn it, you cannot overturn it. I do not think anyone thinks he got it. I do not think anyone in the stadium thinks he got it. I do not think Ray Rice thinks he got it. I do not think anyone on their team thinks he got it. But he got it. They just did not have a camera view to overturn it. That's what the referee said. He felt bad that they could not because he did not have a view. He knew his knee was down on the 35-yard line."

But it doesn't matter what Rivers thinks. Upon review, the officials gave Rice and the Ravens a first down. That play propelled Baltimore to a game-tying 38-yard field goal from kicker Justin Tucker to send the game to overtime.

In the extra period, both teams punted on their first possessions, with the Chargers going three-and-out on their second. Baltimore took over with 4:56 left and was able to have Tucker make a game-winning, 38-yard field goal with over a minute left in overtime. Somehow, some way, the Ravens pulled out a 16–13 win. If it wasn't for the miraculous fourth-and-29 play from Rice, the Ravens would have likely flown cross-country back to Baltimore with a loss.

Following the game, Rice referred to the play as, "Hey diddle diddle, Ray Rice up the middle."

"On that play, it was just will, man," Rice said. "Once I made the first guy miss and I cut back across the grain, I actually saw that the defense had to flip their hips. I was just eyeing the first down. I looked and I said, 'Should I keep running to the sideline or should I keep trying to get up field?' That's what I did. I just kept trying to get up field."

15 Firing Cam Cameron

Something seemed off right before halftime of the Ravens-Redskins game during the 2012 season. Baltimore had under a minute to try and drive down the field to possibly add a field goal, or maybe more, to its 21–14 lead. But on the first play of the drive, from Baltimore's 13, Ray Rice was given a handoff that went nowhere. The Ravens immediately called a timeout, which didn't appear to make much sense considering they were backed up in their own territory. Out of the timeout, Joe Flacco completed a nine-yard pass to Dennis Pitta and then elected not to call timeout. Flacco ran for a five-yard scramble the next play for the first down, with the Ravens calling a timeout after that. On the final play of the half, Flacco completed a short pass to Ray Rice, and that was that.

But during that sequence, coach John Harbaugh laid into offensive coordinator Cam Cameron on the sideline, in a manner that hadn't publicly been seen before. Cameron looked past Harbaugh during the berating, and eventually Harbaugh let him be. So when the second half and overtime ended with Baltimore scoring only once more, enough was apparently enough. Cameron was let go the following morning, with the Ravens 9–4. Nationally, it was a bizarre story—a playoff contender leading the AFC North firing its offensive coordinator. In Baltimore, a large faction of the fan base had been waiting for this particular day for quite some time. To them, Cameron was seen as a hindrance to the offense performing the way it's capable of.

Harbaugh addressed the media the day after the decision and was inclined not to say much about the details on Cameron's dismissal.

"People are going to believe what they want to believe," Harbaugh said. "It's what I believe is best going forward for our offense and for our football team. That's not to say anybody can't do the job or didn't do the job. Cam was doing a heck of a job here—doing a heck of a job here for a long time. Nobody knows that better than me, and nobody has stated that more times. I believe that. I also believe that right now at this time, the timing says this is the best thing, and this is what we're going to do."

But was it Harbaugh's decision? Though he's maintained that to this day, there were reports indicating otherwise. Drew Forrester at radio station WNST (1570 AM) detailed what he heard from a source within the organization.

"The Ravens dropped an unthinkable game in Washington on Sunday afternoon. At some point on Sunday night, [owner Steve] Bisciotti stepped in and said, essentially, 'Cam needs to go…now,'" Forrester wrote. "It must have been more demanding than that, because Harbaugh apparently didn't fight the owner on it, simply saying, 'Let's meet at the facility in the morning and decide where to go from here.'"

It was also an open secret within the organization that Cameron and Joe Flacco did not have a good working relationship. When asked if the Ravens were pleased with the move the following Wednesday, one Ravens starter on the offensive side of the ball told me, "Oh yeah," and grinned from ear to ear. The disapproval for Cameron wasn't personal. By all accounts he was a great person to be around in a non-football setting. But when it came to the game, a philosophical disconnect developed that hurt the team.

The front office has denied involvement in Cameron's dismissal. When asked by USA Today Sports if he or Bisciotti had anything to do with firing Cameron, general manager Ozzie Newsome offered nine no's in response.

"John has to stand before his coaching staff and his players," Newsome said, "and if, at any one point, do they think that he is overly influenced by Steve or I, then he loses his staff and his players. It has to be him."

Before the Redskins game, the Ravens had five games in 2012 in which they didn't reach 300 total yards of offense. This was the year Flacco was supposed to elevate his game to the next level, and it wasn't happening yet. By removing Cameron from the equation, Flacco now had a chance to prove his former offensive coordinator was hindering his progress.

After an all-around poor showing against Denver, in interim offensive coordinator Jim Caldwell's first game, Flacco began to come into his own. In Week 16, Flacco had a spectacular day against the Giants in a 33–14 win. After resting the majority of Week 17's game against Cincinnati, Flacco went to work in the postseason. In four games, he threw for 1,140 yards, 11 touchdowns, and zero interceptions. He helped Baltimore win its second world championship and was named Super Bowl MVP.

Whether it was Bisciotti barking orders or Harbaugh's decision alone, one thing is apparent. The move to fire Cameron was the correct one to make. The results speak for themselves.

16 2000 and 2012: Some Similarities, Yet Different

Oftentimes in sports, pundits and prognosticators will draw parallels between different teams, players, or coaches to compare and contrast the similarities and differences. In professional basketball, LeBron James' Miami Heat are often compared to Michael Jordan's Chicago Bulls. As far as NFL coaching, greats such as Vince Lombardi, Tom Landry, and George Halas are oftentimes spoken in the same vein.

And then, of course, teams themselves are compared from one season to another, especially those that win championships. Baseball historians will dissect the various nuances for each of the 27 New York Yankees World Series titles.

The Ravens are no different, with their 2000 and 2012 Super Bowl seasons compared by both fans and the media alike. It's easy when so many eye-popping similarities poke out. Yet possibly more intriguing are the differences each team possessed in its route to a title.

First, the similarities: we'll start with adversity. Each team needs to overcome some level of adversity to win a title. And both the 2000 and 2012 teams were no different. Both teams endured three-game losing streaks where the offense struggled to move the ball. The 2000 team lost three games in a row to Washington, Tennessee, and Pittsburgh, scoring a combined 15 points in the process. Nothing was working right offensively, and despite a strong defense, it was tough to overcome. The 2012 team did just the same, though later in the season in December. Two of the same foes were the same, as Baltimore lost consecutive games to Pittsburgh, Washington, and Denver.

Though Baltimore was able to score 20 against Pittsburgh, 28 against Washington, and 17 against Denver, it was the offense that let it down in each contest. The best example could be the Washington game, in which the Baltimore offense put up 21 in the first half. In the second half, the offense unraveled and was only able to score one touchdown in a 31–28 overtime loss. Offensive coordinator Cam Cameron was fired shortly thereafter.

Each team began their Super Bowl season 5–1 and became instant title contenders. The humbling experiences that later followed helped mold the teams into what they eventually became. They were briefly grounded due to the losing streaks, only to overcome the obstacles when it mattered most.

Baltimore entered the 2000 and 2012 playoffs as the No. 4 seed and was forced to play in the wild-card round. It got to host one game before going on the road the next two rounds. In the first round of the 2000 playoffs, Baltimore beat Denver 21–3. In 2012 the Ravens beat Indianapolis 24–9. Both Ravens teams then had to beat the No. 1 and 2 seeds in the AFC playoffs to reach the Super Bowl.

The only difference in the end was that in 2000 the New York Giants were the NFC's No. 1 seed and in 2012 the San Francisco 49ers were seeded No. 2. In both Super Bowl games, the Ravens scored 34 points in victory.

One constant was present on those 2000 and 2012 teams, and that was Ray Lewis. Lewis had recently become one of the vocal leaders of Baltimore's 2000 team. By 2012 he commanded the

Ravens' locker room. Nothing changed on that front, except for the type of seasons Lewis put together.

Here's where the differences start to come together. In 2000 Lewis had 137 tackles and three sacks in 16 games. In 2012 Lewis tore his right triceps in Week 6 and was forced to miss the remaining 10 games of the regular season. Lewis did make it back for the postseason, however.

Sticking with the defensive side of the ball, Baltimore's defense in 2000 will go down in history as one of the best to ever compete in an NFL season. The 2012 defense, not so much. The Ravens ranked 17th in total defense during its second Super Bowl title run, allowing 350.9 yards per game. But the defense was opportunistic and timely with turnovers. In the postseason, the Ravens created six interceptions and forced five fumbles through four games. Without the defense stepping up, it's unlikely the Ravens would have won the Super Bowl.

In addition, the Ravens' offense in 2000 was dreadful. All that was required was for quarterback Trent Dilfer to not make many mistakes. Joe Flacco tied an NFL record held by Joe Montana by throwing 11 touchdowns in a postseason without an interception. Flacco was named Super Bowl XLVII MVP, whereas Lewis was named Super Bowl XXXV MVP.

There were some unique similarities both teams shared en route to a world championship. But both teams certainly had different identities.

17 Joe Flacco, Ray Rice, and the 2008 Draft

Entering the 2008 draft, the Ravens were in dire need of a quarterback. The organization had struggled finding a quarterback to take the offense to the next level, and coach John Harbaugh and the organization were well aware of the type of talent NFL teams need if they wanted to compete for Super Bowl championships.

The top two quarterbacks in an otherwise weak quarterback class were Matt Ryan, out of Boston College, and Joe Flacco, out of Delaware. The next best quarterback was Michigan's Chad Henne, and he wasn't considered a first-round quarterback by most scouts. In addition, it was assumed Ryan would wind up as a top five pick, meaning Baltimore's shot at a quarterback hinged on drafting Flacco in the first round or trading back to take a quarterback in the second round.

So the Ravens sent a crew including Harbaugh, general manager Ozzie Newsome, newly hired offensive coordinator Cam Cameron, and scouting executive Eric DeCosta to observe Flacco working out on Delaware's campus to see if he could be the kind of player that could lead the Ravens under Harbaugh's watch.

The Ravens continued to do their due diligence, inviting Flacco to meet with the organization in Baltimore before the 2008 draft. Again, Flacco impressed. If Baltimore had the opportunity, it was clear whom the organization wanted.

"I just felt like he was a guy that would do whatever it took to overcome whatever to be the best that he was going to be," Harbaugh said. "That's proven to be true. He's a guy that no matter what happens, no matter what criticism he felt in front of him, no matter what disappointments he might have, he steps up and he bounces back and he comes back and goes to work."

So with the 18th overall pick in the first round, the Ravens selected Flacco to run the offense. Sure, Flacco had his ups and downs. But by year five, Flacco won the city of Baltimore over, bringing a second Super Bowl title home and earning a five-year, $120.6 million deal that became the largest contract in NFL history. Flacco's 63 regular and postseason wins in his first five years are also an NFL record. He also was able to lead Baltimore to a postseason win in each of his first five seasons, which is an incredible feat when compared to other great NFL quarterbacks of his era.

But when the Ravens selected Flacco in the first round of that particular draft, they weren't done addressing offense. Sitting available at the 55th overall pick in the second round was running back Ray Rice, who played college football at Rutgers.

Rice became a household name nationally during his sophomore season when he ran for 1,794 yards and 20 touchdowns. He helped place Rutgers, never known for its football, on the national stage by leading it to a top 10 ranking by mid-November. After a 2,000-yard season as a junior, Rice declared for the draft.

Despite his skill, Rice wasn't thought of as a first-round prospect. A lot of that was based on his size. Despite an almost 200-pound frame, Rice only stood 5'8", making him one of the smaller backs in the class. One of the negatives consistently listed by draft experts was that he couldn't move the pile, that he was a one-dimensional back who couldn't handle contact.

However, a strong combine performance elevated his status to the second and third rounds, which still seems like an incredible value today.

With the Ravens needing to address the running back position, they took Rice with their second-round pick. This draft, Harbaugh's first, proved to be an abundance of riches with the first two picks. In combined passing, rushing, and receiving totals, Flacco and Rice accounted for 26,331 yards and 148 touchdowns in their first five years together.

The only other draft class that compares is the first one in Ravens history, when Baltimore selected tackle Jonathan Ogden and linebacker Ray Lewis in the first round. Once again, the Ravens hit a home run with a draft class that ultimately led them to a Super Bowl championship.

18 The Historic First Game

The Baltimore fans weren't going to disappoint their new team when the Ravens were set to kick off their inaugural season at home on September 1, 1996.

When the Colts played their last season in Baltimore, fans and owner Robert Irsay were at odds with each other. The product on the field was sloppy, and drafting John Elway only to get nothing close to fair compensation when he bailed for Denver was aggravating. Fans stopped going to Memorial Stadium in protest of the regime, not necessarily in anger or apathy toward the team.

Then Irsay packed the team's bags and moved to Indianapolis. Baltimore fans were devastated. With the Ravens the city's new team, they were sure to come out and support the team in the opener no matter what.

A crowd of 64,124 fans arrived at Memorial Stadium to cheer the Ravens on. Turnouts were in the low 30,000s, or even less, during the end of the Colts era. (One Associated Press report stated that the last Baltimore Colts game, against the Houston Oilers, drew only 18,000 fans.) The excitement was back in Baltimore.

The Ravens wanted to do their part to reward the fans for their support. The first game was against the Oakland Raiders, a team hoping to build on an 8–8 season the year before. The packed stadium of fans donning purple and black was reminiscent of the past, when attendees would let loose during the glory days of Johnny Unitas, Lenny Moore, Art Donovan, and other Colts legends.

Vinny Testaverde made history by scoring the first touchdown in Baltimore Ravens history. The score came at the end of the first quarter on a nine-yard run, giving the Ravens an early 7–0 lead, much to the crowd's delight. However, Oakland would respond with 14 unanswered points thanks to two touchdown receptions by Raiders receiver Tim Brown, with quarterback Billy Joe Hobert tossing both. The Raiders would use those scores to head into half-time with a 14–7 lead.

The Ravens were able to add two field goals thanks to Matt Stover to cut the game to 14–13 in the third quarter, keeping the home fans on the edge of their seats.

After Oakland punted to start the fourth quarter, Testaverde completed two consecutive passes for 52 yards. Then the ground game got going, and Baltimore's second scoring drive was capped with a one-yard Earnest Byner touchdown run. The Ravens were now up 19–14 with a raucous crowd behind them. With under five minutes remaining in the game, Oakland faced a fourth-and-4 from its own 36 and elected to punt. Baltimore executed its four-minute offense and ran out the clock, not giving the Raiders a chance to come back. The Baltimore Ravens won their first game in franchise history.

It would be one of only four wins that season, but a monumental one at that. The 64,124 fans who showed up to watch the city's new team win received their money's worth. Football was back, and the love affair between it and Baltimore was stronger than ever.

19 Hiring Brian Billick

As fate would have it, one of the best things that could have happened during the Ravens' coaching search in early 1999 was Minnesota suffering a stunning defeat to Atlanta in the 1998 NFC Championship Game. The Vikings had only lost one game all season

Brian Billick, shown here during his second training camp with the Ravens as head coach in July 2000, took Baltimore to the promised land at the end of the season, winning Super Bowl XXXV over the New York Giants.

and were favorites to be the NFC's representative in the Super Bowl. Yet they lost and had to head home earlier than most expected.

Had the Vikings won, they and offensive coordinator Brian Billick would have been preparing for the biggest game of their lives. The Baltimore Ravens would never have had the opportunity to interview Billick for the coaching job that was suddenly open due to the organization electing not to re-sign Ted Marchibroda. The Ravens were reportedly also interested in either George Seifert or Mike Holmgren, but Seifert took a job with the Carolina Panthers, and Holmgren canceled a trip to Baltimore before accepting the coaching job at Seattle.

Pittsburgh defensive coordinator Jim Haslett had also interviewed for the job, but it was Billick who stood out. During the 1998 regular season, the Vikings scored an astonishing 556 points and accrued 6,264 total yards. Those were impressive numbers that Art Modell wanted to bring to Baltimore.

Billick accepted the job on January 20, 1999, becoming Baltimore's second head coach in franchise history. He signed a six-year contract.

"Six years is a minimum gamble," Ravens owner Art Modell said at Billick's introductory press conference. "This is a good man. We waited for the opportunity to interview Brian, and we're glad we did. He has a wonderful passion for the game."

The move proved to be an immediate success. The Ravens recorded their first non-losing season in 1999, posting an 8–8 record that included a four-game winning streak in Weeks 13 to 16. The defense was beginning to jell as one of the best in the NFL, with the offense continuing to work out its various kinks.

Billick would reach his pinnacle in 2000 as Baltimore reached the postseason for the first time under his guidance. To help his team focus, he forbade the team from uttering the words "playoffs" or "Super Bowl." Maybe the gimmick worked, as the Ravens

Brian Billick Highlights

Years as NFL Head Coach (all with the Ravens): 9 (1999–2007)
Record: 80–64 (.556)
Playoff Appearances: 4
Playoff Record: 5–3 (.625)
Division Championships: 2
Average Wins Per Season: 8.9
10+ Win Seasons: 4
Super Bowl Record: 1–0

defense overpowered all four opponents en route to a Super Bowl XXXV win over the New York Giants.

Now that the Ravens had won a Super Bowl in year five of their existence, it was time to keep winning games. Baltimore returned to the postseason in 2001 but lost in the divisional round of the playoffs to Pittsburgh. In 2002, with a huge roster turnover, Billick's Ravens went 7–9 and failed to reach the postseason. However, given the lack of talent on the roster, the season was deemed a success.

However, the longer Billick was removed from the Super Bowl championship season, the more people forgot about the achievement he was a part of. As an offensive guru in Minnesota, he could never put together a consistent offensive team in Baltimore. Then again, Minnesota had Cris Carter and Randy Moss at receiver, Robert Smith at running back, and Randall Cunningham (in his last productive season) at quarterback. There was a reason that offense was as prolific as it was. The Ravens never came close to matching that kind of talent on the offensive side of the ball during the Billick era. When the Ravens took quarterback Kyle Boller with the 19th overall pick in 2003, he was looked at as the guy to get Billick over the hump. What transpired was the reverse, something Billick later admitted to.

20 Firing Brian Billick

A day after the Ravens ended their 2007 season, Brian Billick's contract was terminated by the organization. He had spent nine years as the coach of the Ravens, delivering a Super Bowl title in 2000 and making three other postseason appearances.

But it was the reported internal discord within the organization that did Billick in. Even though the Ravens had a 13–3 record in

2006, the best in franchise history, the 5–11 campaign experienced in 2007 was too much to overcome. The worst part about Billick's final season was that during a nine-game losing streak, the Ravens fell in overtime to the Miami Dolphins. The Dolphins hadn't won a game all season, and notched their only victory against Billick's Baltimore squad.

Owner Steve Bisciotti bought a majority stake in the franchise in 2004, and his philosophy was that you can't reward past success when the present and future are at stake. Bisciotti didn't like the direction the organization was heading in, which is why he pulled the trigger on Billick's dismissal.

What was strange, however, was that a *Baltimore Sun* report just weeks prior to Billick's firing cited an anonymous source close to Bisciotti giving the head coach a vote of confidence, and saying that he'd be back for the 2008 season. In fact, Ravens beat reporter Aaron Wilson, who's now with the *Baltimore Sun* but with the *Carroll County Times* during the Billick years, wrote that Billick was told he'd return for at least another year.

"From a general standpoint, I think my record speaks for itself," Billick said in mid-December 2007. "It has been a tough year clearly, but I don't know how dramatically I've changed. If I was a good coach last year when we went 13–3, how is that different now one year later?"

However, on December 31, 2007, Bisciotti addressed reporters about his decision to can Billick after a disappointing 5–11 campaign.

"I believed that it was time for a change, I believed that we have the nucleus of a team that can get back to the Super Bowl, and we felt that in the next five years we had a better chance with a new coach than leaving Brian in that position," Bisciotti said.

He added, "It's a gut feeling. I have one job here, and that's to have a leader that I think gives us the best chance. We have been losing more than winning lately." It wasn't just Billick who was let go, either. It was the entire coaching staff, including defensive coordinator Rex Ryan, who was becoming a trendy name for potential head coaching positions.

Players were surprised with the decision. Former Ravens receiver Mark Clayton received a text message from a friend with the news, and he told a *Baltimore Sun* reporter he didn't believe it.

"Whenever you have a bad year, somebody's got to be held accountable," offensive tackle Jonathan Ogden told the *Baltimore Sun* the day Billick was let go. "By no means is it ever [the fault of] the head coach, but they take the fall unfortunately. Things happened to us this year, but it's just the unfortunate nature of the way this business is. Produce or you're not going to be here."

Billick's tenure ended with an 80–64 record over nine seasons.

"Brian Billick had clearly lost the locker room support and was being openly challenged by veteran players," Wilson said. "It was a negative situation that the owner, Steve Bisciotti, was aware of. He was also frustrated with the offense not making more progress and the quarterback situation. Ultimately, Brian's message had grown stale with older players who had heard it all from him before. It wasn't all his fault, there was a talent void at key positions, too. However, the coach is always held responsible for how the team performs on the field. The firing was understandable, and Brian has no hard feelings."

21 John Harbaugh and "the Team, the Team, the Team"

After making the tough decision to fire former Super Bowl champion Brian Billick, owner Steve Bisciotti needed to find a coach he could trust and rely on. It didn't have to be a well-known commodity, as long as the coach could get the job done.

Ravens head coach John Harbaugh directs training camp in June 2013, fresh off of winning the franchise's second Super Bowl. Harbaugh is the only coach to lead his team to at least one playoff victory in each of his first five seasons.

So when the Ravens hired John Harbaugh, a defensive backs coach and special teams coordinator during his assistant coaching days in Philadelphia, there were a lot of puzzled looks around Baltimore. Who was John Harbaugh? Did they mean Jim Harbaugh, the former NFL player who'd had a one-year stint with the Ravens? Who is this guy?

Baltimore fans soon learned. A team-first oriented coach, Harbaugh put his stamp on the program early.

"I'm a football coach. That's what I wanted to be, and that's what I am. I'm excited to be the head coach of the Ravens," Harbaugh stated on the Ravens' team website. "It's a big job that provides the opportunity to work with some outstanding people. I grew up as a coach's son, and I understand the core and fundamental principles that define a great football team. At the heart of football are three foundations: first is the team, second is the team, and third is the team. We'll stick with that from beginning to end. We will take care of one another. We will stand shoulder to shoulder. We will push each other to the highest levels. We will lift each other up. Our style of play will be tough, fast, physical, and smart."

There were a few names up for the job in addition to Harbaugh. They were Dallas Cowboys offensive coordinator Jason Garrett, Ravens defensive coordinator Rex Ryan, and New York Jets offensive coordinator Brian Schottenheimer. In a 2011 interview with the *Baltimore Sun*, Bisciotti explained why he hired Harbaugh over someone like Ryan, hinting there might have been a fractured locker room at the time.

"From a chemistry standpoint...we really liked John and we thought it was going to be tougher for Rex to bring the whole team together after him spending 10 years on one side of the ball that was the dominant side of the ball," Bisciotti told the *Sun*.

Being that Harbaugh wasn't a highly sought-after name when he was hired, he had a lot to prove. And he needed to do so early in a city like Baltimore. In 2008, his first season and with a rookie quarterback in Joe Flacco, Harbaugh helped guide his team to an 11–5 record and playoff berth. The Ravens then reached the AFC Championship Game before falling to Pittsburgh.

Harbaugh kept up his winning ways, reaching the playoffs not only in his first season, but in his first five seasons. In that time span, he recorded 54 regular season wins and a 9–4 playoff record, which included three AFC Championship Game appearances and one Super Bowl title. Since the 1970 NFL-AFL merger, Harbaugh is the only coach to direct a team to a playoff win in each of his first five seasons.

Bo Schembechler's Influence

When John Harbaugh was a child, his father, Jack Harbaugh, was an assistant coach on Bo Schembechler's coaching staff at the University of Michigan. Therefore, Harbaugh, and his brother, Jim (who later played under Schembechler), were around him quite a bit. Schembechler's mantra "the team, the team, team" is something John Harbaugh has borrowed and brought to Baltimore. In the hallway leading to the indoor practice facility, those words are displayed prominently on the wall. Before Super Bowl XLVII, Jack Harbaugh said, "I see Bo's fingerprints all over the Ravens football team and all over the San Francisco 49ers team, and there could not be anyone that you could better emulate."

After winning Super Bowl XLVII, Harbaugh reflected on Bisciotti's decision to hire him a day later. "For Steve Bisciotti to hire me…I mean, who else would've done that?" Harbaugh said. "To me, Steve Bisciotti is just a different kind of thinker. He doesn't look at things the way everybody else does. You sit down with him for five minutes, and you can see that. That's why he's been so successful."

In terms of his leadership, one quote stood out after a devastating 23–20 loss to New England in the 2011 AFC Championship Game. He invoked the famous mantra of former Michigan football coach Bo Schembechler, making the case that you win as a team and you lose as a team. It's likely one of the traits that got him hired in the first place.

"It's what we do, it's how we play," Harbaugh said. "The team, the team, the team. That's not going to change."

22 "In Ozzie We Trust"

History has shown Baltimore made the right decision in taking Ed Reed 24th overall in the 2002 NFL Draft. Thing is, it barely happened. The Ravens staff gave Reed a slight edge over Florida cornerback Lito Sheppard on its draft board, with both players still available at the 24th overall pick.

Steve Bisciotti was still a minority owner at the time, but present for the decision. As Bisciotti recalls, the Ravens assigned the same number grade to Reed and Sheppard, but Reed was listed one spot higher. With cornerbacks deemed more valuable as a whole, Bisciotti wondered why the Ravens would prefer Reed to Sheppard if they graded the same.

"I don't understand this. If they both have the same grade, why would you not take a corner over a safety?" Bisciotti said he told general manager Ozzie Newsome.

Newsome replied, "Because I am true to my board."

The board worked in this instance, much like it has throughout Ozzie Newsome's career in Baltimore. Newsome was promoted to Baltimore's general manager position in that 2002 off-season when the organization picked Reed in the first round. Since then, Newsome has excelled as one of the standout general managers in the entire NFL.

There's an old slogan around the Under Armour Performance Center, which is, "In Ozzie We Trust." When the Ravens released running back Willis McGahee, tight end Todd Heap, wide receiver Derrick Mason, and nose tackle Kelly Gregg in 2011, the answer inside the organization was always, "In Ozzie we trust."

When Reed and safety Bernard Pollard were released early in the 2013 off-season, and when wide receiver Anquan Boldin was traded to San Francisco, the answer was still the same. Newsome is always thinking ahead with a plan. The moves in 2011 turned out fine as Baltimore reached the AFC Championship Game. After letting some key players from the 2012 Super Bowl championship team go, Newsome was able to sign outside linebacker Elvis Dumervil, safety Michael Huff, and defensive tackle Chris Canty. When Newsome makes a move, it's well calculated. Bisciotti learned that during the

2002 draft when Newsome expressed his desire to take Reed. Since then, Bisciotti has stepped back to allow Newsome and his team to call all the shots in the personnel department.

"Ozzie's credibility is what stands out the most," Ravens coach John Harbaugh stated on BaltimoreRavens.com. "And it's not just about what he has accomplished. To me, it's his commitment and focus while striving to do more."

Newsome has had a long and successful NFL career. Newsome was selected by the Cleveland Browns in the first round of the 1978 draft after a standout college career at Alabama. Newsome went on to become one of the better tight ends in league history, recording 7,980 receiving yards and 47 touchdowns during a 13-year career. Only Tony Gonzalez and Shannon Sharpe have recorded better career numbers as tight ends.

After retiring, Newsome's first non-player NFL job was with the Browns, where he became an assignment scout in 1991. By 1994 Newsome was the Browns director of pro personnel and then received the new title of vice president of player personnel when the organization moved to Baltimore in 1996.

Even though it took another six years for Newsome to become the NFL's first black general manager, Newsome played a pivotal role in each Baltimore draft class. He helped the organization select tackle Jonathan Ogden and Ray Lewis in the first round of the 1996 draft. Newsome also had his hand in picking these key players prior to becoming GM: Peter Boulware (1997), Jamie Sharper (1997), Duane Starks (1998), Chris McAllister (1999), Jamal Lewis (2000), and Todd Heap (2001). Newsome's had a knack for evaluating talent, which has kept Baltimore in contention in most years since winning Super Bowl XXXV.

Newsome's formula has proven to work. As they say inside the Castle in Owings Mills, Maryland: "In Ozzie we trust."

"I think we have a process in place, and we'll stay true to the process," Newsome said. "The process is what has gotten us the success, and I think the process will be where we'll maintain it. So we'll stay true to that."

23 Ravens Uniforms through History

The first Baltimore Ravens uniforms were revealed in a ceremony at the Inner Harbor Gallery Mall, with quarterback Vinny Testaverde, defensive end Rob Burnett, and wide receiver Michael Jackson acting as the organization's models.

It was June 5, 1996, with the organization recently announcing it would be known as the Ravens on March 29, after a fan vote decided it. Now, they'd need their colors, after going through training camp wearing generic black attire.

So there they were, the colors of the Ravens: purple, black, and gold. Testaverde, Burnett, and Jackson were donning both the home and road jerseys. The original home tops were purple, worn by Testaverde and Jackson, with white numerals and lettering. The numbers had a gold outline around them. The white jerseys were in the same mold, with purple numerals and lettering, but with a double outline of white and black around the numbers.

The logo on the helmet, which was black, resembled a shield with a stylized *B* in the middle. Raven wings sprouted from the shield with the word *Ravens* typed out over the stylized *B*.

The Ravens wore black pants, with one white stripe down each side, with both the home and away tops during the inaugural season, becoming the first NFL franchise to wear an all-dark color scheme since the Vikings did in 1964.

The uniform changed slightly in 1997, with the numerals presented with a drop shadow effect. The Ravens decided to go with white pants with the purple jerseys, electing only to wear black pants with the road whites. In 1998, the Ravens decided to go with white pants for both sets of tops.

In 1999 the helmet changed to show a cartoon raven head as opposed to the shield with the stylized B. This was due to the fact that the Ravens lost a lawsuit from local artist Frederick E. Bouchat, who claimed he designed a logo eerily similar to what the Ravens used on their helmets. Bouchat sent his design to the Maryland Stadium Authority and was never compensated for it. Therefore, the Ravens dropped it from the helmet and placed the new raven head on it instead.

Up until 2000 there was a raven with its wings spread on each shoulder of the jerseys. This was removed, and in its place was a coat of arms, located on the pants previously, with the Maryland state flag designed into it. With the coat of arms gone, a stylized *B* was now worked into the pants.

No major changes were made until 2004, when the Ravens added an all-black alternate uniform. The black pants were solid and the top was styled just like the purple one. In 2008 the Ravens began mixing and matching uniform combinations, with the team wearing black pants with white tops and white pants with black tops.

In 2012 the Ravens added a black patch to the upper left of each jersey top that read "Art." This was to honor former owner

When Wearing All Black

In a day and age when players want to look good each game, Baltimore's roster typically gets excited when it brings out the all-black uniforms. When the Ravens decided to wear the all-black uniforms in 2012 in a home game against Pittsburgh, Jacoby Jones, in his first year with the franchise, couldn't contain his excitement to one of the team's reporters. "Man I've been waiting to wear those black jerseys all year," Jones said. "That black is pretty solid. It's mean. It makes a statement." The Ravens generally have success in the attire. Since its inception, the Ravens are 9–3, and 6–1 under John Harbaugh, when wearing all black.

Art Modell, who died at the age of 87 on September 6, 2012. The organization wore the patch on the jersey from Week 2 through the Super Bowl win.

24 Joe Flacco's 2012 Postseason Run

It was year five for Joe Flacco. He had been to two AFC Championship Games already and had a full understanding of the offense, even if there was some discord between himself and former Ravens offensive coordinator Cam Cameron at times. Flacco was thought to be poised for a breakout year when he'd surpass the 4,000-yard mark for the first time and prove that the Ravens could win with offense for the first time in team history.

Flacco put in a stellar training camp and preseason before the 2012 season opener against Cincinnati. And then Flacco showed the NFL his prowess, throwing for 299 yards and two touchdowns in a 44–13 win over the Bengals.

Sometimes things don't go according to the plan. With people across the NFL landscape buying into Flacco as an upper-tier quarterback all of a sudden, Flacco's numbers reverted back to what NFL fans were accustomed to. He was able to lead the Ravens to 10 wins in the 2012 regular season, but threw for 3,817 yards and 22 touchdowns—both numbers lower than what the expectations had called for, even though the yardage total was a career high.

However, when you reach the postseason, you're granted a new season. The Ravens won the AFC North and earned the No. 4 seed, giving Flacco and the offense ample time to regroup and start over. And the offense was already feeling better about itself with Jim Caldwell assuming offensive coordinator duties in Week 15 against Denver. Though the offense was out of sync for Caldwell's debut, it

Ravens QB Joe Flacco looks to throw during the first half of Super Bowl XLVII vs. the San Francisco 49ers. During the Ravens' 2012 postseason run, Flacco passed for 1,140 yards and 11 TDs with no picks in Baltimore's four victories, culminating in a championship and Super Bowl MVP honors for Flacco.

looked outstanding in a 33–14 thrashing of the New York Giants, which saw Flacco throw for 309 yards and two scores.

Though Baltimore lost four of its final five games (which included the season finale against Cincinnati with most of its starters resting), there was some momentum brewing that was moving under the radar.

Baltimore was fortunate as the No. 4 seed to open with Indianapolis at home. Heading into the contest, it looked to be a favorable matchup for the Ravens. The Colts had a rookie quarterback, Andrew Luck, under center, and the defense wasn't one many pundits thought could get after Flacco consistently. In addition, the Ravens decided to start Bryant McKinnie at left tackle after spending the season on the bench. One of the reasons for the move was that left guard Jah Reid was placed on season-ending injured reserve with a toe injury, which required the starting line to shift.

The Ravens could have gone with Bobbie Williams or Ramon Harewood at guard, both of whom had started games during the 2012 season. However, the Ravens went with McKinnie, who started each game in 2011 but lost his job after a tumultuous off-season.

With McKinnie at left tackle, Michael Oher moved from left to right tackle, and Kelechi Osemele moved from right tackle to left guard. Matt Birk stayed at center, and Marshal Yanda remained at right guard. As it turned out, this offensive line proved to be the best five Baltimore could have trotted out there.

With a reshaped line in front of him, Flacco excelled against the Colts. Though he only completed 12 of 23 passes, Flacco threw for 282 yards and two touchdowns in a 24–9 wild-card round win. Flacco was only sacked one time and made all the decisions you'd want your quarterback to make. For Flacco, step one was completed.

Now it was time to go on the road and face a Denver Broncos team led by Peyton Manning, which had won 11 games in a row. Very few reporters and analysts were giving the Ravens a chance, considering they'd have to defeat Manning and the Broncos in a freezing atmosphere in Denver.

Down 7–0, thanks to a 90-yard punt return for a touchdown by Broncos specialist Trindon Holliday, Flacco used his arm to get the Ravens back in the thick of things. On a second-and-2 with just over 10:30 left in the first quarter, Flacco dropped back to pass and saw a streaking Torrey Smith splitting Denver's cover 2 defense down the middle of the field. Flacco let loose a deep throw and hit Smith in stride, with Smith finishing off a 59-yard touchdown to tie the game.

Denver would take a 21–14 lead in the second quarter with the home crowd growing increasingly louder inside Sports Authority Field at Mile High. Manning had already thrown two touchdowns as the Denver offense was beginning to click against an improving Baltimore defense.

But Flacco and Smith weren't ready to go away. With 43 seconds left in the first half, the Ravens had moved the ball to the Denver 32-yard line, which was helped by a missed Matt Prater field-goal attempt.

From the 32, Flacco dropped back to pass, looking for Smith again. In textbook fashion, Flacco lofted a fade down the right side-line to Smith, with Broncos cornerback Champ Bailey in coverage. The ball was thrown to give Smith the best chance to make a play on the ball, which the young receiver did. Smith jumped up to snag the ball with Bailey appearing to have made a bad judgment on it. Smith then trotted the additional five yards into the end zone to tie the game heading into halftime.

The Ravens and Broncos traded scores in the third quarter, with Holliday returning the opening kickoff 104 yards for a touchdown. Ray Rice tied the game late in the quarter with a one-yard touchdown run. With defenses tightening up, it wasn't until 7:11 to go in the fourth quarter that Denver was able to pull back ahead with a 17-yard touchdown pass from Manning to Demaryius Thomas.

Flacco and the Ravens moved the ball down to the Denver 31 with just under four minutes to go. But on fourth down, Flacco's pass to tight end Dennis Pitta fell incomplete. It looked bleak for Baltimore at the time, though there was still enough time if the defense could give Flacco just one more chance.

After giving up one first down on Denver's ensuing possession, the Ravens were set to get the ball back with 1:09 remaining. Denver fans were beginning to celebrate inside Sports Authority Field at Mile High. It didn't appear possible the Ravens could rally, right?

Wrong. All it takes is a little time and a strong arm, both of which worked in Flacco's favor this January night.

Facing a third-and-3 from the Baltimore 30 and just 42 seconds left, Flacco took the snap out of shotgun and began dropping back. With a perfect pocket developing, he stepped up and saw Jacoby Jones with a shot at getting behind the Denver secondary. Flacco cocked his arm back and let loose his patented deep throw. What happened next can be looked at in one of two ways: 1) it was an amazing throw from Flacco to Jones, one that got just enough air to get over the secondary and into the arms of a deep threat that scored the game-tying touchdown; 2) it was a horrible defensive play from Broncos safety Rahim Moore, who admitted as much after the game, telling the *Denver Post* the "season ended on me."

With both teams heading to overtime, the game was going to come down to which quarterback didn't make the first mistake. It just so happened that the signal caller to mess up would be Manning, one of the NFL's greatest quarterbacks to ever play. His interception late in the first overtime period gave Baltimore a chance to win the game.

Baltimore capitalized on Manning's mistake. Using the ground game, the Ravens got down to Denver's 29 in the second OT and called on kicker Justin Tucker to win the game. Tucker made a 47-yard attempt and sent Baltimore to the AFC Championship Game.

Once again, the Ravens weren't expected to win. After all, they were facing Tom Brady and the New England Patriots. The Patriots were looking to avenge a regular season loss in Baltimore, one that the Ravens won with a game-winning field goal. But the Ravens were a team of destiny, led by Flacco and his suddenly superb level of play. Baltimore won 28–13 and earned a berth in Super Bowl XLVII.

And in the Super Bowl against San Francisco it was more of the same. Flacco got the Ravens out to an early lead thanks to three

Good Joe Flacco vs. Bad Joe Flacco

Up until the 2012 postseason, there wasn't a level of consistency present in Joe Flacco's game. Sometimes he'd look like a top five quarterback. Other times, not so much. Due to Flacco's inconsistencies, there was always a worry over which Flacco would show up: Good Joe or Bad Joe. Here are two examples each of Good Joe and Bad Joe throughout Flacco's career:

Good Joe No. 1 In a 34–3 win over Cleveland in 2009, Flacco was able to carve up the Browns secondary with ease. He finished the day 25-of-35 for 342 yards and a touchdown.

Bad Joe No. 1 Flacco might not have played a worse game in his career than he did against Jacksonville in 2011. He finished 21-of-38 for 137 yards, a touchdown, and an interception. He averaged just 3.6 yards per attempt, with 90 of those yards coming with under 5:22 remaining in the game.

Good Joe No. 2 Flacco played astonishingly well in the 2012 season opener against Cincinnati. He was efficient and showcased pinpoint accuracy. He finished 21-of-29 for 299 yards and two touchdowns.

Bad Joe No. 2 In a 15–10 loss to Cincinnati in 2010, Flacco only completed 43.6 percent of his passes (17-of-39) for 154 yards, a touchdown, and four interceptions. The four interceptions are a single-game high for Flacco.

touchdowns and 287 yards of passing. Up 28–6 early into the second half, the Ravens were able to hold on despite a long power outage in New Orleans' Superdome, which arguably led to the 49ers being able to regroup for a comeback attempt. But the Niners' bid fell short as the Ravens held on for a 34–31 win to stake their claim as Super Bowl champs.

All in all, Flacco completed 58 percent of his passes for 1,140 yards in the postseason. Flacco threw 11 touchdowns and zero interceptions, joining Joe Montana as the only other quarterback to accomplish that feat.

Flacco was rewarded with a five-year, $120.6 million contract after his postseason. Flacco may not have had the grandest regular season. But he won when it mattered most, putting in a postseason Ravens fans will never forget.

25 Dominance: The 2000 Defense

Very few teams can stake their claim as to having the best defense ever. One of the first to come to mind is the 1985 Chicago Bears, led by linebacker and NFL Defensive Player of the Year Mike Singletary. Another stellar defense in the running would be the 1976 Pittsburgh Steelers, which held teams to single digits in eight of their last nine regular season games.

The 1977 Atlanta Falcons' defense, dubbed the "Gritz Blitz," put pressure on quarterbacks all game, making life difficult for opposing offenses. It also gave up an average of only nine points per game.

The most recent defense to jump into the discussion was the one the 2000 Baltimore Ravens fielded. From start to finish, with the lone exception in Week 2 against Jacksonville, the Ravens rarely ceded ground. By the end of the season, the Ravens held teams to an average of 10.3 points per game, which was the best mark set by a defense since the Falcons' Gritz Blitz, which played a 14-game season. Baltimore's 10.3 points per game number holds the top spot since the NFL expanded to a 16-game season.

The Ravens also hold the record for fewest rushing yards allowed in a 16-game season at 970. Think about that: through 16 games, the Baltimore Ravens held opponents to under 1,000 yards on the ground. Even the 1969 Dallas Cowboys, which hold the record for fewest rushing yards allowed in a 14-game season, gave up 1,050 throughout the season. (This mark is also better than 17 defenses from the strike-shortened 1982 season that featured NFL teams playing just nine games each.)

The Ravens shut out four opponents in 2000—Pittsburgh, Cincinnati, Cleveland, and Dallas. Five additional teams failed to score 10 points. Only Jacksonville (36), Tennessee (23), and the New York Jets (20) reached the 20-point barrier.

In Week 4's 37–0 blowout over Cincinnati, the Ravens held the Bengals to 94 total yards. Cincinnati's leading rusher for the day was Corey Dillon, who picked up nine yards on 12 carries. The Bengals were only able to pick up seven first downs in 60 minutes of play. When the Ravens were at their best on defense, this was the kind of game they were capable of playing.

Despite playing with an offense that struggled mightily at times—including a five-game stretch where it couldn't score a touchdown—the Ravens' defense was able to dictate the time of possession battle. Even though the offense was forced to punt 86 times, opponents only averaged a time of possession of 26:41.

In four playoff games, the Ravens' defense only allowed 23 combined points. In fact, Baltimore's defense and special teams outscored Denver, Tennessee, Oakland, and the New York Giants 28–23 (Anthony Mitchell, a 90-yard TD return of a field-goal block vs. Tennessee; Ray Lewis, a 50-yard interception return for a TD vs. Tennessee; Duane Starks, a 49-yard interception return for a TD vs. New York Giants; and Jermaine Lewis, an 84-yard kickoff return for a TD vs. New York Giants).

The Ravens' franchise has described their play as "relentless" over the years, and it began with this unit. Not since the 1985 Bears did a defense intimidate its opponents the way the 2000 Baltimore Ravens did. Simply put, the defense was just *that* good.

26 Steve Bisciotti Buys the Ravens

Stephen J. Bisciotti was a C student while attending his alma mater of Salisbury State University. But Bisciotti's entrepreneurial spirit, as well as the motivating factors surrounding his life, are proof that collegiate accolades don't always define long-term success.

Bisciotti grew up in suburban Maryland and often attended Colts and Orioles games with his father. He'd venture out to Westminster with his family to see the Colts practice during training camp. A lifelong sports fan, being in the position he's in now was a pipe dream as a child.

But when Bisciotti was 23, he founded the business Aerotek with his cousin Jim Davis. The goal was to provide temporary staffing help to the aerospace and technology companies. They essentially began this business out of their homes with two full-time employees. Yet, in the first year of the company's existence, Bisciotti and Davis made $1.5 million in sales. Both men knew immediately they had a future with Aerotek.

Aerotek later became the Allegis Group, which became the largest privately owned staffing company in the United States.

Even though the city of Cleveland voted to raise tax revenue of $175 million to go toward the remodeling of Cleveland Stadium, owner Art Modell—who asked for the revenue raise—believed it wasn't enough to keep the Browns in Cleveland in the end. He moved the team, to secure the financial interest in the organization with his family.

However, he still had financial burdens to deal with. In 2000 Bisciotti bought a minority stake in the franchise. According to the

Ravens organization, Bisciotti's money in 2000 went toward securing free agents of interest that helped lead the team to a Super Bowl XXXV title.

Four years later, in 2004, Bisciotti purchased the majority stake in the Ravens and became the principal owner. Bisciotti is living out a boyhood dream to be involved in sports, though he prefers a behind-the-scenes approach. He's not the kind of owner who wants to be seen meddling in the affairs of his team. He prefers to put the right people in place and let them go to work.

"I'm okay if I'm one of the least known owners in pro sports," Bisciotti is quoted as saying on the Ravens' website.

Bisciotti's biggest project, from a financial standpoint, was building the Ravens' practice facility at 1 Winning Drive in Owings Mills. Dubbed "the Castle" for its medieval look, the Ravens work each day in a state-of-the-art and gorgeous building, with a private practice field in the backyard. On site is an indoor facility where the team practices in case of bad weather. It cost the organization $31 million and opened in October 2004. In 2012 Bisciotti allowed athletic apparel company Under Armour to purchase the naming rights to the facility, which is now officially called the Under Armour Performance Center.

One of the more risky decisions that Bisciotti made was hiring John Harbaugh to be Baltimore's head coach in 2008. Here was Harbaugh, a special teams coordinator and defensive backs coach in Philadelphia, who was relatively unknown to the public. Based on advice Bisciotti received, he interviewed Harbaugh and came away impressed. That decision, one the Baltimore fans were initially puzzled with, turned out to work in the long run. As of 2013 Harbaugh has accrued five consecutive trips to the playoffs, three AFC Championship Game appearances, and a Super Bowl championship.

Bisciotti was forced to make tough decisions as a 23-year-old head of an upstart staffing company. Now he sits in the M&T Bank

Bisciotti Wanted Jason Garrett First

The Ravens couldn't have been more fortunate to land John Harbaugh as their head coach in 2008. Harbaugh has taken Baltimore to the playoffs five consecutive years and delivered the organization a Super Bowl title. But Harbaugh was not owner Steve Bisciotti's first choice. Bisciotti wanted then–Cowboys offensive coordinator Jason Garrett, who was becoming a hot commodity due to the potency of his offenses.

After interviewing for the open job in 2008, Garrett decided to stay in Dallas. He ended up becoming the Cowboys' head coach but has dealt with a lot of distractions during his tenure. In 2012 Dallas and Baltimore met in Week 6, and Garrett addressed turning down the job to the Baltimore media in a conference call.

"Just at that time, I just felt, and my wife felt, it was the best thing for us to stay in Dallas," Garrett said. "We certainly have no regrets, and I'm sure the Ravens don't have any regrets, either. John Harbaugh has done a fantastic job with that team. They are one of the elite franchises in the league."

Stadium owners' suite, watching his decisions play out between the white lines of the football field.

Not bad for a C student out of Salisbury State.

27 Baltimore's First Postseason Game

It took five years and a second coach to do it, but Baltimore finally reached the playoffs after the first 16 games of the 2000 season.

The town was electric and ready for Baltimore's first second season to begin. Finishing second to Tennessee in the AFC Central, Baltimore earned a wild-card spot as the No. 4 spot. It opened by hosting Denver at PSINet Stadium.

Denver entered the game boasting the NFL's second-best offense, with running back Mike Anderson leading the way. Anderson ran for 1,487 yards (fourth best in the NFL) and 15 touchdowns (second best) during the 2000 regular season.

Early in the contest, Denver saw why the Ravens defense was so tough to go against. On Denver's first possession, quarterback Gus Frerotte threw an interception to Ray Lewis on just his second passing attempt of the game. The game would remain scoreless through the first quarter, but Jamal Lewis would give Baltimore a 7–0 advantage with a one-yard plunge early in the second quarter.

Denver answered with a 31-yard Jason Elam field goal, but that would be all the Broncos would muster offensively. The most bizarre play of the day came next on Baltimore's ensuing possession. Dilfer threw a pass to Jamal Lewis in the flat, which was bobbled. The ball then skidded off of Denver defensive back Terrell Buckley's hands. Tight end Shannon Sharpe was in the right place at the right time and snagged it himself. He then darted to the sideline and sped 58 yards to the end zone to put the Ravens up 14–3.

Jamal Lewis would add a 27-yard touchdown to his day in the third quarter, giving Baltimore a 21–3 lead that would eventually be the final score. But the bigger story of the day was how pedestrian the Ravens' defense made Denver's offense look that day. Anderson, who had the big regular season, was held to 40 yards on 15 carries. Frerotte finished 13-of-28 for 124 yards and an interception. It was the first time in 28 Denver postseason games that the Broncos went without a touchdown.

"I didn't really believe they ever saw a defense like ours," Ray Lewis said after the game.

28 Jamal Lewis, Baltimore's Bell Cow

When Phil Savage, a former Ravens player personnel staffer, returned to Owings Mills, Maryland, from a recruiting trip at the University

Jamal Lewis leaps over a Cleveland defender on his way to amassing 295 rushing yards on September 14, 2003. He went on to run for 2,066 yards that season.

of Tennessee, he came away impressed with a player eligible for the 2000 NFL Draft.

He reported to Ozzie Newsome, then the vice president of player personnel, with some news. The Tennessee running back who ran for 1,364 yards as a freshman, but tore his anterior cruciate ligament as a sophomore, was looking strong during a rehabilitation workout. Savage marveled at the athleticism this particular player showed, even if it wasn't in everyday football drills.

His name was Jamal Lewis, and he would be high on the Ravens' radar throughout the entire 1999 college football season.

"[Savage] came back, and he was talking about this player who was rehabbing an ACL injury and who was working out in a sand pit, and he marveled at how this player was working," Newsome recalled. "He came back and said, 'They have a player down at the University of Tennessee by the name of Jamal Lewis.' Well, the following year, it was during the bye week, Alabama played Tennessee the [third] Saturday in October. Jamal and I know that date quite well. I had the opportunity to go to the game…. There were probably, maybe, a dozen first-round picks in the game; Jamal was in the game, and so was Shaun Alexander. As the game went on, it was a very close game, but when a play needed to be made, Jamal stepped up and he had, I think, a 50- or 60-yard run to seal the game for the University of Tennessee."

The Ravens were hopeful of landing Lewis. With the way the 1999 NFL season played out, Baltimore became extremely lucky to have the opportunity to do so. Baltimore had traded its 1999 second-round pick to the Atlanta Falcons for their 2000 first-rounder. After reaching the Super Bowl in 1998, the Falcons had an unremarkable 1999 season and finished 5–11. The record gave the Falcons the fifth overall pick in the draft, which had just become Baltimore's.

The Browns had the first overall pick and chose Penn State defensive end Courtney Brown. The Redskins had the next two picks and chose Penn State linebacker LaVar Arrington and Alabama offensive tackle Chris Samuels. Selected fourth by the Bengals was Florida State receiver Peter Warrick.

Lewis was available, and the decision became a no-brainer for a team looking for a premier running back to add to the roster.

Coming off an 8–8 season that featured an outstanding defense, the Ravens wanted a back that could take on tacklers and run through them. Interestingly enough, the Ravens had Priest Holmes on the roster but still felt the need to upgrade. Baltimore selected Lewis, who was able to step in and contribute to Baltimore's legendary Super Bowl run. (Baltimore also acquired the 10th overall pick and selected receiver Travis Taylor. With the defense set, the Ravens had a clear focus on improving the offense.)

Lewis received 10 carries and totaled 23 yards in his first two games. Holmes, Baltimore's starter, ran for 119 yards on 27 carries in the season opener against Pittsburgh. Yet in Week 3, Lewis was handed the starting role. He was given nine carries and ran for 76 yards in a 19–6 loss to Miami. It was the next week, against Cincinnati, that saw Lewis break out onto the NFL scene.

Lewis began the game grinding yards out, picking up small gains before picking up a six-yard rush with a little over four minutes left in the first quarter. On the first play of the second quarter, Lewis ran in his first career touchdown from 11 yards out. However, with success comes failure, as Lewis lost his first career fumble later in the period.

Lewis began wearing down the defense, and his yards-per-attempt began increasing. He had a 15-yarder, an eight-yarder, a nine-yarder. It looked like he scored another touchdown, an eight-yarder, but it was nullified due to a holding penalty. Lewis finished the day with 116 yards and a touchdown in a 37–0 blowout.

Lewis started each game the remainder of the season, except for a Week 6 game against Jacksonville, and recorded double-digit carries in each contest. After a five-game offensive slump that saw the Ravens fail to score a touchdown, Lewis played a big part in getting the Ravens back on track. At Cincinnati on November 5, 2000, Lewis ran for 109 yards and caught three passes for an additional 70 yards. In the final six games of the regular season, Lewis ran for 725 yards, bringing his season total to 1,364. He then ran for 338 rushing yards in four playoff games, including 102 in Baltimore's 34–7 Super Bowl win over the New York Giants.

But Lewis wouldn't get to play during the 2001 season. During a training camp practice, nose tackle Kelly Gregg's helmet collided with Lewis' left knee, tearing his ACL and spraining his MCL. Lewis was done for the season, and Priest Holmes was no longer with the Ravens. Baltimore's repeat hopes were dashed early.

"I can sum this up by saying that the reason why we were able to win the Super Bowl in 2000 was because of Jamal Lewis," Newsome said. "But, I think the reason we didn't win in 2001 was that Jamal got hurt and we weren't able to replace him."

Lewis bounced back in 2002 with a 1,327, six-touchdown campaign. But it was 2003 that took Lewis' career into the upper echelon. Lewis ran for 2,066 yards, becoming the fifth running back to break the 2,000-yard mark. The second-best rushing year ever at the time, his season remains the third best in NFL history, behind Eric Dickerson's 2,105 yards with the Rams in 1984 and Adrian Peterson's 2,097 yards with the Vikings in 2012.

Lewis ran for 1,006 yards and seven touchdowns in 2004 (in 12 games played) but had a season-worst in Baltimore in 2005, rushing for just 906 yards and three touchdowns. With Steve McNair taking over as the starting quarterback in 2006, some pressure was lifted off of Lewis as he ran for 1,132 yards and nine touchdowns. On February 28, 2007, the Ravens released Lewis, though Newsome told reporters he was interested in re-signing him. However, Lewis ended up signing a deal with Cleveland, where he played his remaining three NFL seasons.

In Baltimore, Lewis carried the ball 1,822 times for 7,801 yards and 45 touchdowns in six seasons, all of which are franchise records. In his nine-year career, Lewis totaled 10,607 yards and 58 touchdowns. Lewis became the seventh Raven to enter the Ring of Honor, which became official with a ceremony at halftime of Baltimore's 2012 home contest against Cleveland.

"For a 20-year-old coming out of Atlanta, Georgia, to a city that I'd never been to, better yet a part of the country I'd never been to, it was just a great honor to play here for the years that I was here," Lewis said. "I learned a lot, was around a lot of great players."

29 From Trent Dilfer to Elvis Grbac

Hindsight is often 20/20, and with what transpired in the quarterback transition from Trent Dilfer to Elvis Grbac, a case can be made that this was one of the worst decisions made in Ravens history.

After the 2000 Super Bowl season, the Ravens were looking to upgrade the quarterback position, a spot it took Baltimore a long, long time to nail down. The Ravens started Tony Banks to open the 2000 season, and Banks got out to a solid start, throwing six touchdowns in his first two games (five coming in Week 2's thriller over Jacksonville). But as the season continued, Banks began to struggle. Coach Brian Billick went to his backup Trent Dilfer and never looked back. While Dilfer certainly didn't set the league on fire, he managed games appropriately and kept Baltimore in smart situations.

Dilfer would wind up being the team's quarterback for Super Bowl XXXV and earned a championship ring as a result. Then the off-season came and Dilfer certainly wanted to remain a Raven. Two thousand was his only season with the Ravens, and he felt he had done enough to stay around. He'd been a team player, backing up Banks for eight games. He'd turned the offense around to help the defense. And yet, there he was being dismissed from the organization for another quarterback. Dilfer handled the exit with class, however, telling reporters he'd cherish his time in Baltimore. "It's the great culmination of a wonderful year," he said. "The ring will eventually rot away. I'm proud of it, but the relationships I've made with these guys are far greater than the ring."

The Ravens, looking for a downfield passer, turned to former Chiefs quarterback Elvis Grbac. Grbac was coming off a career-best season in Kansas City, throwing for 4,169 yards and 28 touch-downs. The Ravens were impressed and signed Grbac to a five-year, $30 million contract.

When Grbac was announced to the Baltimore media, he expressed confidence that he'd be the guy to take Baltimore's offense to the next level. "It's time that a quarterback comes in here and provides leadership, a go-to guy, a vertical passing game," he said. 'This is a great team. I can make it better.'"

Any quarterback will tell you a strong running game is needed to be successful in the passing game. Perhaps Grbac could have had a better 2001 season in Baltimore if he'd had a running back to shoulder his fair share of the carries. But in training camp, Jamal Lewis tore his ACL and was out for the season before it started. The top two running backs became Terry Allen and Jason Brookins, and already, Baltimore's offense was in trouble.

Grbac threw for 262 yards and a touchdown in Baltimore's season-opening win over Chicago. Then he followed it up with three picks a week later in a 21–10 loss to Cincinnati. The lack of a running game put a lot of pressure on Grbac, which slowly brought him out of favor with the Baltimore fans. His numbers weren't too bad early in the season, though he threw six touchdowns and six interceptions in the first five games of the season.

And then came the Week 6 game at Cleveland. The new Browns, brought back by expansion in 1999, hadn't beaten Baltimore since entering the league. Art Modell's decision to move the Browns to Baltimore was still fresh in Cleveland's mind, and the city was dying for a win over the Ravens.

Grbac, a Browns fan as a child, completed 80 percent of his passes (16-of-20) but for only 142 yards, and tossed two interceptions in a

24–14 loss. With about five minutes left in the third quarter, Grbac was sacked by Jamir Miller, which injured the quarterback's chest. Backup Randall Cunningham finished the game for Grbac. With Grbac on the sideline, cameras caught him appearing to cry, something he later claimed to be sweat. Baltimore fans and media began to ridicule Grbac following the incident.

Cunningham played the next two games due to the chest injury Grbac sustained against Cleveland. Baltimore won those games against Jacksonville and Pittsburgh. When Grbac returned to the lineup against Tennessee in Week 9, fans booed him. Writers were no longer giving Grbac the benefit of the doubt and openly second-guessing the decision to replace Dilfer with him.

"It was a disastrous, ill-fated decision," said *Baltimore Sun* Ravens beat writer Aaron Wilson, who was covering the team for the *Carroll County Times* in 2001. "It was unpopular in the locker room, and Elvis was never embraced by his teammates."

The Ravens would finish the regular season 10–6 and win a wild-card playoff game against Miami, 20–3. Baltimore would lose the next week to Pittsburgh 27–10, with Grbac throwing three interceptions. Grbac finished the regular season with 15 touchdowns against 18 interceptions, and threw just one touchdown against three interceptions in two playoff games.

Despite his five-year, $30 million deal, Grbac retired after the 2001 season.

"He left Baltimore after one year despite his ability," Wilson said. "He just never fit in with the Ravens. It was a huge misstep by the organization. It affected team chemistry."

Luke Jones, a Ravens beat writer and talk show producer for WNST (1570-AM), thought the Grbac move was bad during the 2001 season. However, looking back on it, he doesn't think the move was as bad as it's been made out to be. Though Grbac threw more interceptions than touchdowns, he was fighting an uphill battle with Baltimore's running game missing all year. Jones actually made the argument that Grbac getting the Ravens to the playoffs might have been more than Dilfer could have accomplished in 2001.

"Thinking with a clear head 12 years later, the Ravens probably don't make the playoffs if Dilfer's the quarterback, considering Jamal Lewis was out for the season," Jones said.

30 "Heeeeaaapppppp"

Each Sunday, from 2001 through 2010, there was a familiar collective sound that would echo throughout M&T Bank Stadium.

"Heeeeaaapppppp!" fans would scream.

Tight end Todd Heap quickly became a fan favorite in Baltimore. Part of the reason was his reliability. Another reason was the grit and toughness he showed each play. If Heap was asked to risk a big hit by cutting across the middle of the field for a pass, he'd do it. Time and time again, Heap would take a crushing hit only to stand up after completing a catch.

Heap was selected by the Ravens with the 31st overall pick in the 2001 draft, just after the organization won its first Super Bowl championship. Heap, who played college football at Arizona State, would see some action as a rookie, hauling in 16 receptions for 206 yards and a touchdown. He'd quickly become more involved in the offense during his second season.

Heap, who became a top target for quarterbacks Jeff Blake and Chris Redman, caught 68 passes for 836 yards and six touchdowns. His yardage total was just 33 shy of receiver Travis Taylor, who led the Ravens in receiving yards that season. The season was ultimately a disappointment, though, as the Ravens finished 7–9.

Heap was a model of consistency in Baltimore, and fans clamored to him. Maybe it was Heap's blue-collar work ethic and preferred

Ravens tight end Todd Heap turns upfield after catching a pass during a game against the Denver Broncos at M&T Bank Stadium in 2009.

low profile that caused fans to adore him. As Kris Jones, longtime Ravens fan and writer at RussellStreetReport.com, noted, the city got to see Heap grow up in front of its own eyes.

"He was the first draft pick following the first Super Bowl," Jones said. "He made tough catches but was also the primary receiving outlet for most of his career because he never had any supporting cast on offense for the most part."

In 2005, Heap set career highs with 75 receptions, 855 yards, and seven touchdowns, though the Ravens finished 6–10. During the 2006 season, when the Ravens posted a regular season best 13–3 record, Heap caught 73 passes for 765 yards and six touchdowns. He was Mr. Reliable with the Ravens, and instrumental to the offense's success based on the notion that there weren't many other options to rely on.

Good quarterbacks were a rarity in Baltimore ever since the Ravens came to town. Through his career, Heap caught passes from quarterback busts Elvis Grbac and Kyle Boller, as well as Steve McNair near the end of his career and Joe Flacco at the beginning of his.

"He would have been a better tight end if he had a better quarterback," Jones said. "He made the most of having Boller."

Heap was the consummate team player, though, never complaining when things weren't going his way. Sure, a case could be made that Heap would have excelled better with a more efficient and reliable quarterback. But Heap made the most of what was presented to him, which was another reason why fans flocked to him. He and Boller were actually close friends, and Heap was not happy with the criticism his buddy would take.

When the Ravens drafted Flacco in 2008, the then youngster leaned on Heap early in his career. In 2008 and 2009, Flacco completed 88 passes to Heap for 996 yards and nine touchdowns. But as it goes for a lot of players reaching the end of their careers, Heap was beginning to become injury-prone with all the hits he took during his career.

After a bizarre 2011 off-season marred by a lockout, the Ravens surprisingly released Heap, much to the chagrin of Flacco. It was time, in the organization's eyes, to get younger at the position. Baltimore had recently drafted tight ends Dennis Pitta and Ed Dickson, who were both ready to contribute in bigger roles.

Heap eventually signed with Arizona, which had a road game in Baltimore during the season. Heap ended up unavailable for the game due to a hamstring injury. According to RussellStreetReport. com, Heap met with Steve Bisciotti prior to the Ravens-Cardinals game on October 30, 2011. During their on-field conversation, Bisciotti pointed to Baltimore's Ring of Honor and told Heap, "Pick where you'd like your placard to be."

Prior to that Cardinals game, Heap bought an ad in the *Baltimore Sun* to show his appreciation to the fans who supported him in Baltimore for 10 long seasons.

"I would like to personally thank Art Modell for all that he has done, not only for me, but also for the passionate people of Baltimore," Heap wrote. "Mr. Modell brought football back to the city and restored fans' pride in cheering for their home team. Our thoughts are with Mr. Modell as he mourns the passing of his wonderful wife Pat. I would also like to thank not only Steve Bisciotti for his great leadership of the Ravens organization, but also all of those within the organization who have been like family to me. I have played with so many great teammates over the years and am honored and proud to have stepped onto the field with each of you."

Replacing Todd Heap

When Todd Heap was released before the start of the 2011 season, there was a concern as to who would be able to take over his starting tight end spot. Heap had played a vital role with the organization for 10 years, catching 467 passes for 5,492 yards and 41 touchdowns. Dennis Pitta became the player Baltimore would turn to. Pitta, who is close friends with quarterback Joe Flacco, worked his way into the No. 1 tight end role by early 2012. In 2011 and 2012 combined, Pitta caught 101 passes for 1,074 yards and 10 touchdowns.

31 Matt Stover, the Reliable One

When Baltimore needed a crucial kick, it could turn to Matt Stover, the longtime kicker who spent the majority of his career with the Ravens organization.

Technically, Stover was a part of four NFL teams from 1991 to 2009, though he was with Cleveland before the move to Baltimore. All in all, he spent 18 years with the Browns and Ravens, every bit a key contributor in each season.

It was an uncertain time when Stover came with the Ravens to Baltimore. There was a lot of resentment in Cleveland for the departure, and Baltimore was in need of a makeover. They weren't going to be the Browns as Cleveland was allowed to keep its history to give to the expansion team it would receive in 1999. Stover remembers moving to Baltimore, with early workouts conducted in black-and-white attire with no idea what the team name or identity would be.

Soon enough, they'd be the Ravens. And soon enough, Stover would become a fan favorite. Stover was no stranger to the clutch kick, having made 12 game-winners with Baltimore (14 in his entire career), according to BaltimoreRavens.com.

One of the better kicks Stover ever made in a Ravens uniform came at Cleveland in 2006. Heading into the fourth quarter, the Browns held a 14–3 lead over Baltimore. However, the first play of the final period was a three-yard touchdown pass to Todd Heap. A two-point conversion fell incomplete, allowing Cleveland to keep a 14–9 lead. Stover then cut into the lead with a 43-yard field goal with 4:38 remaining to make it 14–12.

With the Browns threatening to score from the Baltimore 4-yard line, quarterback Charlie Frye threw an interception to Chris McAlister in the end zone. The Ravens then ran 10 plays and reached the Cleveland 33-yard line. Stover was then asked to kick a 52-yard game-winner from the right hash in one of the toughest stadiums in the NFL for a specialist.

Stover handled pressure through his career and remained calm in this situation. His kick, with 24 seconds remaining, cleared the uprights and gave Baltimore a 15–14 victory.

But perhaps Stover's greatest kick of them all came against Tennessee in the 2008 divisional round of the playoffs. Tennessee kicker Rob Bironas had tied the game up at 10–10 with 4:26 remaining in the game. After a couple of runs, Joe Flacco hit Heap for a 23-yard reception on third-and-2. A couple of plays later, Willis McGahee scampered for an 11-yard pickup, putting the ball at the Tennessee 34. Three plays later, Flacco found Mark Clayton for an eight-yard gain. The Ravens were one yard short of a first down and had a decision to make. They could send in youngster Steven Hauschka, the designated long-range field-goal kicker, or ask Stover to make the kick from 42 yards away.

The coaching staff went with Stover, which turned out to be a great decision. Sure enough, Stover knocked the field goal in, and Baltimore advanced to the 2008 AFC Championship Game. The Tennessee game-winner turned out to be the last of Stover's career, as the Ravens lost 23–14 to Pittsburgh in the conference title game.

Stover was released during the off-season and played one more NFL season with Indianapolis in 2009. Stover made 354 of his 471 career field goals with the Ravens and holds the team record for kicking percentage in a season (93.3 percent in 2006). Stover ranks 13th all-time in field-goal percentage, having made 83.7 percent of his career kicks, and checks in at fifth all-time in career field goals made. More impressive than any percentage or kicking stat might be the fact that Stover never missed a game due to injury in his career.

Getting Their Kicks In

With the Ravens being the second newest franchise in the NFL, Matt Stover has hogged most of Baltimore's kicking records. When the organization moved from Cleveland, Stover came, too, and kept kicking exceptionally well.

Stover holds the franchise record for most points scored (1,464), which means he should have some bloated numbers compared to the other kickers in Ravens history. After all, Stover did kick in Baltimore from 1996 to 2008.

Stover was one of the best kickers in the 1990s and 2000s, and the numbers prove it. Stover could regularly be counted on to make a crucial kick, no matter the circumstance.

Most FGs Made, Career:
354 Matt Stover (1996–2008)
66 Billy Cundiff (2009–2011)
30 Justin Tucker (2012–present)

Most FGs Made, Season:
35 Matt Stover (2000)
33 Matt Stover (2003)
30 Justin Tucker (2012)
30 Matt Stover (2005)
30 Matt Stover (2001)

Longest FG Made:
56 Justin Tucker (2012)
56 Wade Richey (2003)
54 Justin Tucker (2012)
54 Steve Hauschka (2008)
52 Matt Stover (2006)

Best FG Percentage, Career (Min. 30):
.909 Justin Tucker (30-of-33) (2012)
.847 Matt Stover (354-of-418) (1996–1998)
.795 Billy Cundiff (66-of-83) (2009–2011)

These days, Stover acts as an analyst with Comcast SportsNet Baltimore, offering his opinion on the cable channel after each game.

Stover was inducted into the Ravens Ring of Honor on November 20, 2011. He became the sixth former Raven to earn the distinction.

"There are a lot of people in my Ravens family who played with me, who assisted the team, all these people all played a huge part in what happened with my career and why the success came about," Stover said. "The fact that it was bigger than just the game, it was bigger than just kicking for me. It was always about the other guy, helping the other person to be the best they could be; not only on the field, but off the field. That's really what my main mission was."

32 Ray Lewis in the Community

Like a lot of professional athletes, Ray Lewis took it upon himself to give back to the community that supported him. As a member of the Baltimore Ravens for 17 years, Lewis had the means to lend a helping hand to those in need. The city of Baltimore has a soft spot for those deeply involved in paying it forward, which is why Lewis will always be remembered fondly in Charm City.

Each Thanksgiving, Lewis hands out an estimated 800 turkeys to families that otherwise wouldn't be able to afford one for the holiday. He's usually present, greeting each person who arrives to pick one up. It's just another way for the city to see Lewis' generosity off the field.

Lewis created the Ray Lewis Foundation early in his career in Baltimore, which has grown substantially since the early days. He and his mother are constantly looking for ways to give to the less fortunate. They raise money for charities, offer scholarships, and provide grants.

One of the fundraising events Lewis participates in is called Ray's Summer Days. Money has been raised for various organizations, such as elementary schools, the Maryland State Boys Choir, the Girl Scouts of Central Maryland, and local high school football programs. Celebrities ranging from Magic Johnson to boxer Evander Holyfield have helped lend Lewis a hand in these efforts.

Lewis also runs a program called Kids of Character, designed to honor children aged five to 18 who have demonstrated a positive attitude in various aspects of everyday life, despite the circumstances they may have dealt with. The program requires these youths be involved in assisting their peers who are in need emotionally, physically, or financially.

Other community initiatives include Lewis handing out over 200 filled book bags to needy students each year. Lewis was able to partner with Wal-Mart to help provide basic school supplies for students, to ease the financial burden on their parents. During the holidays, Lewis organizes a toy drive, as well as a coat and blanket drive.

Lewis' involvement isn't limited to the various programs and initiatives he's created. He'll regularly receive letters from the community, seeking inspiration from the hero they watch on Sundays. One great example of Lewis latching on to a member of the Baltimore community was seen in the NFL Network's *A Football Life* episode that focused on him.

In it, Lewis welcomed Sergeant First Class Allen Wiseman, who was injured in Iraq, to a Ravens practice. Wiseman usually wore his Ray Lewis jersey when he was on duty overseas. The one day he was unable to do so, his helicopter was shot down. Wiseman also sustained a bullet wound that day and was later awarded a Purple Heart. To show thanks to Lewis for his community efforts, as well as being the Baltimore Ravens' leader, Wiseman gave Lewis his Purple Heart.

Another relationship showcased was one Lewis had with Dundalk, Maryland, resident Bill Warble, or "Papa Bill" as Lewis called him. Warble was diagnosed with terminal cancer, and Lewis decided to take a keen interest in him. Lewis would visit him at home, to pray with and comfort him. Lewis invited Warble to practice and introduced him to the team.

"Papa Bill changed my perspective about what you complain about, what you don't complain about," Lewis said on the show.

Lewis retired after 17 years of football and community work in Baltimore. Though his football days are done, his involvement in Baltimore's community will surely continue.

33 Ravens Honor the Baltimore Colts

When the Baltimore Colts packed their belongings in the dead of night on March 29, 1984, a little bit of the city died. Some fans never followed the NFL again, even when the Ravens came to town in 1996. The Colts were Baltimore's team. To this day, many Baltimoreans have never accepted the fact the Colts now belong to Indianapolis.

Baltimore, like cities such as Pittsburgh, Buffalo, Green Bay, and Cleveland, is a blue-collar town that believed its football team embodied all the characteristics that made the city unique. Rain or shine, win or lose, the fans came out to support the team.

But when Colts owner Robert Irsay couldn't convince the city to build him a new stadium by 1984, he took the team with him to Indianapolis. The Baltimore Colts were no more. The only thing left were memories and the remaining players still living in the area.

The best Colt of them all was Johnny Unitas, arguably the greatest quarterback to ever play the game. Unitas played 17 seasons with the Colts and set 22 NFL records during his tenure. He was the NFL's MVP three times and was the only Colt to be on the 1958 and 1959 championship teams and the Super Bowl V title team.

Lenny Moore was a dynamic running back for Baltimore's Colts, totaling 5,174 yards and 63 touchdowns in 12 seasons. He also hauled in 363 receptions for 6,039 yards and 48 TDs during his career. Moore is a regular around the Ravens' training facility, having adopted them as his team when Baltimore got football back, as Moore doesn't associate himself with the Indianapolis Colts.

Raymond Berry was also a legend in Baltimore. A receiver, Berry caught 631 passes for 9,275 yards and 68 touchdowns during a 13-year career. His best game came in the 1958 NFL championship game, catching 12 passes for 178 yards and a touchdown. John Mackey was an exceptional tight end, as both a dominant blocker and pass-catcher. Mackey was one of the first tight ends to be used as a receiver, hauling in 331 catches for 5,236 yards and 38 touchdowns in his career.

Other greats include offensive lineman Jim Parker, defensive tackle Art Donovan, defensive end Gino Marchetti, and linebacker Ted Hendricks. Parker played both left tackle and left guard during an 11-year career, becoming a decorated lineman in the process. Donovan was a 26-year-old rookie after serving in World War II. A locker room leader, Donovan was named to five Pro Bowls due to his versatility on the defensive line.

Ask an elder Colts fan, and he'll tell you Marchetti was the greatest defensive end to ever play the game. He constantly drew double and triple teams, yet could still be effective getting after the passer. When the NFL named its 50th anniversary team in 1969, Merchetti drew the distinction of being the best to ever play his position.

Hendricks played five of his 15 years with the Colts, totaling 11 interceptions from 1969 to 1973. Hendricks made the Pro Bowl as a Colt in 1971, 1972, and 1973.

All of the aforementioned Colts are in the Pro Football Hall of Fame and an important part of Baltimore football history. Fans that adopted the Ravens as Baltimore's team consider them an extension of the old Colts. Despite the fact that the Colts are in Indianapolis,

Ravens and Orioles Unite

During the 2012 season, the Ravens and Major League Baseball's Baltimore Orioles made it a point to support each other, given that both were having successful seasons. The Orioles reached the playoffs for the first time since 1997, with the city of Baltimore awestruck. Ed Reed and Anquan Boldin started wearing Orioles hats to practice each day. Orioles players and Manager Buck Showalter made it out to the Ravens' game against Dallas. "The Ravens are big fans of the Orioles," John Harbaugh said in mid-September 2012. "We're cheering them on in this pennant race."

Baltimore still does its best to claim the Colts from 1983 and before. Even the Ravens have played their part in doing so.

In 2002 those eight Colts—Unitas, Moore, Berry, Parker, Donovan, Mackey, Marchetti, and Hendricks—were inducted into the Ravens' Ring of Honor. Their pictures are present on the Ravens' wall, and the surviving members of that group are welcomed to the team's facility at any time, as if the Ravens franchise had been in Baltimore this whole time.

Baltimore has grown to love its Ravens, through the ups and downs, wins and losses. But it will never forget its history and what the NFL's Colts meant to the city from 1953 to 1983.

34 Ozzie Newsome's Right-Hand Man, Eric DeCosta

For quite some time, Eric DeCosta has been one of the most highly sought-after candidates to take over a general manager position in the NFL. The skill is there, having studied under Ozzie Newsome since 1996 when he took an entry-level position with the organization.

It's been a steady climb for DeCosta. First, he was promoted to be an area scout in 1998. From then until 2002, DeCosta scouted the Midwest, analyzing draft day trades with duties to target free agent possibilities. A quick study, he became the director of college scouting in 2003.

DeCosta has received a lot of credit for assisting Newsome in the stellar drafts Baltimore's had under the front office's leadership. Terrell Suggs, Haloti Ngata, Ben Grubbs, Marshal Yanda, Ray Rice, and Joe Flacco were all drafted before DeCosta's next promotion, which was to director of player personnel.

More success followed, and by 2012 DeCosta became the assistant general manager. A lot of front office employees in his position would have left by now. DeCosta is genuinely happy with the Ravens. It seems each year the organization is releasing a statement indicating DeCosta is remaining with the organization. Through hard work and dedication, DeCosta has gone from being the first intern the Ravens hired when the organization moved to Baltimore to Newsome's second in command.

DeCosta grew up in Taunton, Massachusetts, and played linebacker and fullback for his varsity football team. He attended Colby College in Maine, where he was a three-year letter-winner at linebacker. He's developed a special knack for evaluating talent, which likely makes up for the lack of talent he had as a player. In multiple interviews, DeCosta has joked about how poor of a player he was when asked to give a scouting report on himself.

"He'd probably say he was an instinctive player, but he was a reject physically," DeCosta told the *Boston Globe* once. "I was an overachieving, try-hard guy who made a lot of plays. I couldn't run and I wasn't big. That's not a good combination for a linebacker."

It's clear DeCosta enjoys the role he has with the Ravens organization. If he had a desire to become a general manager as soon as possible, he'd already be out of Baltimore. That hasn't happened, and it's likely DeCosta will remain a Raven for life. Though the numbers aren't public, it's believed that DeCosta is earning one of the highest salaries in the NFL for his position.

Whenever Newsome, 57 as of the fall of 2013, decides to retire, a plan is in place to hand the reins over to DeCosta. It's unknown when that time will come, considering Newsome isn't exactly aging or in bad health. In the meantime, DeCosta is enjoying his job enough to the point that there's no reason to leave.

"It's a relationship business," DeCosta told the *Baltimore Sun* in a 2013 interview at the NFL Scouting Combine in Indianapolis. "I'm fortunate to work with a bunch of great guys. It's a great place to work. I appreciate that side of the business. Individual achievement comes and goes. At the end of the day, you look at the guys you work with, and the friendships you develop, and that's the most important thing."

35 Ravens Get Lucky Drafting Terrell Suggs

"With the seventh overall pick in the 2003 NFL Draft, the Baltimore Ravens select Marshall quarterback Byron Leftwich."

Wait, what?

That almost happened in 2003. Needing a quarterback, the Ravens, holders of the No. 10 pick in the first round, were looking to trade up to select their guy. Leftwich had just finished a remarkable career at Marshall, where he threw for 11,903 yards and 89 touchdowns. He finished sixth in Heisman Trophy voting in 2002 and threw for over 4,000 yards in each of his final two seasons in college.

After struggling to find a consistent quarterback, it was only natural for the Ravens to want to select Leftwich. However, it was unlikely that Leftwich would fall to No. 10. General manager Ozzie

Newsome knew the Ravens needed to trade up if they were going to get the tall signal-caller with the strong arm.

Baltimore reached an agreement with Minnesota to trade up to the No. 7 spot so it could select Leftwich. The Ravens waited. And waited. And waited. The NFL never announced the move, and time ran out on the Vikings. Therefore, if Jacksonville, positioned at No. 8, wanted to select someone at No. 7, it could, but it had to do so quickly before Minnesota could regroup and turn in a pick. And if Jacksonville was able to draft someone fast enough, Carolina, originally slated at No. 9, could then make a selection at No. 8, as long as it was before Minnesota turned in a draft pick.

Jacksonville, seizing the opportunity, immediately selected Leftwich. "I remember having phone talks with Ozzie, and it was pretty much set in stone," Leftwich said. "I guess the debacle happened during the draft and everything. I remember being at the draft. I think I had three teams with my name on a card trying to shove it in. I remember that part because I was at the draft. I thought I would be a Raven."

The Panthers then rushed in their pick, which was Utah offensive tackle Jordan Gross. By then, the Vikings knew they needed to make a pick and took defensive tackle Kevin Williams out of Oklahoma State.

Baltimore was shocked and looking to adjust its plan. At the 10th overall pick, the Ravens selected Terrell Suggs, an outside linebacker out of Arizona State.

Following the snafu, Minnesota claimed its calls to the NFL office for the trade went unanswered. The Ravens were obviously bothered by the situation but moved forward with the hand they were dealt. They decided to aggressively pursue a quarterback in that draft and traded up to pick 19 to take California's Kyle Boller.

Boller never panned out in Baltimore, but Suggs certainly did. So for the sake of comparison, here's how Suggs and Leftwich's careers turned out:

The Ravens got lucky in drafting future Pro Bowl linebacker and Defensive Player of the Year Terrell Suggs (center) with the 10th overall pick of the 2003 NFL Draft (not so much with No. 19 selection Kyle Boller).

From 2003 to 2012, Suggs became a mainstay and big-time contributor on Baltimore's star-studded defense. In his first 10 seasons, Suggs totaled a combined 588 tackles and 84 1/2 sacks (a franchise best). He won the 2011 NFL Defensive Player of the Year award and was named to the Pro Bowl five times.

After three years as a starting quarterback in Jacksonville, Leftwich became a journeyman backup. After leaving the Jaguars following the 2006 season, Leftwich made stops in Atlanta, Pittsburgh, and Tampa Bay, respectfully, before returning to Pittsburgh. His career numbers include 58 touchdowns and 42 interceptions.

Defensive Players of the Year

The Ravens have had a long history of defensive success, with a number of individuals earning accolades from the NFL. This includes winning the coveted Associated Press NFL Defensive Player of the Year. A Baltimore player has won it in four separate years. Ray Lewis won it in 2000 and 2003, Ed Reed won it in 2004, and Terrell Suggs earned the honor in 2011. The four AP Defensive Player of the Year awards ties Baltimore with the New York Giants for second most, with Pittsburgh claiming seven different defenders who have won the distinction.

The Ravens were upset on draft day in 2003. They wanted Leftwich to become the organization's quarterback of the future. Yet, in a twist of events, the Ravens ended up ahead when it was all said and done. They got a top-tier pass rusher who has wreaked havoc on opposing quarterbacks his entire career. Maybe Leftwich would have had a different career if he had been in Baltimore. Perhaps he would have had a lot more success playing on a team with a defense that was consistently among the NFL's best.

Then again, Suggs was one of the main reasons why Baltimore's defense was so dominant in the 2000s. In the grand scheme of events, Minnesota's failure to finalize a draft day trade turned out to be a blessing for the Ravens in the long term.

36 The Kyle Boller Era

If you're ever in the mood to see a Baltimore Ravens fan slap his or her forehead, bring up the name Kyle Boller. You're more than likely to receive a long-winded response as to why Boller should be in consideration for the worst quarterback in NFL history.

Let's be fair to Boller for a minute, though. He was Baltimore's second choice at quarterback in the 2003 draft. The Ravens wanted to trade up and snag Byron Leftwich but were unable to when the Vikings failed to reach the NFL office with news of the agreement. Therefore, the Ravens drafted Terrell Suggs at No. 10 overall and then made a trade with New England to take Boller with the 19th pick in the first round. Head coach Brian Billick was fond of Boller during the draft, which is one of the reasons why Baltimore made the move.

But over the years, even Billick reconsidered his decision to draft Boller.

"I am living proof that if you miss on a first-round quarterback, as I did with Kyle Boller, you end up broadcasting games and writing about the NFL instead of coaching," wrote Billick in a FoxSports.com column in 2011.

But how did Boller become the Baltimore whipping boy? It all seemed to happen so fast.

Boller started nine games as a rookie and didn't have the results he would've hoped for. The highest completion percentage Boller had in a game he started that season was 57.69 percent, in a 17–10 loss to Kansas City. Despite a season-high completion percentage, Boller threw three interceptions in the loss. The only multiple-touchdown game he threw as a rookie was against Cincinnati, when he completed 15-of-27 passes for 302 yards and two touchdowns. Oddly enough, that was the only game of Boller's 2003 season that saw him throw for over 156 yards. Boller injured his thigh against St. Louis in Baltimore's ninth game and didn't start a game the remainder of the season. He finished 2003 with seven touchdowns and nine interceptions.

The ensuing off-season featured the Ravens looking to add an elite downfield threat for Boller. In fact, the Ravens traded a draft pick to San Francisco for receiver Terrell Owens. However, Owens objected to the trade, reportedly because he didn't want to play with

Boller. Ultimately, Baltimore got its pick back and Owens continued his career in Philadelphia instead.

Boller's 2004 season, everything considered, wasn't that bad. It was the only time he started all 16 regular season games in his career. He threw for 2,559 yards and 13 touchdowns, both of which were career highs. But he also tossed 11 interceptions and coughed the ball up another 11 times. Against pressure, Boller also had a tendency to panic. You never knew what you were getting, though. On one play, Boller would hold the ball and take a crushing hit. The next, he'd lob a pass into double coverage and risk an interception.

The inconsistencies helped wear Boller's welcome out in Baltimore quick.

It was thought that Boller was poised to break out in 2005 with it being his third season in the NFL. Boy, how some analysts jump to conclusions too quickly. In the season opener against the Indianapolis Colts, Boller got off to a dreadful start. On Baltimore's first possession of the game, Boller capped an otherwise decent drive with an interception to Colts linebacker Gary Brackett.

Boller was serviceable the rest of his time in the game. He didn't throw any picks or make any horrible decisions. Then again, Boller wasn't doing enough to move his team down the field. Late in the third quarter, though, Larry Tripplett sacked Boller for a 10-yard loss. Boller sustained a severe turf toe injury that ultimately forced him to miss the remainder of that game as well as the next seven. Making matters worse for Boller was that the home crowd in Baltimore cheered when he sustained his toe injury. It would be an uphill battle to gain the fans' support after the rocky start he endured.

One notable Boller critic was longtime Broncos tight end–turned CBS studio analyst Shannon Sharpe. Sharpe also played two seasons with the Ravens in 2000 and 2001, and was quick to sound off on Boller all season. After Boller aimed the quip, "I wish I could have been perfect," Sharpe's way, the former NFL tight end sounded off during a pregame show before Baltimore's 16–13 overtime win over Pittsburgh.

"Kyle, you do have a valid point, you shouldn't be listening to me," Sharpe said on the broadcast. "Go down the hallway to Brian Billick's office or Ozzie Newsome's office and ask them what kind of player they really think you are. You're right. You do have your teammates behind you: your fullback and your halfback, and that's only because they have to be."

To conclude the 2005 season, Boller put together two solid performances against Green Bay and Minnesota, respectively. Against the Packers, Boller threw for 253 yards, three touchdowns, and zero interceptions. The following week against the Vikings, Boller threw for 289 yards, three touchdowns, and one interception. Could it be that Boller was finally coming into his own as the prognosticators predicted to start the season?

Not quite.

His 2005 finale was a dud as he completed just 15 of 36 passes for 151 yards and two interceptions. Boller was back to being Boller and back to being on Baltimore's bad side.

To address the problem Boller presented at quarterback, the Ravens brought in Steve McNair for the 2006 season. McNair led Baltimore to its best regular season in team history (13–3) and accounted for 3,050 yards, 16 passing touchdowns, and 12 interceptions. No, those weren't earth-shattering numbers, but they also weren't Boller's. That was saying something at the time.

In 2007 groin, back, and left shoulder injuries limited McNair to just six starts during the season, giving Boller ample opportunities to prove he could lead the Ravens into the future. Boller started eight games and appeared in 12. He only threw for more than 200 yards twice in his starts and posted nine touchdowns against 10 interceptions.

Boller's last chance came in 2008 after McNair retired. There was a three-way battle for the Baltimore starting quarterback job between Boller, Joe Flacco, and Troy Smith. Boller had an early lead and was named the starter for the preseason opener against New England. In Baltimore's second preseason game against Minnesota, Boller injured his shoulder. On September 3, 2008, Boller was placed on injured reserve, and Flacco was named the starter.

Boller became an unrestricted free agent in 2009 and signed with the Rams. He had one more stint as a backup in Oakland, where he actually started a game and appeared in another after an injury knocked starter Jason Campbell out for the season.

Boller signed with the Chargers as a backup before the 2012 season but chose retirement instead of playing through another season. Not counting his limited action with St. Louis and Oakland, Boller finished his Baltimore career at quarterback 746-of-1,311 for 7,846 yards, 45 touchdowns, and 44 interceptions. He also accounted for 36 fumbles in five years.

Boller was a rare miss for a Baltimore organization known for having success in the draft.

"Kyle Boller was everything you wanted in a quarterback on paper, but when you watched him play on a weekly basis, you wanted to tear that paper to shreds," said Luke Jones, a Ravens reporter and talk show producer for Baltimore radio station WNST. "He'd show a flash of brilliance every so often that made you think he was figuring it out, only to trip over his own feet and fumble without anyone touching him in the next moment. And, yes, that actually happened."

37 Ed Reed: The Greatest Safety Ever?

Plenty of safeties have come and gone throughout NFL history. John Lynch, Darren Woodson, Jack Tatum, Steve Atwater, and

Ronnie Lott are a handful of the best to ever play the position. So where does Ed Reed rank among the best safeties? Could he even be considered the best ever?

Reed came to Baltimore via the 2002 draft as the 24th overall pick. Some pundits didn't think Reed was a first-round player, that it might be a reach to take a safety in the first round. The Ravens begged to differ, selecting Reed with hope he would be a long-term cornerstone of Baltimore's defense.

Here's some of what Reed has been able to accomplish during his 11 years in Baltimore: 605 total tackles, 109 pass deflections, 61 interceptions, 1,541 interception return yards (the most in NFL history), and seven defensive touchdowns. He became a starter as a rookie and soon became one of the best in the game during his time. Reed's ability to decipher defenses hasn't been matched by many, drawing the attention of coaches around the NFL.

During the 2012 season, the Baltimore media participated in a conference call with Denver Broncos quarterback Peyton Manning, whom the Ravens would have to defend in Week 15 of the season. A reporter asked Manning if he enjoyed the challenge of facing Reed because he was one of the best safeties in the NFL. Manning quickly felt the need to correct the reporter.

"I thought you said he was one of the best safeties, and I was going to correct you," Manning said. "He is the best safety in the league and has been really for this past decade. You can kind of go on and on. [He has] unbelievable ball skills, unbelievable range, great hands. You can tell what kind of athlete he is by what he's done once he's got the ball in his hands—returning [turnovers] for touchdowns. [He's a] smart player. The list goes on and on."

Those who do believe Reed is in the conversation to be the best safety ever often compare his career to Lott's. Lott played the majority of his career in San Francisco before late stints with the Raiders and Jets. Lott's career numbers included 63 interceptions, 730 interception return yards, and five defensive touchdowns. Ask

Ravens safety Ed Reed (20) is flanked by teammates Samari Rolle (22) and Ray Lewis (52) after intercepting a pass against the Philadelphia Eagles in November 2008. His 1,541 interception return yards is the most in NFL history.

any longtime NFL fan, and Lott's name will come out immediately when this conversation begins. Reed went to nine Pro Bowls and was the 2004 NFL Defensive Player of the Year. Lott was named to 10 Pro Bowls but never earned a Defensive Player of the Year award.

But both players were different with what they were great at. Lott was easily the most intimidating safety to ever play the game. Receivers didn't dare cross the middle with Lott patrolling the field. Reed is much more of a cerebral safety, relying on his instincts in coverage to confuse quarterbacks.

In an episode of NFL Network's *A Football Life* that featured Patriots coach Bill Belichick, he and Tom Brady were discussing Reed in Belichick's offense, and how challenging it can be to scheme against him.

"Everything he does, he does at an exceptional level," Belichick said.

Brady added, "The thing about playing against Ed is you are always so aware of where he is…. Every time you break the huddle, that's who you're looking at."

Even at age 34 in 2013, Reed has plenty of football left in him. Shoulder injuries have pained him later in his career, but he's managed to play through them. He's still someone quarterbacks have to fear, even if he's not the same physical tackler he was early in his career. Reed wound up leaving Baltimore after the 2012 season, signing a three-year, $15 million contract with the Houston Texans.

38 Derrick Mason, Baltimore's Best Receiver

Derrick Mason spent eight seasons with Tennessee and six with Baltimore. When it came down to deciding which team to retire with, the decision was easy. He chose Baltimore.

"My heart was here," Mason said. "Tennessee is a good place, it's a great place, and like I said, they gave me an opportunity to start my career, and I will always thank the brass there. But my heart was here. You can't do something somewhere else when your heart is in another place. My heart was here, so it was an easy choice for me."

That was a bold statement from a guy who played on a team inches away from winning a Super Bowl in 2000. He was also on the other side of the early Ravens-Titans rivalry games, before realignment moved the teams into separate divisions.

After totaling 6,114 yards and 37 touchdowns with Tennessee, Mason signed as an unrestricted free agent with the Ravens in 2005. He went from public enemy No. 1 to embraced by Baltimore's diehards.

Mason quickly built a reputation of toughing out multiple injuries and playing through pain. With the Ravens, Mason appeared in every game he was eligible to play in. Whether it was a broken finger or knee injuries, Mason was suiting up.

"I grew up, and you couldn't quit; you just couldn't no matter what the situation is, you couldn't quit," Mason said at his retirement press conference in June 2012. "I can remember playing in a parking lot with some grass with my brothers, and I hit my head on the concrete, had a big knot on my head. I'm walking home crying, and my brother grabs me by my neck and says, 'You're not quitting.' So I had to play, and that's where it comes from. I was born and raised that way."

That kind of toughness went a long way when John Harbaugh became the Ravens coach in 2008.

"I don't remember [Mason] ever missing a practice that I can recall," Harbaugh said. "From 2002 to 2011, [he] played in 149 straight games. As a special teams guy, [he] posted 5,000 return yards and 10,000 receiving yards—the only player in NFL history, ever, in the history of the game, to do that."

Mason had some big games for the Ravens. He became a reliable option early on in Joe Flacco's career. When Flacco was a rookie in 2008, Mason's performance against the Browns in early November was one to remember. Mason hauled in nine passes for 136 yards and a touchdown to help give Baltimore a 37–27 win. Later that postseason, Mason caught the lone touchdown in Baltimore's win over Tennessee in the AFC divisional round of the playoffs.

In 2009 Mason topped the 100-yard mark twice, recording 118 yards in an early-season win over Cleveland and 142 yards in a close loss to Indianapolis. In six seasons with Baltimore, Mason topped the 1,000-yard mark four times.

When Mason was a free agent, he almost signed with the New England Patriots. It would have been hard to argue going to a franchise like New England, as it was coming off back-to-back Super Bowl titles, with NFL titles in three of the previous four seasons. When it came down to his decision, Mason felt Baltimore was the place for him.

"It was something about this place," Mason said. "Having played this team for so many years, I knew what this team was about, and—it might sound kind of crazy, but being an offensive player, when you play against a defensive that is so tough, you want to be a part of that defense because you don't want to play them anymore."

Mason had a great six years in Baltimore. But a business decision was made right before the 2011 season began, which resulted in Mason's release. Mason's tenure in Baltimore ended with 471 receptions for 5,777 yards, both of which are Ravens records. Mason had stints with the New York Jets and the Houston Texans during the 2011 season before announcing his retirement during the 2012 off-season.

Ravens fans will always remember the gritty receiver they grew to love but once hated when he was a Tennessee Titan.

"I have always said this: [Baltimore fans] took a guy and his family that [they] rooted against for eight years—and I can remember playing at old Memorial Stadium—and [they] rooted against us coming into that building. Eight years after that, coming here, and [the fans] embracing me. That felt good. That truly felt good. There are not too many places you can go, and a place really embraces you the way that the city of Baltimore embraced me. I will be forever indebted to this city."

39 Jamal Lewis Runs for 295 against the Browns

It was September 14, 2003, and the Ravens were running toward the locker room when left tackle Jonathan Ogden grabbed running back Jamal Lewis. Baltimore was hosting the Browns at M&T Bank Stadium and jumped out to a 16–3 lead at the half.

Ogden leaned in and told Lewis, "Let's go get it. We can get 300 yards."

The statement would seem a bit odd if it wasn't for the fact that Lewis already had 180 yards on 16 carries through two quarters. Lewis ripped two huge runs early and then paced himself the rest of the half with some solid gains.

It all started on the second play of the game, when Lewis took a handoff and burst through for an 82-yard touchdown run. When the Ravens got the ball back on the ensuing drive, Lewis immediately ripped off a 23-yarder, giving the bulldozing back 105 yards on two carries. Lewis added five more rushing yards before a missed field goal ended the possession.

Lewis didn't find much room in the third quarter, however, with his biggest run being a six-yard gain. But with starting quarterback Kyle Boller getting injured late in the third quarter, Lewis knew his team would be depending on him down the stretch. Patience can be a virtue, as Lewis quickly found out when the fourth quarter brought play back onto the football field.

On the first play of the fourth quarter, Lewis ripped off his third big play of the day. This time it was a 63-yard run Lewis took to the end zone. The timing for the touchdown was perfect, given that the Browns had cut Baltimore's lead to 16–13. Lewis put Baltimore

Best Rushing Days in Ravens History

The Ravens have long been a run-first ballclub on offense, which has led to quite a few big days from Baltimore running backs. The No. 1 day that sticks out is Jamal Lewis' 295-yard outburst against Cleveland, which set an NFL record for most yards in a single game. The Ravens have had plenty of other big days, which are listed below (Cleveland and Cincinnati have taken the brunt of the beatings against Baltimore's running game):

November 22, 1998, vs. Cincinnati: Priest Holmes ran for 227 yards on 36 carries.

December 21, 2003, vs. Cleveland: Jamal Lewis ran for 205 yards on 22 carries.

December 4, 2011, vs. Cleveland: Ray Rice ran for 204 yards on 29 carries.

January 1, 2012, vs. Cincinnati: Ray Rice ran for 191 yards on 24 carries.

October 6, 2002, vs. Cleveland: Jamal Lewis ran for 187 yards on 26 carries.

November 19, 2000, vs. Dallas: Jamal Lewis ran for 187 yards on 28 carries.

September 26, 2004, vs. Cincinnati: Jamal Lewis ran for 186 yards on 18 carries.

December 7, 2003, vs. Cincinnati: Jamal Lewis ran for 180 yards on 30 carries.

October 26, 1997, vs. Washington: Bam Morris ran for 176 yards on 36 carries.

September 27, 1998, vs. Cincinnati: Priest Holmes ran for 173 yards on 27 carries.

back up by 10 with a record-setting day unfolding for the fans that made it out to M&T Bank Stadium.

Lewis added 22 more rushing yards on three carries when Baltimore regained possession, though the Ravens were forced to punt. When Baltimore got the ball back, Lewis added another 15 yards to his total. This, along with a 30-yard Alan Ricard run, helped set up a 21-yard field goal from Matt Stover, which put the game away. Safety Ed Reed would add another touchdown to the total with a 54-yard interception for a touchdown at the end of regulation to give Baltimore a 33–13 win.

Lewis finished with 295 rushing yards and two touchdowns on 30 carries. This set an NFL record for rushing yards in game, besting former Bengals running back Corey Dillon's total of 278 in 2000. Lewis' record has since been beaten by Vikings running back Adrian Peterson, who ran for 296 against San Diego in 2007.

What's fascinating about Lewis' big day was that he practically predicted it. During the week leading up to the game, Lewis spoke with Browns linebacker Andra Davis on the phone. Davis teased Lewis, saying he hoped the star back in Baltimore got 30 carries against his Browns. Lewis replied that, if he was given 30 carries, he'd break Dillon's record.

That Lewis did. As a team the Ravens ran for 343 rushing yards, a franchise record that still stands today.

"This is the most disgusting feeling I ever had in my life," Browns safety Earl Little told reporters after the game. "He said what he said, and then he did it. It's in the history books."

40 From Willis McGahee to Ray Rice

Whether it was Ted Marchibroda, Brian Billick, or John Harbaugh, the Ravens have always looked to establish the run first and foremost. Each roster Baltimore has had is built for it, possibly due to the fact the organization never had a top-tier quarterback until Joe Flacco came to town in 2008. But even with Flacco, the Ravens' philosophy has been to run the ball.

Lewis had finished his seventh year in Baltimore when the organization released him in February 2007. There was some hope to re-sign Lewis, but he eventually inked a deal with division rival Cleveland instead. The Ravens were in the market for a running back to help set the tone in the ground game.

The Ravens turned to Willis McGahee, who had just completed his fourth year in Buffalo. However, McGahee had only played in the latter three seasons. He missed what would've been his rookie campaign due to a horrific knee injury sustained in the 2003 Fiesta Bowl when he was with the University of Miami. However, McGahee was proving why Buffalo was right for taking a chance on him with the 23rd overall pick in the 2003 draft by running for 1,128 yards and 13 touchdowns in 2004, and 1,247 yards and five touchdowns in 2005. In 2006 McGahee's yardage total dropped to 990, though he still accounted for six touchdowns.

McGahee was falling out of favor with Buffalo, though, and made some disparaging remarks about the city. The organization began shopping him around, and in came Baltimore. The Ravens gave the Bills two 2007 draft picks and a 2008 pick for McGahee.

McGahee was a monster for Baltimore in 2007, despite the team succumbing to a 5–11 record. He started 15 games and ran for 1,207 yards and seven touchdowns, earning a Pro Bowl roster spot in the process. McGahee topped the 100-yard mark five times, with a season-best 138 yards and a touchdown against New England late in the year.

It didn't take long for McGahee to learn he wouldn't be the top running back in the foreseeable future, though. With the Ravens firing Billick and hiring Harbaugh, the Ravens had the opportunity of drafting a running back fairly high in the draft. Rutgers running back Ray Rice was available in the second round, and the Ravens pounced on the opportunity.

A lot of NFL teams overlooked Rice due to his short stature. To the Ravens, Rice was a strong, powerful back with a low center of gravity who could also be a weapon out of the backfield. It seemed certain Rice had a bright future ahead.

Injuries hampered McGahee during the 2008 season, as he dealt with eye, knee, shoulder, and ankle ailments. He missed three games in the regular season and finished with 671 yards (a career worst at the time) and seven touchdowns. Rice and fullback Le'Ron McClain were eating into his carries as well, as McGahee failed to record 200 carries for the first time in his career.

In 2009 the shift began to take place. Rice was named the starter with McGahee the complimentary back. Rice would snag most of the headlines, running for 1,339 yards and seven touchdowns, and also catching 78 passes for 702 yards and a touchdown. But McGahee carved a niche for himself, totaling 14 touchdowns (12 rushing, two receiving) during the season. He also had a career-best game against Oakland, which saw McGahee rumble for 167 yards and three touchdowns.

McGahee spent one more year in Baltimore as Rice's backup. His numbers dropped considerably to 380 yards and five touchdowns. The transition was practically complete. Rice was the starter with the Ravens expressing a long-term interest in him. McGahee had fared well in Baltimore, though his services would no longer be needed. Before the 2011 season, McGahee was released. Eventually, McGahee would land on his feet and join the Denver Broncos as a free agent.

Rice posted single-season bests in 2011 in rushing yards (1,364), rushing touchdowns (12), receiving yards (704), and receiving touchdowns (three) in 2011. This earned him a five-year, $40 million contract.

In four years with Baltimore, McGahee ran for 2,802 yards and 31 touchdowns. Though he left the organization somewhat unceremoniously, McGahee will always be remembered as the hard-nosed back who served as the buffer between Jamal Lewis and Ray Rice. His role may have diminished after his first season with the Ravens, but the player he became for Baltimore remained just as important.

41 Jacoby Jones Dances into Super Bowl Lore

It was almost as if Jacoby Jones knew he was auditioning for the ABC competition *Dancing With the Stars* all season. During the Ravens' 2012 season, Jones was always planning a touchdown celebration to unleash if he had the opportunity to reach the end zone for six points.

In Week 2 against Philadelphia in a 24–23 loss, Jones caught a touchdown pass from Joe Flacco and unleashed a dance called the "Choppa City Juke," which was first popularized by NFL running back Chris Johnson and receiver Mike Sims-Walker.

When Jones returned a kickoff 108 yards for a touchdown against Dallas, he broke out into a celebration reminiscent of what Deion Sanders did in his prime. A few weeks later against Oakland, Jones took a kickoff 105 yards for a touchdown. Following this score, Jones broke out a modernized version of the old dance called the "Cabbage Patch."

The one time Jones didn't dance during the 2012 season was when he caught a 70-yard bomb for a score to take the AFC divisional round game against Denver into overtime. Overcome with joy, he kneeled down and said a quick prayer.

"I didn't even dance," Jones said following the game. "I had to thank God. And you know I'm a dancing fool."

So when the Ravens reached the Super Bowl, Jones knew he'd need something planned in case he was able to reach the end zone on the biggest stage in all of sports. With the world watching, Jones was only hoping he could reach the end zone once. Twice would just be icing on top.

In the second quarter and with under two minutes to go, the Ravens were looking to add to their 14–3 lead. Joe Flacco dropped back to pass and saw Jones running down the middle of the field in between San Francisco's defenders. Jones adjusted on the ball and needed to dive and fall to the ground in order to catch it. Never hearing a whistle, Jones got up and put a juke move on 49ers corner Chris Culliver before running toward the goal line and diving into the end zone.

Jones immediately got up and began dancing a jig with his teammates circling around him in celebration. The Ravens were now up 21–3 and in control of the game.

Then the second half opened, and Jones was back to take the ensuing kickoff. A low line drive was kicked into the end zone. This allowed Jones to take a couple of steps and get a head start before catching the ball. Fullback Vonta Leach and running back Anthony Allen gave two key blocks right up the middle of San Francisco's coverage. Jones ran through the blocks en route to a 108-yard kickoff return for a touchdown.

Naturally, it was time for Jones to dance again. And this time it was in tribute.

Jones broke out the "squirrel dance," made famous by Ray Lewis when he introduced it during pregame introductions before home games. Lewis said a childhood friend used to perform that dance, and he originally made it part of his pregame routine to honor him.

And besides the fact that Super Bowl XLVII was Lewis' last game, maybe there was another reason to honor him with the celebration. Before the special teams play, Lewis ran over to Jones and placed both hands on his chest. Lewis explained that God told him to do so after the game.

"I was just told to put my hand on his chest, and I rubbed my hands down his chest, and then I saw him break through," Lewis said.

Ravens wide receiver Jacoby Jones breaks out Ray Lewis' "squirrel dance" after returning a kickoff 108 yards for a touchdown in the second half of Super Bowl XLVII against the San Francisco 49ers in New Orleans.

Baltimore ended up winning the Super Bowl 34–31, withstanding a furious San Francisco comeback after a power outage delayed the game for 34 minutes in the third quarter. Jones played an integral role in Baltimore leaving New Orleans champions.

And Jones, who all along may have been preparing for *Dancing with the Stars*, ended up on the show. He competed during season 16 alongside professional Karina Smirnoff. Funnily enough, Smirnoff had to convince Ravens coach John Harbaugh to allow Jones to join the show.

"Once she came in and made the case, I was okay with it," Harbaugh said.

Snoop Dogg Visits Practice

During the dog days of summer, the Ravens received a visit from another kind of dog—rapper Snoop Dogg. It was a thrill for many of the players who grew up listening to his songs. At the end of practice, Snoop Dogg broke the Ravens' huddle down with a chant he learned from Ray Lewis. Lewis introduced him to the media as "a new coach out here today." During his media session, when one reporter asked Snoop Dogg if he could offer some "Ravens shizzle," referencing the rapper's style of slang, Snoop replied, "Slow down, nephew."

42 Heartbreak in Foxborough

Throughout the 2011 regular season, there was little doubt which two teams were the best in the AFC. You had the 13–3 New England Patriots and the 12–4 Baltimore Ravens.

The Patriots were winners of nine in a row, including eight regular season games and the divisional round playoff game. Their only losses were to Buffalo, Pittsburgh, and the New York Giants. The loss to Buffalo was somewhat perplexing, though the Bills had started the 2011 season hot before cooling off. The other two losses weren't bad, considering both the Steelers and Giants reached the postseason.

The Ravens were somewhat enigmatic. Sure, they won 12 games, but their four losses were to inferior teams. They lost an early season contest to Tennessee and reached a season low after losing 12–7 to Jacksonville. Road losses to Seattle and San Diego were also somewhat perplexing, though it's admittedly tough to travel across the country to play West Coast teams.

But one thing about the 2011 Ravens was certain: they played up to the competition. When Baltimore faced an elite team, it brought its A game. There was little doubt that the Ravens would give the Patriots everything they had in order to reach the Super Bowl.

After exchanging three-and-outs, the Ravens were still unable to get their offense going. On its second possession, Baltimore was forced to punt after running just three plays. New England was first to capitalize; moving down the field and having kicker Stephen Gostkowski make a 29-yard field goal to go up 3–0.

Baltimore's offense had mostly been sluggish throughout the first quarter and ended the opening period scoreless. However, its last possession of the first quarter had been successful, which culminated with the Ravens reaching the New England 3-yard line. However, that was as close as the Ravens would get, as coach John Harbaugh elected to take the points on fourth down. Billy Cundiff knocked in an easy 20-yard field goal to tie the game.

Both teams began to pick up the pace and exchanged touchdowns on their next possessions. BenJarvus Green-Ellis ran in a seven-yard touchdown for the Patriots, and Ravens tight end Dennis Pitta caught a six-yard touchdown. The difference in the first half came down to a Gostkowski field goal made late in the second half to give New England a 13–10 halftime advantage.

New England opened with the ball in the second half and methodically moved down the field. Tom Brady found Gronkowski for a 21-yard gain. Tight end Aaron Hernandez picked up 12 yards on a reception. New England set up a first-and-10 from the Baltimore 14-yard line but was only able to add a field goal to its scoring total, lengthening its lead to 16–10.

The Ravens would answer with a long drive of their own. Plays made from Ed Dickson, Lee Evans, Dennis Pitta, and Ray Rice helped get the ball down to the New England 29-yard line. From there, Flacco found rookie receiver Torrey Smith for a 29-yard touchdown, which was upheld after an officials' review. Baltimore now held its first lead of the game at 17–16.

Things looked even brighter for the Ravens as Cundiff kicked the ball off to Patriots' running back and return specialist Danny Woodhead, who then fumbled on the play. Baltimore recovered, poised to score again. But the New England defense rose to the challenge and forced a field goal try. Cundiff's 39-yard kick was good, and the Ravens were now ahead 20–16.

It looked like Baltimore had come up with another big play shortly after when cornerback Cary Williams intercepted Brady. However, Terrell Suggs was called for an offside penalty, keeping the ball in New England's hands.

Brady and the offense would drive down to Baltimore's 1-yard line and elect to go for it. Brady took the snap and pushed his way forward, forcing his way into the end zone on a quarterback sneak. He crossed the line and put the Patriots back in front 23–20.

The Ravens were able to move the ball again but momentarily looked dead in the water after Flacco threw an interception to New England linebacker Brandon Spikes while looking for Dickson down the middle of the field. But Brady gave the Ravens life again when he decided to test Baltimore deep for a kill shot. Both safety Bernard Pollard and cornerback Jimmy Smith were in coverage, with Pollard tipping the ball to Smith for the pick. Smith was then able to run to Baltimore's 38-yard line to give the offense another shot.

But once again, Baltimore's offense couldn't convert, as a fourth-and-6 pass to Pitta fell incomplete. With 2:46 remaining, all New England needed to do was convert a first down, and the game would be over. Brady completed a seven-yard pass to Deion Branch on first down. The defense buckled up on second down and forced Green-Ellis into a one-yard loss. Brady's third-down pass fell incomplete, and once again, Baltimore's offense was in business.

From the Baltimore 21, Flacco completed a five-yard pass to Pitta on second down before picking up 13 more yards with a completion to Anquan Boldin. After an incomplete pass on first down, Flacco found Boldin on consecutive plays for nine and 29 yards. Flacco hit Boldin again and looked to have picked up a first down. But Boldin fumbled the ball out of bounds, and the ball was ruled just one yard short of the first down.

And here's where the heartbreak came.

On second-and-1, Lee Evans, who had an injury-plagued season, broke free from the New England secondary. If Flacco could throw the ball over the Patriots' secondary, then Evans would have a great chance of giving Baltimore the lead and possibly a Super Bowl berth. The ball couldn't have been thrown more perfectly. Evans turned to catch the ball, with his outside shoulder at a 45-degree angle pointing toward the right sideline. The ball was in Evans hands, for just a second. It looked like the Ravens were heading to Indianapolis to play for a Super Bowl championship.

But just like that, Patriots cornerback Sterling Moore reached his arm in and knocked the ball out of Evans' hands. The pass was ruled incomplete.

"I threw my hands up and started running that way," Flacco said after the game. "Then I saw the ref give an incomplete sign."

Said Evans in the locker room postgame: "I feel I let everyone down."

On third-and-1, the ball fell incomplete to Pitta, setting up a seemingly easy, 32-yard field goal for Billy Cundiff. If Cundiff makes the kick, the Ravens and Patriots head to overtime for the right to play two weeks later in the Super Bowl.

But there was some confusion on the sideline. Cundiff was a down off in his routine. There was some speculation that the scoreboard was off, which threw Cundiff off. With fourth-and-1 on deck, Cundiff was not prepared and had to run onto the field. Despite the fact that it appeared Cundiff was rushing on the field to get ready for the field goal try, the Ravens elected not to call their final timeout.

The ball was snapped with one second remaining on the play clock. The line gave Cundiff good protection. The snap came from Morgan Cox, and punter Sam Koch was unable to spin the ball with the laces facing toward the uprights. Instead, the hold showed the laces facing to the side. Still, it was a 32-yard try slightly off of center.

Cundiff's leg connected with the football. And immediately, the ball began hooking left. The Patriots fans went wild. New England would hold on with a 23–20 win and head to the Super Bowl. The Baltimore sideline was in disbelief, saddened with what transpired in an otherwise epic AFC Championship Game.

"There's really no excuse for it," a despondent Cundiff said. "It just didn't go in."

Maybe it was the way they lost. But Ray Lewis, who had just completed his 16th NFL season didn't want to go out that way. He immediately announced he'd return for a 17th season, giving the Ravens some positive news during a night that was full of despair.

"For us to be here now, I am hungry again, I am thirsty again," Lewis said. "Is this my last time as a Raven? Absolutely not, it's just too much."

43 Vinny Testaverde vs. St. Louis in 1996

Though the Ravens stumbled to become a consistent winner early in team history, the inaugural season showcased a veteran quarterback still savvy enough to create excitement inside a football stadium.

Vinny Testaverde, about a month shy of turning 33 years old, posted the best season statistically for a quarterback in the Ravens' first year in Baltimore. He finished with 4,177 yards and 33 touchdowns, a number only Joe Flacco has come close to matching.

Testaverde was forced to throw the ball around in 1996 because the defense had trouble keeping points off the board. In five of Baltimore's first seven games, the Ravens gave up 26 points or more, with all those games resulting in losses. Testaverde had already eclipsed the 300-yard mark twice during that span, but to no avail.

In Week 9, the Ravens were in need of a win with St. Louis on the schedule. Early on it was more of the same, however, with the Rams jumping out to an early 13–0 lead midway through the second quarter. Up to this point, Testaverde had only thrown for 41 yards and an interception, so it wasn't looking good for Baltimore early on.

Something happened in Testaverde after that as he began to catch fire. Testaverde completed a 25-yard pass to Michael Jackson on third-and-14. Passes of nine and six yards to Jackson and Derrick Alexander, respectively, set Baltimore up at the St. Louis 13. Testaverde was sacked for a 14-yard loss on the next play. Never mind the loss of yardage, though. Testaverde got up and executed a 27-yard touchdown pass to receiver Floyd Turner. The extra-point attempt failed, and the Ravens trailed 13–6 at the half. (The missed extra point was the only time that ever happened in kicker Matt Stover's Ravens career.)

The halftime break seemed to have thrown Testaverde off his rhythm a bit in the second half as his first two drives ended in a punt and interception. The pick was thrown to Rams defensive back Todd Lyght, who returned it 25 yards for a touchdown to put St. Louis up 20–6. Stover added a 50-yard field goal with under 10 minutes left in the third quarter to cut the Rams' lead to 20–9.

The Rams were forced to punt, and Testaverde went back to work. He completed two passes to running back Earnest Byner, the second completion going for 40 yards, putting the Ravens at the Rams' 3-yard line. Two plays later, Bam Morris ran in a short touchdown, and Testaverde tossed a two-point conversion to receiver Derrick Alexander to cut the Rams' lead to 20–17. St. Louis then lengthened the lead to 23–17 with a 30-yard field goal to start the fourth quarter.

The Ravens began their next drive in great field position, thanks to a 29-yard kickoff return by Jermaine Lewis, as well as an additional five yards from a face mask penalty. The ball was at the Baltimore 40, and Testaverde went right at the St. Louis defense. His first play of the drive was a 37-yard completion to Byner. Byner then ran for 10 yards combined on the next two carries, before Testaverde found receiver Derrick Alexander in the end zone for a 13-yard score. The Ravens were now ahead 24–23.

On St. Louis' ensuing possession, safety Stevon Moore gave Baltimore the ball back after picking off quarterback Tony Banks. On the next Ravens possession, Testaverde completed three passes for 39 yards before Morris capped the drive off with a 10-yard touchdown run. The Ravens were now up by eight, 31–23.

The Rams wouldn't go away, though, and were able to tie the game up with just over three minutes remaining in the game. Running back Harold Green ran for a one-yard touchdown and also punched in the two-point conversion to tie the game at 31–31. The game ended up going into overtime after Stover missed a 32-yard field-goal attempt that would have won the game in regulation.

The Rams won the toss and elected to receive. In the process of its first overtime possession, St. Louis was able to hold the ball for 9:17, methodically moving the ball downfield. On third-and-7 at the Baltimore 15, kicker Chip Lohmiller came in to attempt an easy opportunity. The snap was then bobbled and fumbled, with Moore recovering the ball. Testaverde completed three passes for 38 yards on the next drive before being sacked and fumbling the ball away, giving the Rams another chance to win with 3:14 remaining.

At fourth-and-1 from the Baltimore 40, the Rams chose to go for it and failed. Banks' pass to Eddie Kennison fell incomplete, and the Ravens regained possession with 1:05 left. After a false start penalty, Testaverde found a groove when it mattered most. He hit Jackson for a 23-yard gain. He then completed a seven-yard pass to tight end Brian Kinchen. His third completion in a row went Jackson's way for 13 yards.

Just 20 seconds remained, and the Ravens were hoping now was the time to win the game. The initial call was for Testaverde to execute a quarterback sneak, call timeout, and allow Stover to kick a game-winner. Testaverde didn't like the call. He changed the play and instead dropped back to take a shot into the end zone. Facing pressure, Testaverde threw the ball off his back foot towards Jackson. Jackson was just breaking into his route when he saw the ball come his way. Testaverde figured that the pass was high enough to be incomplete if Jackson couldn't come down with it. But Jackson did, and it won the game for Baltimore.

Testaverde finished the afternoon 31-of-51 for 429 yards, three touchdowns, and two interceptions. The 429 yards passing still stands as a single-game record in Ravens history.

44 Torrey Smith Breaks Out against St. Louis

When Torrey Smith was drafted in the second round of the 2011 draft, he didn't have any off-season obligations to attend with his new team. The NFL had locked out the players, and therefore players were stuck in limbo. Sure, the league had just held a draft, but would there be an upcoming season?

The Ravens players were preparing like it, forming voluntary practices to prevent rust from building up. Receiver Derrick Mason organized the offense during a workout at Towson University, with the rookie Smith in attendance. Smith even tweeted on his personal account that his last play of the day was a 70-yard reception he caught from Joe Flacco.

By the time the lockout was lifted, all eyes were fixed on what Smith could do. Within a day of the season starting, the Ravens had released receiver Derrick Mason and tight end Todd Heap, two of Flacco's favorite targets. Anquan Boldin would become the primary target in the offense with a bunch of unproven receivers behind him.

Smith, a speedster who attended college at the University of Maryland, struggled early with drops during training camp, which prompted the Ravens to acquire Lee Evans in a trade from Buffalo. But Evans injured his foot early in the season and couldn't play in Baltimore's Week 3 meeting against St. Louis. Up to that point the Ravens were 1–1 with a home win over Pittsburgh and a road loss at Tennessee. The Ravens needed another receiver to take the pressure off of Boldin.

Smith emerged at the right time.

On Baltimore's second offensive play from scrimmage in the first quarter, Flacco dropped back and saw Smith streaking down the right sideline. Flacco hit the rookie in stride with a defender falling. Smith turned on the jets and flew down the field for a 74-yard touchdown. Just like that, Smith recorded his first career NFL catch and touchdown on the same play.

Two Rams and one Ravens possession later, Baltimore had the ball again and was driving on the St. Louis defense. On the second play of the series, Smith took an end around for a 10-yard rush.

Five plays later, it was time for Smith to record his second career catch in the NFL. Flacco gave a play fake to Ray Rice, which helped set up a generous pocket for the strong-armed quarterback. Flacco saw Smith breaking free and launched another deep pass.

Smith was able to get behind two St. Louis defenders and haul in a 41-yard pass for yet another touchdown. Two catches, two touchdowns. Yet Smith wasn't done just yet. The Ravens were able to force a three-and-out on St. Louis' next possession, giving the offense the ball back once more in the first quarter.

On the second play of that particular series, running back Ricky Williams was able to scamper for a 28-yard run to place the football at the Rams' 18-yard line. On the next play, Flacco was under center and faced a heavy St. Louis blitz. Throwing off his back foot, Flacco lofted a pass to Smith, who was in one-on-one coverage down the left sideline. Flacco put up a perfect fade, which Smith jumped up to grab in the end zone.

After two catch-less games, Smith burst onto the scene with three catches, 133 yards, and three touchdowns in the first quarter. Smith would add two more catches during the game to give him a grand total of 152 yards. The Ravens blew the Rams out by a score of 37–7.

"I've been playing football forever, and I've been making plays forever," Smith said after the game. "Having a game like this, it proves to other people that haven't seen me play, it lets them know I can play."

45 Steve McNair to the Rescue

For the majority of the Ravens' history, getting quality quarterback play was a rarity. After Vinny Testaverde's two years, the organization trotted out Jim Harbaugh, Eric Zeier, Tony Banks, Trent Dilfer, Elvis Grbac, and Kyle Boller.

It wasn't pretty.

Boller was arguably the worst, as an entire chapter of this book is dedicated to the years he spent angering fans throughout Charm City. In the summer of 2006, in need of a quarterback, the Ravens gave the Tennessee Titans a 2007 fourth-round draft pick for Steve McNair.

Dubbed Air McNair during his collegiate days at Alcorn State, McNair could flat-out launch the ball downfield. Having spent 11

Steve McNair scrambles against the Tennessee Titans in the second quarter of his first game against his former team in Nashville on November 12, 2006. The Ravens won 27–26 behind McNair's 373 yards passing and three TDs.

years with the Titans organization, McNair totaled 27,141 yards passing and 156 touchdowns. He was beloved by Titans fans, having led their team to a Super Bowl game during the 1999 season.

Baltimore fans were ecstatic about McNair, mainly because it was seen as an upgrade over Boller. McNair led the Ravens to four consecutive wins to start the season, tossing five touchdown passes in the process.

McNair then suffered back-to-back setbacks, throwing four interceptions in two games, while getting injured in the second one. The Ravens dropped both contests and fell to 4–2 to begin the season.

But behind a strong defense and a quarterback as talented as McNair, things began to pick back up. In early November, McNair threw for 245 yards in a win over Cincinnati. The next week, a 27–26 win over McNair's former team, Tennessee, McNair completed 29 of 47 passes for 373 yards and three touchdowns. Down 26–17 heading into the fourth quarter, McNair knew he had to pick the pace up offensively. Baltimore did add a field goal early in the fourth quarter to cut Tennessee's lead to 26–20.

With the score still the same at the 5:09 mark, McNair took over and led Baltimore down the field. He completed a 34-yard pass to receiver Demetrius Williams to place the Ravens at the Tennessee 15-yard line. Two plays later, McNair hooked up with what would be the game-winning touchdown to receiver Derrick Mason from 11 yards out.

"His demeanor, it just never ceased to amaze me," Ravens coach Brian Billick said of McNair following the win. "The calm this man has. At no point have I ever seen him blink there, and there was a few times to blink out there."

The Ravens actually trailed that game by 19 points at one point, making it the largest deficit the organization ever overcame to win a game. That mark was broken when Baltimore came back from a 21-point deficit to defeat Arizona in 2011.

From there on out, McNair was efficient as Baltimore's starter. Interceptions were limited, and McNair played mostly mistake-free football. Against Kansas City in Week 14, McNair threw for 283 yards and a touchdown in a 20–10 victory. The Ravens would go on to post their best regular season record in franchise history at 13–3. But they'd fall in the divisional round of the playoffs to

Indianapolis, 15–6. After a sharp season, McNair threw two interceptions in the loss.

McNair would start six games in 2007 but dealt with injuries throughout. The following April, McNair announced his retirement.

Tragedy struck when a young woman named Sahel Kazemi murdered McNair with multiple gunshot wounds on July 4, 2009. Kazemi was also dead at the scene with one gunshot to her head. Nashville police ruled the case a murder-suicide.

"Steve was such a happy person," said Derrick Mason, McNair's teammate in both Baltimore and Tennessee, in a statement after the shooting. "I even called him 'Smile.' He was always smiling and was always willing to lend a hand to anyone who needed it. I've known him for 13 years, and he was the most selfless, happiest, and friendliest person I have known. His family and my family are close, and it is a blow to us all. It is a devastating day. Steve will always have a place in my heart. My family and I are hurting for his family. Our thoughts and prayers are with them."

46 Billy Cundiff vs. Justin Tucker

There never seems to be a happy medium if you're a place-kicker. It can be the most thrilling experience to kick a game-winner for your team. But it can also be the most alienating. As a kicker, you're not participating in drills with your teammates. You're doing your own work, with a long snapper and punter. You're off to the side, so to speak, while your teammates beat each other up in practice.

The instant you become an inconsistent kicker, the easier it becomes for your teammates to turn their backs on you.

During the 2010 season, Ravens kicker Billy Cundiff was almost automatic. He made 26 of his 29 attempts for a career-best 89.7

kicking percentage. His performance warranted him a new contract with Baltimore, which was worth $15 million over five years. From that moment, it seemed Cundiff was the long-term kicker in Baltimore.

But Cundiff didn't live up to those expectations during the 2011 season. He struggled from long range, hitting just one of six kicks from 50 yards or further. He finished the year 28-of-37, good for just a 75.7 percentage.

But perhaps the worst moment of his 2011 season was in the AFC Championship Game against New England. With 15 seconds left on the clock, he rushed onto the field after a mix-up on the sideline. The Ravens didn't call a timeout and had Cundiff attempt a 32-yarder to send the game into overtime. Cundiff's kick hooked wide left, and New England ended up reaching the Super Bowl as a result.

The Ravens are a calculated franchise, so they weren't going to release Cundiff for the miss. Sure, his season wasn't strong, but he'd still have every opportunity to retain his job. In early February 2012, one high-ranking team official said it would remain Cundiff's job to lose. But the official said he'd have competition to prove his missed kick was a one-time blip, and that he could handle pressure.

Once the three-day draft extravaganza was finished in April, the Ravens brought in rookie Justin Tucker out of Texas for a workout. He wasn't signed immediately, which may have given Cundiff a belief that the Ravens would stick with him no matter what.

"The team doesn't have anybody else here," Cundiff said on May 23, 2012. "The team believes in me. The coach has been really positive with me throughout the whole off-season."

Not so fast, Billy. Six days after saying that, the Ravens agreed to terms on a deal with Tucker. There would be a competition after all. Even so, the job was still Cundiff's to lose. Tucker wasn't a highly ranked kicker coming out of Texas. How could an inexperienced kicker just out of college take a veteran's job in one preseason?

"[Cundiff's] done nothing to make us think he can't handle that kind of competition," Ravens coach John Harbaugh said after the

Tucker signing. "There's always competition. Obviously, Billy has the edge. Everybody's fighting for their job."

But when Tucker came into off-season workouts and training camp, one thing became apparent: the kid could kick. Rarely would he miss, and his range was drastically better than Cundiff's. During the 2012 training camp, Tucker made 95 percent of his kicks attempted in front of the media. Cundiff didn't come close.

In Baltimore's third preseason game against Jacksonville, Cundiff was benched, and all of the kicking duties were given to Tucker. Tucker made kicks from 33 and 53 yards and boomed touchbacks out of the end zone. It didn't take long for the Ravens to realize they had a new kicker they needed to go with. Three days after the preseason game against the Jaguars, Cundiff was released.

"Billy had a great camp, the best he has had with us," Harbaugh said. "He showed, like he always has, a toughness and an ability to come back and a be a top-flight NFL kicker. These decisions are never easy, and this one was difficult for all of us."

The move proved to be a good one. Tucker hit regular season game-winners against New England and San Diego and defeated Denver in the postseason with a field goal in double overtime. Up 28–6 in the Super Bowl against San Francisco, the 49ers began a furious rally in the second half. Tucker made two key fourth-quarter kicks to aid Baltimore in becoming Super Bowl champions.

Tucker finished his rookie campaign 30-of-33 (90.9 percent) with a long of 56. By 2012 Baltimore had a new long-term kicker. His name was Justin Tucker.

"I really do appreciate the front office and the coaching staff putting their faith in me," Tucker said. "I will do everything I can to bring my lunch pail to work every day, and I know that sounds cliché. I've said it probably a hundred times before, but that's really the attitude that everybody has around here. This is a blue-collar atmosphere, and we are just trying to bring our lunch pail to work every day."

47 Cursed Quarterbacks

By this time, you've read about the woes of Trent Dilfer, Elvis Grbac, and Kyle Boller. You've also read about the solid season Steve McNair had in 2006. Not to leave anyone out, Baltimore had a few more quarterbacks over the years who were dreadful. Ever since the Ravens moved to Baltimore in 1996, good quarterbacks have been few and far between.

Vinny Testaverde posted the best regular season in franchise history in 1996 with 4,177 passing yards. A season later, his passing total fell to 2,971 yards, though he only started 13 games.

Eric Zeier, a star quarterback at the University of Georgia, was Testaverde's backup and started three games in 1997. And when he was in ball games, he had some decent moments. In the three starts and five games he appeared in, Zeier accounted for 958 yards, seven touchdowns, and one interception. It appeared the Ravens had an up-and-coming quarterback they could count on.

But in 1998 coach Ted Marchibroda tabbed Jim Harbaugh to be Baltimore's starter, after the Ravens traded draft picks to acquire him from Indianapolis. It reunited Harbaugh and Marchibroda from when the two were quarterback and coach with the Colts. Harbaugh disappointed in his lone season with Baltimore, however, throwing for just 1,839 yards, 12 touchdowns, and 11 interceptions. It was just the third time in his career that Harbaugh threw for less than 2,000 yards. Zeier stayed on as Baltimore's backup but did start four games. Zeier's run in Baltimore would end as he left for Tampa Bay the following season. Harbaugh was out, too, as he continued his playing days with San Diego in 1999.

Tony Banks was next in line in Baltimore, with the Ravens getting the young quarterback in a trade with St. Louis. The Ravens began the year with Scott Mitchell and Stoney Case starting at quarterback, with neither looking the part. Case finished the season with three touchdowns to eight interceptions, and Mitchell tossed just one touchdown to four interceptions. Banks started the last 10 games and had the most success out of the three quarterbacks. He finished the year with 2,136 yards, 17 touchdowns, and eight interceptions. Not bad for a guy practically run out of town in St. Louis.

The 2000 season was a different story for Banks, who returned to his blundering ways as a quarterback. Banks started the first eight games of the year but averaged an interception each game. He had a strong five-touchdown performance against Jacksonville, which inflated his stats, considering he threw just three touchdowns in the remaining seven games he started. Baltimore did not score a touchdown in the last four games Banks started in 2000, causing coach Brian Billick to defer starting quarterback duties to Trent Dilfer.

Dilfer wasn't much better, throwing 12 touchdowns and 10 interceptions in his eight regular season starts. He only surpassed the 200-yard mark three times, though he was a little more efficient as a game manager. Baltimore's defense was too good that year. Dilfer didn't have to do much as the Ravens were still able to win the Super Bowl.

The following year was the Elvis Grbac experience, which backfired considerably. In 14 starts, Grbac posted 3,033 yards but only converted 15 touchdowns to 18 interceptions. His run lasted just one season in Baltimore. Including two playoff games, Baltimore only scored 20 or more points seven times with Grbac at quarterback.

Next up were quarterbacks Chris Redman and Jeff Blake. Redman began the season the starter, and put up okay numbers. He only threw three interceptions in six starts, but was abysmal in Baltimore's Week 2 shutout loss to Tampa Bay. An injury derailed Redman's season, and Blake stepped in to start. Blake started the last 10 games, finishing the year with 2,084 yards, 13 touchdowns, and 11 interceptions. It seemed par for the course as far as Baltimore quarterbacks were concerned.

Two thousand three brought in the Kyle Boller era, which brought a lot of frowns to Baltimoreans by the time the 2007 season ended. Anthony Wright started 14 games during the Boller era due to injury.

It took a long time, but drafting Joe Flacco in 2008 finally ended the quarterback woes Baltimore dealt with for years. When folks want to criticize Flacco for not being up to their standard, remember what preceded him.

48 Anquan Boldin, Strictly Business

During his three years in Baltimore, Anquan Boldin was a focus-first, talk-second kind of player. Rarely would he make himself accessible for media interviews during the week, opting to spend his time away from the spotlight that comes with being a professional football player.

For Boldin, what mattered most to him was winning games. After spending his first seven seasons with Arizona, Boldin, along with a fifth-round draft pick, was traded to Baltimore for third- and fourth-round selections. With Boldin on board, Baltimore was thought to finally have a receiving group that could terrorize NFL secondaries. Along with Boldin was Derrick Mason, and the Ravens also brought in veteran T.J. Houshmandzadeh. Todd Heap was still a receiving threat as a tight end, making it seem the Ravens were about to blow up yardage-wise.

For Boldin, it was an ideal situation to play in an offense more suited to his physical style of play. The trade paid off in a big way early. Boldin was a key part in Baltimore's season-opening 10–9 win against the New York Jets, totaling 110 receiving yards. Boldin's best game in 2010 came in Week 3 against Cleveland, where he exploded for 142 yards and three touchdowns. Boldin and Joe Flacco built an early rapport that led to the receiver churning out 837 yards and seven touchdowns in year one with Baltimore.

As the next two seasons unfolded, Boldin became a mentor for a suddenly young receiving corps. The Ravens didn't bring back Houshmandzadeh and released Mason and Heap. Boldin placed it upon himself to help instruct rookies like Torrey Smith, Tandon Doss, and LaQuan Williams to get them up to speed with the offense.

"He is the definition of a pro," Smith said. "Faithful, religious, a great father. He has always been willing to help me in any way. And he is one of the great route runners of all-time, so I have certainly benefitted from that."

Boldin remained Flacco's go-to target, hauling in 887 yards and three touchdowns in 2011. In 2012 Boldin recorded 921 yards and four touchdowns. It was late in the postseason, though, when Boldin began showing how focused he was. Against Indianapolis, Boldin caught five passes for 145 yards and a touchdown. Two weeks later against New England in the AFC Championship Game, Boldin caught two touchdown passes. He couldn't hide from reporters much longer, especially during Super Bowl week.

Soft-spoken and tight-lipped, Boldin expressed the kind of confidence he had in himself and his teammates to win Super Bowl XLVII.

"For me, I just want to make it another game," Boldin said the Tuesday before the Super Bowl. "I know there's a lot that's going on around the game, but there's still a game to be played. For me, I'm here for that reason and that reason only."

Boldin would go on to catch six passes for 104 yards and a touchdown in Baltimore's Super Bowl championship win over the 49ers. It was an unbelievable moment for the veteran wide receiver.

But with Baltimore looking to put together its 2013 roster, it needed Boldin to take a pay cut due to salary cap constraints. Boldin refused, and the Ravens traded him to the same 49ers squad he beat up on.

After the transaction was complete, general manager Ozzie Newsome released a statement thanking Boldin for his three years in Baltimore, in which he totaled 2,645 yards and 14 touchdowns.

"Managing and assembling your roster is difficult and among the most important things we do," Newsome said. "It is not always pleasant, and in the case of Anquan, it is unpleasant. We know he can still play at a high level. What he has done in his three seasons with us goes well beyond the numbers, and his numbers are very good. He fit in as a Raven from day one. His leadership, just by the way he played and prepared, was a powerful force for us. And when we needed the tough catch in important times, he made those. Look at his production in our Super Bowl run. He stepped up in a big way. When he wasn't targeted, or when we weren't passing, his blocking was outstanding. We all thank 'Q' for what he did for the Ravens over the last three years."

49 Haloti Ngata: Another Piece to an Elite Defense

It didn't take long for Haloti Ngata to become one of the NFL's premier defensive tackles. He had it in him from the beginning. He's a prototypical space-eater in a 3-4 defense. At 6'4" and 340 pounds, Ngata has become an immovable force on the line. His presence in the trenches frees linebackers up to make plays in opposing backfields.

But his game is better than just being a space-eater up front. He has enough power to where he can get after the quarterback,

Switching Jerseys on Fridays

Each Friday at practice, the Baltimore Ravens will switch jerseys with one another, wearing a different number they normally don't put on. It can sometimes result in hilarity, especially when a defensive lineman swaps jerseys with a defensive back. For example, it wouldn't be out of the question for Lardarius Webb—5'10", 182 pounds—to swap with Haloti Ngata,—6'4", 340 pounds. The jersey on Ngata would be extra tight, and Webb's would be rather loose. Some media members speculate the team does this to try and disguise who's practicing and who's not. If that's the case, it rarely works. More than likely, it's a camaraderie thing.

even when he's fighting through double teams. Offensive linemen hate going against Ngata as his combination of power, strength, and speed rank at the top of elite defensive linemen.

Ngata was drafted in the first round with the 12th overall pick of the 2006 draft. It was the first time the Ravens used a first-round pick on a defensive lineman. Ngata proved his value in his first season. He started every game as a rookie and recorded his first sack against Pittsburgh in Baltimore's 15th game of the season.

Ngata quickly became a focal point on the defense. In 2007 he sacked opposing quarterbacks three times and tallied 63 combined tackles. And that was on a struggling unit that finished the season 5–11. Once John Harbaugh took over the team in 2008, Ngata began dominating opponents.

Though Ngata's play on the field is violent, he's quiet off the field. One of the more laid-back players on the team, Ngata has an easy-going personality and gets along with his teammates quite easily. That's helped with team chemistry up front, especially between the defensive line and inside linebackers. Ray Lewis has stated multiple times that Ngata's addition in 2006 helped him tremendously because, if Ngata wins a battle up front, he'll make a play in the backfield. If he doesn't win the battle, Ngata's good enough to occupy the blocker, which allows Lewis to run in to make the play.

In 2010, Ngata set a career best with 5½ sacks and tied a career-high with five pass deflections. That same season, Carolina Panthers center Ryan Kalil told ESPN reporter Jeffri Chadiha that there's only one defender he hates going against.

"That was the only time in my life that I've ever been frightened of another player on a football field," Kalil told Chadiha. "But that's why Haloti's presence alone is such a big thing. He has the size, the strength, and the quickness to do whatever he wants out there."

From 2010 to 2012, Ngata has sacked quarterbacks 15½ times—5½ in 2010, five in 2011, and five in 2012. With Lewis retired and Ed Reed leaving for Houston in the 2013 off-season, Ngata will be asked to take more of a leadership role on defense.

"I think I've got to get out of my comfort zone and be more vocal," Ngata told BaltimoreRavens.com in March 2013. "Especially if we're going to have a younger defense, show them what it's about and give them somebody to look up to. With what I've done in Baltimore and things I've accomplished individually, I think it comes with the territory. I'm definitely up for the challenge."

50 The Ravens vs. Peyton Manning

Let's be frank about this. Peyton Manning has historically been a thorn in the side of the Baltimore Ravens since he entered the NFL in 1998. Once Manning got going as one of football's greatest to ever play, he's been extremely tough for Baltimore to defeat.

The Ravens won the first two games against Manning, a 38–31 victory in 1998 and a 39–27 win in 2001. That's when things get murky.

Manning won his first game against the Ravens on October 13, 2002. The Ravens and Colts were in a tough game throughout the entire 60 minutes, with the game tied at 13–13 heading into the fourth quarter. Colts kicker Mike Vanderjagt made two field goals to go ahead 19–13 before Ravens running back Jamal Lewis scored a go-ahead touchdown, putting Baltimore up 20–19 with 9:08 remaining. The Ravens were able to force Indianapolis to turn the ball over on downs to regain possession with a chance to put the game away.

Baltimore was unable to do so, being forced to punt with 2:37 remaining in the fourth quarter. Manning went to work, completing three consecutive passes before being sacked by Ravens linebacker Peter Boulware. Never mind the 13-yard loss, as Manning rifled a 16-yard completion to Marvin Harrison, bringing up fourth-and-5. However, a false start penalty brought the Colts back to fourth-and-10.

Manning's next pass fell incomplete to Qadry Ismail, who played the previous three seasons with Baltimore. But a defensive pass interference penalty was called, which turned out to be a 22-yard gain for the Colts. A 15-yard pass to Harrison got the Ravens closer, with running back Edgerrin James getting Indianapolis to the Baltimore 20. With nine seconds left, Vanderjagt kicked a game-winning field goal and gave Manning his first victory over Baltimore.

The two teams would meet again in 2004 and 2005, with Manning coming out victorious in both. In the 2004 meeting, Indianapolis won 20–10, with Manning accounting for 249 yards and a touchdown. In 2005 the Colts won 24–7.

The next time Manning would face off against the Ravens would be in the 2006 postseason. It was the first time the Ravens defense had been able to stifle Manning since the first two times Baltimore matched up against him. Manning was limited to 15-of-30 passing for 170 yards and two interceptions. Manning was erratic all game, with Indianapolis held to five field goals. Yet the Ravens' offense was worse. Ravens quarterback Steve McNair threw for 173 yards and tossed two picks of his own, negating Manning's poor showing. Indianapolis won a field goal battle, defeating Baltimore 15–6.

In the 2007 regular season, Baltimore's worst since 1996, Manning's Colts destroyed the Ravens 44–20. In embarrassing fashion, Manning threw for 249 yards and four touchdowns. A year later in John Harbaugh's inaugural season, Manning threw three touchdowns in a 31–3 beatdown.

On November 22, 2009, Baltimore played Manning closely. He was able to post 299 passing yards but only threw one touchdown and tossed two interceptions. But it was Matt Stover, Baltimore's longtime kicker who was released before the regular season and now with Indianapolis, who kicked what would be the game-winning field goal in the fourth quarter. Manning and the Colts won again, this time besting Baltimore 17–15.

The two teams would meet again in the divisional round of the playoffs, with Indianapolis winning 20–3. Manning went 30-of-44 for 246 yards, two touchdowns, and one interception. That was the last time Baltimore would face Manning as a Colt. During those days, Manning went 8–2 against the Ravens.

Manning missed the 2011 regular season with a nagging neck injury that required surgery. The Colts released him following the season and drafted rookie quarterback Andrew Luck with the first overall pick in the 2012 draft. Without Manning, Baltimore finally ended its eight-game skid against Indianapolis, defeating a Manning-less Colts squad 24–10 on December 11, 2011.

When Manning hit free agency, he ultimately decided on playing for the Denver Broncos. After a 3–3 start, Manning's Broncos caught fire, winning the next 10 games of the season. That included a 34–17 win over Baltimore in Week 15. Manning only threw for 204 yards and a touchdown, though running back Knowshon Moreno was able to do a lot of damage by running for 115 yards.

Manning was now 9–2 against the Ravens, having owned them the majority of his career.

For all the misery Manning gave Ravens fans over the years, Baltimore will gladly take the one win it was able to get over Manning since 2001, however. It was the divisional round of the 2012 play-offs, with Denver a clear favorite heading into the matchup.

The Ravens weren't able to fully stop Manning, as he threw for 290 yards and three touchdowns. But the defense was able to pick off two passes, one of which helped set up the game-winning field goal. Baltimore's offense made just a few more plays than Denver's, as the Ravens escaped with a 38–35 win and advanced to the AFC Championship Game.

In Manning's first 12 meetings against Baltimore, he went 9–3. But, if you're a Ravens fan, that third loss Manning experienced might make up for all the havoc he caused for just over a decade.

51 Ray Lewis Announces His Retirement

It seemed unusual at first that multiple Ravens players were interested in what Ray Lewis had to say at a usual Wednesday press conference. But five minutes into Lewis' presser on January 2, 2013, it became clear why his teammates were watching their leader answer question after question from the media contingency.

Lewis was formally announcing his retirement. His team had found out only two hours prior to this news announcement. In a team meeting, coach John Harbaugh asked Ray if he had anything to share. Lewis stood up to address the team, speaking to them about the importance of loyalty and commitment. Lewis committed himself to strenuous rehab to get back on the field. Lewis' message was that with dedication, anything is possible. Then he told his teammates, "This is my last ride."

The 2012 NFL season would be the 17th and final season for Ray Lewis, one of the greatest middle linebackers to ever play the game. A sure first-ballot Hall of Famer, Lewis was initially thought to miss the remainder of the 2012 season. But Lewis convinced general manager Ozzie Newsome to place him on the injured reserve–designated to return list, giving him the slight chance of returning for the postseason.

"He talked to me about a lot of different things," Smith said. "We've been through a lot of similar things in life. Growing up and even now. To have him as someone to talk to and lean on, as an older guy and a mentor, has been a blessing."

It didn't appear Lewis was giving retirement that much of a thought until he tore his triceps against the Cowboys in Week 6. Lewis began most of the rehab in his home state of Florida, where he got to spend time with his children. His oldest son, Ray Lewis III, pledged a football commitment to the University of Miami, Lewis' collegiate team. The amount of time Lewis spent with his son made him realize it was time to honor a promise and spend more time with him as he becomes a college football player.

"It was probably when I had to look at my son," Lewis said, when asked the moment he knew it was time to retire. "It's hard to look at him and know that he's going through some of the things that I'm going through and see the warrior side of him, but see, ultimately, what he needs. My decision was kind of made up from the first day that I went down [to Florida], and I was in the cast, and I watched his game. I said, 'You know what? You have to go back and finish it.' You have to go finish it, because I've always taught my children if you start something, finish it. That was my whole goal, so my mind was kind of made up then that I had to come back and make this one last run."

The locker room was abuzz that day, as Baltimore's leader had finalized his decision. His teammates were getting used to the idea that Lewis would never retire.

"It caught me by surprise because we all thought the great Ray Lewis was going to play forever," linebacker Terrell Suggs said. "I thought he was going to surpass Brett Favre and still be out there doing it well into his forties."

It rallied the troops, you could say. There was a different level of focus that day, and it was evident throughout the postseason. Lewis could do that. He had a unique ability to inspire those around him. His teammates wanted nothing more than to send Lewis out on a high note.

"When he says something, your eyes and mind—everything just zones in," linebacker Josh Bynes said. "You know it's going to be from his heart, from something he's experienced. You want to take in everything you can from him. Hearing him speak still blows your mind. There are so many things you can take from Ray."

Said kicker Justin Tucker: "Anything he has to say, you're going to listen to and take to heart. I think that's what everybody did today."

The ensuing Sunday would be the last time Lewis ran out of the tunnel at M&T Bank Stadium in a Ravens uniform. As he typically does, Lewis did the squirrel dance, something he made popular much earlier in his career. It was the last time the city of Baltimore would ever see that.

With the clock ticking down and the offense running the clock out, the crowd began chanting Lewis' name. Feeling the moment, Harbaugh sent Lewis in for the final play of the game. After the final kneel down, Lewis broke out one more squirrel dance for the home fans, to their glee.

Lewis' season didn't end that day. Or the week after that, or the week after that. It ended in Super Bowl XLVII, with the Ravens defeating the 49ers 34–31. Lewis announced his retirement the first week of January. He officially retired a month later as a champion.

"What better way to go out?" Lewis said. "And, I think, more importantly, it was my teammates in the way I went out—the things we've been through all year. I was tested through this journey, it was an up-and-down roller coaster, the injuries, the people, and we stayed together. And now, I get to ride off into the sunset with my second ring."

52 Matt Cavanaugh, the Scapegoat

Even with a Super Bowl title under their belts, Brian Billick and Matt Cavanaugh could never maintain expectations for Baltimore's offense.

From 1999 to 2004, Cavanaugh was Billick's offensive coordinator, an extension of the philosophy that made Billick so successful when he was calling the plays with Minnesota in the 1990s. But that kind of offensive explosion, seen in 1998 when Minnesota had receivers Cris Carter and Randy Moss, running back Robert Smith and quarterback Randall Cunningham, never came to Baltimore. The defense could only receive all the headlines for so long. The 2000 season was becoming a distant memory. As long as the Ravens weren't living up to expectations, someone was to blame.

That someone became Cavanaugh. If you tuned into a local sports talk radio show, you probably heard someone ranting about Cavanaugh's vanilla offense. Cavanaugh became an enemy in Baltimore, someone to sling mud at when things weren't going the Ravens' way.

A lot of the issues stemmed from Kyle Boller not turning out to be the quarterback the organization hoped for. But before Boller, Cavanaugh was working with Tony Banks, Trent Dilfer, Jeff Blake, and Chris Redman. It wasn't exactly a who's who of NFL quarterbacks. It could've been construed more as a "who's not."

Entering the 2004 season, there wasn't a seat hotter than Cavanaugh's. And then someone lit another match under it after the season opener against Cleveland, as the Browns defeated the Ravens 20–3. Boller finished the day 22-of-38 for 191 yards and two interceptions. A run-first coordinator, Jamal Lewis was only able to pick up 57 yards on 20 carries. In the first five games of the season, the Ravens only broke 300 total yards of offense once, and that was against Cincinnati in a 23–9 win. Baltimore totaled 380 yards, with Lewis having a big day on the ground, running for 186 yards and a touchdown.

The low point of the season came when New England whipped Baltimore 24–3 in Week 12. Boller finished the day 15-of-35 for 93 yards and an interception. Something had to give, and there was one familiar face to point the finger at.

When coaches take these high-profile positions, the scrutiny will come with the territory. In Cavanaugh's defense, the Ravens dealt with a rash of injuries on offense throughout the year. But Cavanaugh and the offense could never catch a rhythm together. The offense seemed forced and was stagnant at best.

The offense ended 2004 with 4,375 yards for the year, which ranked 31st in the NFL. The defense ranked sixth in total yards surrendered, and gave up a total of 4,803, almost 500 more yards than what the Ravens were able to do through 16 games. That's when you know things are bad.

A few days before the season finale against Miami, television stations WJZ-TV and Comcast SportsNet reported that Cavanaugh would be fired at the conclusion of the season. The Ravens denied the reports initially, as Cavanaugh had to endure coaching the final game against Miami, a 30–23 win. A couple of days after the game, Cavanaugh resigned amid the pressure he was facing. Reading between the lines, Cavanaugh had the choice to resign or be fired.

"Matt and I sat down and had a very frank conversation about where we needed to go, what we needed to do to move forward, what changes we need to make in order to be more productive, particularly on the offensive side of the ball," Billick said. "Matt and I both agreed that part of that change would be at the offensive coordinator's position."

Cavanaugh wasn't a good offensive coordinator in Baltimore. In fact, he was quite the opposite. But he did receive the brunt of the criticism for the offense's failures, even though he never had a capable quarterback under his watch, or an elite receiver to test defenses downfield. Based on the personnel, it made sense to Cavanaugh to run Lewis as much as he could.

But that didn't stop media and fans alike from piling on. Baltimore's *City Paper* summed the city's attitude toward Cavanaugh up best in September 2005:

> These Ravens fans, fed up with the nickel-and-dime, nibble-and-peck efforts of Cavanaugh's "run, and run some more" offense spew such venom that we half expected them to gather in the village square—or Unitas Court—flaming torches in hand, riled and ready to scour the streets demanding the head of the heretic Cavanaugh. Before this actually transpired, Cavanaugh graciously "resigned" at the end of last season; after six years, these fans have finally gotten their wish.

53 Jim Caldwell's 2012 Run

From a national perspective, firing Cam Cameron, Baltimore's offensive coordinator from 2008 through Week 14 of 2012, was a bit much. How could an organization fire its offensive coordinator that late in a season, especially when it was the defense that had been surrendering more yards and points than what Baltimore was used to?

Ask a Ravens fan in the city of Baltimore, and they'll tell you the decision was long overdue. Fans were sick of Cameron, believing he was holding back an offense filled with enough playmakers to do better offensively.

When the Ravens pulled the trigger and fired Cameron, there was a bit of a shock from both perspectives. Baltimoreans didn't expect the Ravens to make that move mid-season, and national followers thought the decision was irrational.

But the decision was made, and now Baltimore needed a replacement. It promoted Jim Caldwell from quarterbacks coach to interim offensive coordinator. Caldwell was previously the head coach in Indianapolis after serving as quarterbacks coach under Tony Dungy. During the 2009 season, Caldwell coached the Colts to a Super Bowl berth, which they lost to New Orleans 31–17. However, when Peyton Manning was forced to sit out the 2011 season, Indianapolis went 2–14, and Caldwell was subsequently fired.

Caldwell had a strong coaching pedigree but was never an offensive coordinator at any level. Could he become a successful one in such a short amount of time?

"Jim is qualified," Harbaugh said. "Jim is a heck of a coach, and we have a heck of staff. They'll do a great job, and I am looking forward to seeing how it plays out."

In his first statement as offensive coordinator, Caldwell said it would take baby steps to improve a Ravens offense that had begun to struggle midway through the season.

"What we're trying to do is just to get about that much better," Caldwell said, motioning his thumb and index finger slightly apart from each other. "That's about it. And that's a difficult task, obviously, trying to get that done in this league."

All eyes were on Caldwell and the offense for Baltimore's next game against Denver. Losers of two in a row, could Caldwell get the offense back on track in such a quick turnaround? Nope. It didn't happen, as Denver used a fast start en route to a 34–17 win. But the Baltimore offense did start producing some plays in the second half, with Joe Flacco and Dennis Pitta having a solid outing. Pitta was able to finish with 125 yards and two touchdowns, though being down 31–3 after three quarters was too much for Baltimore to overcome.

It was on to the next week against a Giants squad for Baltimore's offense to show improvement. With a second week of preparation and familiarity, a difference showed on game day.

Anquan Boldin caught seven passes for 93 yards, and Torrey Smith hauled in five catches for 88 yards. Pitta added 56 receiving yards as Flacco finished the game with 309 yards and two touchdowns. The running game was stellar as well, with Bernard Pierce running for 123 yards, and Ray Rice totaling 107.

For a moment, it was seen as a Giants' blip, given that Baltimore rested its starters in the following week's season finale against Cincinnati.

In the wild-card round of the playoffs, the Ravens accrued 439 total yards, with Pierce totaling over 100 on the ground again. Baltimore defeated Indianapolis 24–9 and advanced to the divisional round to face Denver in a rematch of the regular season game Caldwell made his coordinating debut in.

The offense was night-and-day different than in the first meeting, with Flacco dictating the offense and able to get in a solid rhythm throughout. The Ravens defeated Denver 38–35 in double overtime, with the offense picking up 479 yards against one of the NFL's better defenses throughout the 2012 season. A week later in the AFC Championship Game against the Patriots, Baltimore was able to rack up another 356 total yards en route to a 28–13 win.

The following day, Caldwell was named the official offensive coordinator heading into the 2013 season.

"He's a good person, and he's genuine," Harbaugh said. "He's to the point [where] he doesn't mince words, and he coaches football from the beginning of the day until the end of the day, and the guys appreciate that."

In the Super Bowl, Caldwell called yet another fantastic game, which saw Flacco throw for 287 yards and three touchdowns. His relationship with Flacco grew throughout the season and culminated in success when the offensive play-calling duties became his.

One of the reasons Caldwell was so liked in the Ravens locker room during the run was his ability to listen to the players and adjust his game plan to what they liked to run. The chemistry continued throughout the course of the season's final stretch and ended with the Ravens becoming champions.

"I think we had a good relationship before he became coordinator, so I think he has settled in a little bit," Flacco said. "I think he has had the time to really prepare for it now, and I think we just continue to grow week by week."

54 Joe Flacco Assumes Control

For 17 years, Ray Lewis led the Baltimore Ravens. Lewis was the defining presence in the locker room whom teammates turned to. He was the face of the franchise, having been one of the greatest middle linebackers to ever play the game. Lewis was the focal point of the 2000 defense that won a Super Bowl and was the quintessential team leader. Ask anyone in that locker room, and they'd tell you Lewis could motivate players like no one else they'd ever encountered before.

So when Lewis announced his retirement, there was some speculation as to who would become "the guy" inside the locker room after the 2012 season. Would it be Ed Reed, the longtime safety? Would it be Anquan Boldin? Terrell Suggs, perhaps?

Shortly after the 2012 Super Bowl season ended, Reed was allowed to sign with the Houston Texans. Boldin was traded to San Francisco. Suggs remained with the franchise and would certainly become the leader of the defense.

But it was clear a transition was in the making. The Ravens were now Joe Flacco's team. The way the roster was being rebuilt, to include younger, more energetic players across the board, it made sense to hand the reins to Flacco. Flacco had just been named Super Bowl MVP for a 287-yard, three-touchdown performance against the 49ers. With Baltimore's offense proving it could win a championship, it was only fitting for the quarterback, who'd be entering his sixth NFL season, to become the face of the franchise.

"Regardless of what anyone says, Joe Flacco, he's proven he's one hell of a leader, so I don't have any problems sharing the role with him," Suggs said on NFL Network a week after the Super Bowl.

On March 3, 2013, Flacco was suddenly paid like a leader. The Ravens gave him a five-year, $120.6 million contract, which was the highest NFL contract in the football history at the time.

In the public eye, Flacco has never truly possessed that leader mentality, for whatever reason. Maybe it was because Lewis was so vocal and inspirational that Flacco's style of leadership never radiated like it should have. Players lead in different ways. And by all accounts, Flacco was always a budding leader in the offensive huddle. But with the post–Super Bowl roster makeover, it was time for Flacco to become the leader of the entire team.

"I'm going to be who I am, and I'm going to continue to get better every year and continue to get my guys better around me," Flacco said. "But other than those things, other than continuing to push my teammates and myself, you are going to do everything the same."

The success speaks for itself. Before Flacco became Baltimore's quarterback, the Ravens had been to four postseason trips from 1996 to 2007, with one Super Bowl championship. With Flacco under center, the Ravens have gone to five postseason appearances, three AFC Championship Games, and won one Super Bowl from 2008 to 2012. Whether Flacco was the definite leader or not, his presence made a big difference compared to the Baltimore teams of the past.

Since the Ravens moved from Cleveland in 1996, the organization has been centered around defense. No longer are these Ravens a defense-first team. The torch has now been passed, from Lewis to Flacco. And more success is likely as long as Flacco is a member of the Ravens.

"I love playing here. It's been an awesome five years," Flacco said after signing his $120.6 million contract. "We've had a spectacular team. We have an amazing group of fans. It's close to where I grew up. It's great for my family. There are a lot of really, really good benefits for playing for this organization."

55 O.J. Brigance's Battle with ALS

At almost every practice, O.J. Brigance sits back in his chair to observe the team he once played for. And each day Brigance arrives at work and sits behind his desk, working for the team he once played for. Brigance may be battling the day-to-day realities of amyotrophic lateral sclerosis (ALS), but his mind is still focused on the team he once played for.

Brigance was diagnosed with ALS in 2007, which has taken away muscle function all over his body. He works each day from a motorized chair, which has a computer hooked up to it that allows him to speak through a DynaVox machine.

He's become an inspiration to everyone inside the Under Armour Performance Center, as Brigance continues to fight ALS, also known as Lou Gehrig's Disease.

"O.J. Brigance is the strongest man in the building," Ravens head coach John Harbaugh said after the organization won the 2012 AFC Championship Game against New England. "He sets the tone for all of us."

Brigance, who's the Ravens' senior adviser to player development, always has a smile on his face when you see him around the team's facility. He enjoys working for the team he once helped win a Super Bowl for during the 2000 season.

Brigance, a linebacker, was a special teams standout in 2000, recording a second-best 25 special teams tackles during the regular season. He led the team in postseason special teams tackles with 10, including the first special teams stop against the New York Giants in Super Bowl XXXV.

But that wasn't his only contribution to Baltimore football history. Before getting a shot in the NFL, Brigance, who played college football at Rice University, played in the Canadian Football League. After playing with the British Columbia Lions from 1991 to 1993, Brigance joined the Baltimore Stallions, which joined the league in 1994. A year later in 1995, Brigance helped lead the Stallions to a Grey Cup championship, the equivalent to the NFL's Super Bowl.

Brigance's play with the Stallions caught the attention of the Dolphins, which signed him and kept him on the roster for four seasons. It was in 2000 when Brigance played his only season with the Ravens, rejoining a football team in Baltimore.

It certainly worked in his favor, as he was able to bring Baltimore another football championship—only this time, it was in the country's most popular league. So even when Brigance finished his NFL career with brief stints in St. Louis and New England, he came back to work in Baltimore's front office in 2004.

Brigance first noticed something was wrong during a game of racquetball. His right arm felt weak and he was unable to use the same kind of range of motion he was used to. When Brigance received his diagnosis, he was determined to fight it from the start. He's also dedicated his time and money to ALS research, along with his wife, Chanda. The two founded the Brigance Brigade, which raises money to go toward ALS research. Each year, the foundation hosts a Fiesta to 5K event, which will bring out more than 2,500 participants, which includes members of the Baltimore Ravens players, to help raise awareness for ALS.

"We're just amazed at how the people of Baltimore have come out and supported and helped and done all that they have done in helping bring awareness to this ugly disease," Chanda Brigance told me in April 2012. "I am very excited, O.J. is very excited, we're really, really happy to see the people and the participation."

There isn't one player who isn't inspired by Brigance. Former Ravens receiver Anquan Boldin said, "I think O.J. means a lot to this organization, period. The things that he's been through, the things that he's still fighting through, still his willingness to continue to fight, I think everybody in our locker room is inspired by that."

Said former Ravens safety Ed Reed: "He's been like an uncle to me and like a brother. I love 'Juice.' I'd give everything for him. I would put no other man in his position to go what he's going through."

After the Ravens defeated the Patriots to win the 2012 AFC championship, Brigance presented the Lamar Hunt Trophy to the team. After a brief introduction from CBS sportscaster Jim Nantz, Brigance was the first to introduce the 2012 Ravens as AFC champions.

"Congratulations to the Baltimore Ravens," Brigance said through his computer. "Your resiliency has outlasted your adversity. You are the AFC champions. You are my mighty men. With God, all things are possible."

56 The 2000 Offense: Enough to Get By

The 2000 offense was mostly dull, lulling spectators to sleep. It was one of those rare instances when fans were more excited to see what the defense could do on the field rather than those whose primary jobs are to score points.

The offense was of the game management variety. If it could limit mistakes and let the defense go to work, then the Ravens would be successful for the most part. Kicker Matt Stover remembered defensive players telling the offense, before Super Bowl XXXV, to put up 10 points and that's all. If the offense could do that, the defense would take care of business.

Tony Banks opened the year as Baltimore's starting quarter. He connected on a 53-yard pass to receiver Qadry Ismail in the season-opening, 16–0 win over Pittsburgh. A week later, Banks had a game to remember, throwing five touchdowns in a comeback win over Jacksonville. Banks struggled to open the game but found a groove late. Four of Banks' touchdowns came in the second half.

Banks had six touchdowns in two games. You'd think he'd be on pace for a big year. But Banks went back to his struggling ways in a 19–6 loss to Miami the following week. Baltimore shook up its lineup, inserting rookie running back Jamal Lewis in to start instead of Priest Holmes. Lewis ran for 76 yards on nine carries.

In Week 4, the offense had one of its best outputs of the 2000 season in a 37–0 rout against Cincinnati. Banks threw two touchdowns, one each to Shannon Sharpe and Travis Taylor. Lewis ran for 116 yards and a touchdown, and Holmes added 51 yards of his own. Even fullback Obafemi Ayanbadejo got into the mix, scoring a one-yard touchdown in the fourth quarter.

Then came the skid—sort of.

The Ravens won the following week 12–0, but the offense was beginning to show some struggles. Banks threw 34 passes, completing 18 of them, yet only had 169 yards. Baltimore did get steady production from Lewis and Holmes, yet each time they threatened, they were forced to settle for field goals. A win's a win, though, and the Ravens would take it. The Ravens would win again the next week, 15–10 against Jacksonville. It wasn't pretty, but Baltimore was still winning.

And then it wasn't. A 10–3 loss to Washington began causing some real worry about the direction the offense was heading in. Only six of Banks's 16 completions went for 10 yards or more in what was becoming a predictable, run-first offense. It reached its peak the week after in a 14–6 loss to Tennessee, with Baltimore playing its fourth game in a row without a touchdown. Backup Trent Dilfer replaced Banks in the fourth quarter to hopefully provide a spark, though it wouldn't happen that day. Four games, zero touchdowns—yes, fans were worrying. But coach Brian Billick wasn't panicking yet.

"What happened in the Middle East is a crisis, this is not a crisis," Billick said. "This is something you work through. That is what we have to focus on."

Dilfer earned a start the next week against Pittsburgh but still had to work out some of the rust. He finished 12-of-25 for 152 yards and an interception in a 9–6 loss. Baltimore had just dropped three in a row with no signs of offensive improvement.

But like most slumps, Baltimore's finally came to an end the following week against Cincinnati. Dilfer tossed three touchdowns in a 27–7 win. Next up was a rematch against Tennessee. Dilfer threw two touchdowns, the first one a 46-yarder to Ismail in the first quarter. Lewis ran for 99 yards and a touchdown. With 25 seconds to go in the game, Dilfer linked up with Patrick Johnson for a two-yard touchdown to win the game.

Dilfer, a former sixth overall pick in the 1994 draft, never lived up to the billing that came with the high draft tag. But he was a smart, heady quarterback that could keep an offense out of trouble. With Dilfer at the helm late in the season, the Ravens weren't scaring opposing defenses. But they played smarter, efficient football to let the defense carry the team.

After the Pittsburgh loss, Dilfer threw touchdowns in six of Baltimore's last seven games, with him posting multiple touchdowns in five of those games. Dilfer did struggle in his final two regular season and four playoff games. In the divisional round against Tennessee, Dilfer only completed 31 percent of his passes, though Baltimore was able to win 24–10. In a blowout Super Bowl win against the New York Giants, Dilfer was only able to complete 12 of 25 passes, though he did throw a 38-yard touchdown to Brandon Stokley midway through the first quarter.

Baltimore's 2000 offense struggled to score points, yet the team was able to overcome the setbacks to win a Super Bowl. With Dilfer at quarterback, the offense was good enough and began minimizing mistakes. The best offense, statistically speaking, in Ravens history was in 1996, which saw Vinny Testaverde throw for over 4,000 yards. Baltimore finished 4–12. The city will gladly take a mediocre offense and a Super Bowl over 4–12 any season.

57 Overlooked Contributors

The Ravens have made a habit out of discovering talent out of young prospects who are otherwise overlooked by the rest of the NFL.

Out of Adalius Thomas, Bart Scott, and Jameel McClain, only Thomas was drafted, in the sixth round out of Southern Mississippi. Scott and McClain were undrafted products looking for a shot anywhere in the NFL. Baltimore gave all three a chance, and all three were able to work their ways into the Ravens' starting lineups during their tenures with the franchise.

Thomas was drafted in 2000 and only appeared in three games as a rookie. He had to wait his turn, seeing that Michael McCrary and Peter Boulware were in front of him on the depth chart. A year later in 2001, though, Thomas got to play as a backup in all 16 games, with two of them starts at defensive end. As a reserve, it became apparent Thomas had a bright future on the Baltimore defense. Thomas stayed at defensive end in 2002, where he started 12 games and tallied three sacks. But it was on special teams where Thomas first began to make his mark.

Thomas moved to outside linebacker in 2003 and started 11 games. He totaled 43 tackles and four sacks, but had a team-high 23 special teams tackles, which garnered him a Pro Bowl spot. However, he couldn't participate in the game as he was placed on injured reserve late in the season.

Thomas broke out in 2004 when he recorded eight sacks. A year later in 2005, Thomas continued his pass-rushing prowess, tallying nine sacks. His career peaked in 2006, when he sacked quarterbacks 11 times and earned a second Pro Bowl, but this time for being one of the league's better defenders. Thirty-one teams passed on Thomas until Baltimore picked him with the 186th overall pick in 2000.

Growing up in a rough part of Detroit, Scott had to pass by gang territory on his way to school each day. Unable to qualify for Division I-A football, Scott attended Southern Illinois and played there. But when he was a Saluki, Scott got into an argument with defensive coordinator Michael Vite, which resulted in a six-game suspension. When the Southern Illinois coaching staff was fired before Scott's senior season, members of the staff told incoming coach Jerry Kill that they wouldn't want Scott as a player. Kill's impression of Scott wasn't what was advertised. "Bart played like he was on a mission for us, and he was a captain and leader," Kill told *Sports Illustrated* in 2007.

Not many teams were interested in Scott, as the Ravens were the only team to send a scout to work him out. The Ravens liked what they saw and only hoped he'd be available after the draft, under-standing what kind of value that would be. Scott went undrafted and signed a deal with the Ravens in 2002. For his first three years in Baltimore, Scott was a standout special teams player. He finally got the opportunity to play inside linebacker alongside Ray Lewis in 2005, starting 10 games. In 2006 Scott tallied 9½ sacks and was named to his first and only Pro Bowl. Scott played two more seasons in Baltimore before signing a free agent deal with the New York Jets.

McClain spent most of his younger years fighting an uphill battle. Growing up in Philadelphia, he, his mother, and three siblings went through stretches of homelessness where they'd stay at a Salvation Army shelter. Football became a ticket for himself and his family, as he became a star linebacker at Syracuse University. But in 2008 no one drafted him. The Ravens, however, expressed the most interest in him. The entire front office stayed in touch with McClain before and after the draft, expressing a desire to bring him on board. The decision was easy as a free agent, and McClain inked a deal with Baltimore.

McClain began his Baltimore career on special teams and saw playing time in all 16 games as a rookie. He followed the same route in 2009, and even earned a start in Week 11 against Indianapolis. By 2010 McClain was a full-fledged starter playing next to Ray Lewis on defense.

Thomas, Scott, and McClain may have gone unnoticed by 31 other teams. But all it takes is one team to think a player might be a fit. That was the case, and it paid off for both the players and the team.

58 Super Bowl XLVII's Goal-Line Stand

By no means were the 2012 Baltimore Ravens known for defense. They finished the regular season 17th in total defense, giving up an average of 350.9 yards per game.

Baltimore and defense have been synonymous with each other since 2000, when the Ravens fielded one of the best defensive units to ever line up on a football field.

Even though the 2012 Ravens weren't up to par with the Baltimore standard, Super Bowl XLVII hinged on whether or not they could keep the San Francisco 49ers out of the end zone late in the game. Up 34–29, the 49ers needed a touchdown to take the lead. Baltimore's defense had given up 466 total yards up until the final stand inside Baltimore's 10-yard line.

The 49ers had just reached the Ravens' 7-yard line thanks to a 33-yard run from running back Frank Gore. San Francisco had assumed control over the entire game and looked ready to move ahead with a touchdown.

What happened next will became lore.

On first-and-goal from the 7, San Francisco lined up in the pistol formation, with two tight ends lined up on each side of quarterback Colin Kaepernick and running back LaMichael James behind him. The handoff went to James up the middle, and a brief hole appeared to open. However, it closed quickly with linebacker Dannell Ellerbe and defensive tackle DeAngelo Tyson meeting James after a two-yard gain.

With two minutes remaining, the 49ers ran second-and-goal out of the shotgun, with a bunch formation to the right side of the line. Ravens cornerback Corey Graham had outside coverage out of the bunch and gave the receivers a five-yard cushion. After the snap, it looked like Kaepernick wanted to hit Michael Crabtree, the outside receiver on the play. Crabtree ran a quick out but hadn't turned around yet. Graham saw the play develop and ran to cover him. Kaepernick still had the ball, so Crabtree turned his route up to the end zone. Kaepernick looked quick to the middle of the field before returning to Crabtree in the end zone. Graham stayed with the receiver and knocked the ball out of his hands.

All of a sudden, the 49ers went from poised to take the lead to concerned about the outcome. Third-and-goal from the 5-yard line was now upcoming. It's possible the San Francisco coaches thought the distance was too far to run up the middle, though it's also the kind of distance that can hurt offenses since there's now not as much space for offensive plays to develop.

49ers quarterback Colin Kaepernick (7) throws a pass on fourth-and-goal as Ravens linebacker Dannell Ellerbe (59) closes in during Baltimore's fourth-quarter goal-line stand in Super Bowl XLVII. The pass fell incomplete.

Almost drawing a delay of game penalty, the 49ers called a time-out before the next play. When the 49ers regrouped before the upcoming third-and-goal play, Kaepernick lined up under center, possibly hinting at a run situation. Randy Moss was split out with Crabtree lined up in the slot. Ravens cornerback Jimmy Smith was now taking care of outside coverage, with Graham inside.

Though the 49ers were in a different formation, the play was inherently similar to the previous one. Crabtree broke into a quick out-route off the line, and Graham saw it immediately, though there seemed to be plenty of space for Crabtree to make the catch. Once the ball hit Crabtree's hands, Graham made contact. Shortly after, Smith hit Crabtree in his chest, dislodging the ball from Crabtree's body. San Francisco now had just one play left, and with it being fourth-and-goal from the 5, it was almost assuredly going to be a passing play.

The 49ers went back to the pistol formation, with Gore lined up behind Kaepernick. Two Niners receivers were split to the left with Crabtree isolated on the right with Smith on him in man coverage. Safety Ed Reed recognized the play but didn't want to tip his hand just yet.

Right after the snap, Reed ran to give Smith help over the top. Shortly after receiving the snap, Kaepernick threw a fade to Crabtree in the right corner of the end zone. Part of what seemed like a rushed throw could've been due to the fact that Ellerbe was a free blitzer on the play and bearing down on the second-year quarterback. Smith and Kaepernick tussled a bit with each other, even after the ball was released into the air. The ball wasn't placed well, but the San Francisco sideline was screaming for a defensive pass interference penalty. The referees never threw a flag, and Baltimore prevented a go-ahead score.

After the game, Ravens defensive coordinator Dean Pees explained his defensive calls once San Francisco was at the 7-yard line. He anticipated the 49ers might try to run Kaepernick, which is why his calls were designed to take away that option of San Francisco's offense.

"Here's the thing: we were not going to let them run it in on us, period," Pees said. "We got beat in Washington because we let them run it in on us. We got beat at Philadelphia because I let him run it in on us, the quarterback. They weren't going to run it in on us again."

The Ravens would take a safety on special teams for strategic reasons, which allowed San Francisco one punt return chance at winning the game. Baltimore won 34–31 and became Super Bowl champions.

Certainly the Ravens' offense put the team in position to win the Super Bowl with 34 points scored. But it was the defense's final stand that won Baltimore a second Super Bowl championship.

"We knew what the situation was," Graham said. "Don't let them get in, and we can't lose, it's as simple as that. If they didn't score a touchdown they couldn't beat us. We had to keep them out of the end zone. Guys had to step up. I didn't expect anything different but for us to make that play."

59 Priest Holmes, the One That Got Away

You can't exactly fault the Ravens for drafting Jamal Lewis with the fifth overall pick in the 2000 NFL Draft. The results were proof of what kind of running back he was. With Baltimore, except for 2001 when he tore his ACL in training camp, Lewis only had one season where he didn't run for over 1,000 yards. In 2003 Lewis ran for 2,066 yards, which was the second best mark in NFL history at the time. Drafting Lewis was one of the best decisions the Ravens ever made.

But Baltimore already had a top quality running back on the roster. Priest Holmes, out of the University of Texas, was undrafted in 1997 before signing with the Ravens. Holmes appeared in seven games as a rookie but didn't log any carries. By Week 4 of the 1998 season, Holmes was Baltimore's starter at running back.

In his starting debut, Holmes shredded the Cincinnati defense, gashing it for 173 yards and two touchdowns. In Week 12, again against Cincinnati, Holmes ran for 227 yards and a touchdown on 36 carries. The week after, Holmes ran for 103 yards against the Colts. When the season was over, Holmes' stat line was 233 carries for 1,008 yards and seven touchdowns. It appeared Baltimore had a young, up-and-comer for the foreseeable future in Holmes.

However, his 1999 campaign, in which he entered with a salary lower than that of two backup running backs and a fullback, didn't go as planned. Two weeks into the season and Holmes had a sprained MCL and was forced to miss Week 3's game against Cleveland. Errict Rhett stepped in to fill the starting role for the next five games, as Holmes was unavailable to play.

Holmes finally stepped back in and ran for 40 yards on 10 carries in a 41–9 win over Cleveland. But once again, he was forced to miss the next three games. He played in the final five games of the season, rushing for 412 yards on 66 carries (a 6.2-yard average). Despite the setbacks, the future still seemed bright in Baltimore for Holmes.

Then the Ravens drafted Lewis, a tough-nosed running back out of the University of Tennessee. The Baltimore front office and coaching staff was enamored of Lewis from the start. Despite having Holmes on the roster, it was clear the goal was for Lewis to become the No. 1 back as soon as possible.

"Priest was our running back at that time, and we felt in order for us to grow as an offense, if we could get someone who could be a tackle-breaker, that would be very beneficial for us," Newsome said in 2012.

After Holmes started the first two games of Baltimore's 2000 Super Bowl championship season, Lewis supplanted him—even though Holmes had run for 119 yards in a season-opening win over Pittsburgh. Playing second fiddle to Lewis, Holmes ran for 588 yards and two touchdowns and only carried the ball 18 times for 45 yards in the playoffs.

In the 2001 off-season, Holmes left Baltimore for Kansas City via free agency. It didn't take long to prove what Baltimore was missing out on (not to mention the fact that, with Lewis tearing his ACL in training camp, the team had no proven running back to open the 2001 season with).

Holmes immediately became Kansas City's starter, and after two sluggish games out of the gate, Holmes torched Washington with

23 carries for 147 yards and two touchdowns. Holmes ended 2001 with 1,555 yards and eight touchdowns and earned his first Pro Bowl appearance. Holmes improved on his 2001 numbers by running for 1,615 yards in 2002, and that was without playing the last two games due to injury. More impressive, perhaps, was that Holmes rushed for 21 touchdowns that season. Holmes' yardage total dipped to 1,420 in 2003, but his touchdown total rose to 27. That number still stands tied for second in single-season rushing touchdowns with Seattle's Shaun Alexander (2005), and one behind the 28 Chargers running back LaDainian Tomlinson scored in 2006. Holmes and former Cowboys great Emmitt Smith are the only two running backs to run for 20 or more touchdowns in back-to-back seasons.

The injury bug began biting Holmes in 2004. After eight games that saw Holmes accumulate 892 yards and 14 touchdowns, Holmes injured his hip and missed the remainder of the season. In 2005 Holmes endured a frightening head and neck injury that forced him to miss the remainder of the season after seven games. Holmes retired in 2007, having rushed for 8,172 rushing yards and 86 touchdowns. Two thousand, one hundred two of those yards and 10 of those touchdowns came while he was in Baltimore.

Baltimore didn't necessarily need Holmes once it got Lewis. But sometimes you have to wonder what might have been had the Ravens made an effort to keep Holmes around in 2001.

60 2006: The Ravens' Best Regular Season Squad

Baltimore was finally able to pair a competent quarterback with its defense for a full regular season in 2006. Steve McNair was brought on board after three years of inconsistency with Kyle Boller at the helm.

Baltimore was coming off a disappointing 6–10 season in 2005 and hadn't been to the playoffs since 2003. The Ravens, as well as their fans, were starved for a return to the postseason. Brian Billick, who led Baltimore to a Super Bowl championship in 2000, was beginning to feel the pressure from owner Steve Bisciotti to win immediately.

The Ravens were able to draft three rookies that contributed immediately. Defensive tackle Haloti Ngata was an instant star, taken with the 12th overall pick, thanks to a trade with Cleveland. In the fifth round, Baltimore took safety Dawan Landry out of Georgia Tech, who wound up starting 14 games as a rookie. In the sixth round, the Ravens selected punter Sam Koch, who would start immediately, too.

The Ravens wasted no time proving they hadn't faded into mediocrity. Baltimore jumped out to a four-game winning streak, highlighted by a 27–0 win over Tampa Bay in the season opener. The Ravens won 28–6 over Oakland a week later, with the Ravens coming up with six interceptions in the first two contests.

The next two games weren't as easy, with Baltimore squeaking out a 15–14 win over Cleveland and a 16–13 win over San Diego in consecutive weeks. The Ravens dropped their first game of the season on Monday, October 9, to the Denver Broncos 13–3. A 23–21 loss to Carolina six days later cast some brief doubt as to whether the Ravens were contenders.

"Our momentum has taken a hit," tight end Todd Heap said after the Panthers loss, according to the *Baltimore Sun*. "We started off on a roll and we have hit a little dip. Sitting for two weeks with the taste of a loss in your mouth is not going to be fun. Hopefully, we can all reflect and figure out what we need to do to get better as a team."

A bye week came at the perfect time for Baltimore, which, in addition to dropping two consecutive games in the season, just saw a six-game home winning streak come to an end.

The bye proved worthwhile as the Ravens reeled off five consecutive wins in a row, which included a thrilling come-from-behind win over rival Tennessee, in which Baltimore scored 10 unanswered points in the fourth quarter to win 27–26.

The Ravens suffered their last regular season loss at Cincinnati, a 13–7 defeat, in Week 13. Baltimore then won its last four games by a combined 97–41 margin. The Ravens' 13–3 regular season in 2006 is the best in franchise history, which includes the Super Bowl title teams of 2000 (12–4) and 2012 (10–6). The Ravens lost in the divisional round of the playoffs to Peyton Manning and the Indianapolis Colts 15–6. But even so, the regular season success kept Billick's job safe for the time being.

61 2007: What Happened?

Expectations were back in Baltimore after a superb 2006 season. Brian Billick had another opportunity to prove he was the right man to continue coaching the Ravens.

There would be a different look to Baltimore's backfield, however, with the organization releasing Jamal Lewis during the off-season. Baltimore's hope was to sign Lewis at a reduced rate, but the veteran running back went to Cleveland instead. To replace Lewis, the Ravens made a trade to acquire Bills running back Willis McGahee, who had worn out his welcome in Buffalo with some unflattering comments about the city.

Through six games, the Ravens were in familiar territory at 4–2. That's where they were in 2006 before winning nine of their next 10 games. But in this instance, they had succumbed to some misfortune. Kyle Boller was forced to take over starting duties for a few weeks with McNair dealing with groin and back injuries. Boller was able to pick up a win against St. Louis to get Baltimore its fourth win of the season. From there, it was only downhill. Boller and the Ravens lost to Buffalo 19–14 the next week before the team's bye week. Following the week off, nothing changed. Pittsburgh whipped Baltimore 38–7 in McNair's return. McNair finished with 63 passing yards and an interception in one of his worst performances as a member of the Ravens.

The losses began to pile up as if these Ravens were from the pre-2000 era. They lost to Cleveland 33–30 in overtime. The Chargers blew out Baltimore 32–14, with quarterback Philip Rivers throwing for 249 yards and three touchdowns. Beginning with the San Diego game, the Ravens were now without McNair for the remainder of the season due to a shoulder injury.

After a close 27–24 loss to New England, Baltimore was blown out once again by Indianapolis 44–20. But the boiling point came in Week 15, when the once-feared Ravens traveled to take on the 0–13 Miami Dolphins in a half-empty stadium. At this stage, it was assumed the Dolphins, with first-and-only-year head coach Cam Cameron at the helm, was on track for the first 0–16 finish in NFL history (a mark bestowed upon the Detroit Lions a year later in 2008).

The Ravens jumped out to a 13–3 lead, aided by a Boller touchdown pass to receiver Derrick Mason. Baltimore then proceeded to go scoreless in the third quarter, which allowed Miami the opportunity to tie the game in the fourth quarter. Miami added another field goal and was suddenly on top 16–13 with two minutes left in the game. "This can't be happening," thought Ravens fans everywhere. With Miami 0–13, Baltimore certainly didn't want to be the team to give the Dolphins their first win. It would be nothing short of embarrassing.

Boller sustained a concussion in the fourth quarter, so the Ravens had to turn to Troy Smith, the former Heisman Trophy winner at Ohio State who began the season as the third-string quarterback.

With the game on the line, Smith orchestrated 10 plays to near perfection to get Baltimore to the Miami 1-yard line with 12 seconds left. But it was fourth down, and Billick had a decision to make: tie the game and go to overtime or win it then and there. He chose to kick the 18-yard field goal, which Matt Stover made to send the game into extra time, though he was tempted to go for the win.

"All or nothing in our circumstance, why not?" Billick told reporters afterward. "But we had just driven the length of the field, and there are some things to be drawn from going into overtime and doing those things. Yeah, it would have been fun to try."

Running back Willis McGahee, who ran for 104 yards against Miami, was disappointed, saying, "I wanted a chance."

In overtime, Baltimore's run game got going before stalling at the Miami 26. But then, typical to the 2007 season, Stover missed a 44-yard attempt to win the game. Three plays later, Dolphins quarterback Cleo Lemon hit receiver Greg Camarillo for a 64-yard game-winning touchdown. Dolphins 22, Ravens 16.

That moment was easily the lowest in Ravens franchise history, and made it unlikely for Billick to return to Baltimore for another season.

Internal discord between Billick and some of the players began to build, as well. Veterans got tired of Billick's coaching style, and losing only added to the problems. A select few chose to go over Billick's head and complain to owner Steve Bisciotti. The Ravens ended their season with a win over rival Pittsburgh to finish 5–11, and the next day Bisciotti announced Billick's contract had been terminated.

Record-wise, the 1996 Ravens finished 4–12, yet they aren't remembered as the worst team in franchise history. The 2007 group has gone down in Ravens history with that distinction.

62 Jamal Lewis Joins the 2,000-Yard Club

Dating back to 1920, when the National Football League (then known as the American Professional Football Association) began, only seven running backs have ever run for over 2,000 rushing yards in a single season.

In 1963, Cleveland Browns running back Jim Brown came close, rushing for 1,863 yards in what was then a 14-game season. No one during Brown's era came close, and when Brown retired, this was the NFL record. Then, in 1973, along came Buffalo's O.J. Simpson, who not only broke Brown's record, but also became the first to run for over 2,000 yards by posting 2,003 (also in only 14 games). A new barrier was set for all running backs to try and break through.

And only six others have done so. Eric Dickerson, of the Los Angeles Rams, became the second in 1984 with 2,105 yards in a 16-game season. Dickerson's mark is still the all-time best in the NFL. It took 13 years for it to happen again, with Detroit's Barry Sanders accomplishing the feat with a 2,053-yard season. A season later, Denver's Terrell Davis powered his way for 2,008. Five years later, it became Baltimore running back Jamal Lewis' turn.

In Week 1, Lewis was only able to run for 69 yards on 15 carries in a 34–15 loss. The next week was a different story.

"That next week, I remember [coach] Brian [Billick] saying, 'If we don't give it to him 30 times, it's a problem,'" Lewis said. "And, I just answered the bell."

Lewis ran all over the Cleveland Browns, beginning with an 82-yard touchdown to begin the game. Lewis would set an NFL single-game record with 295 yards, which stood until Minnesota's Adrian Peterson ran for 296 against San Diego in 2007.

The impressive games continued. Beginning with the Cleveland game, Lewis ran for over 100 yards six games in a row. With rookie Kyle Boller at quarterback, the Ravens were dependent on the run. Only once in that span did Lewis not receive 20 carries, which came against Cincinnati in Week 6. He came close, however, getting 19 rushes for 101 yards in a 34–26 loss.

The six-game streak was snapped against Jacksonville as he only rushed for 68 yards. More importantly, though, Baltimore was able to beat the Jaguars 24–17.

The following week against St. Louis, Lewis received 27 more carries, which he turned into 111 yards. After a 91-yard outing in Week 10 against Miami, a 9–6 loss, Lewis had run for 1,449 yards. Through 10 games in 2003, Lewis already had a single-season best, and a mark he wouldn't beat in any of his future seasons.

Lewis' next four games included 117 yards against Seattle, 78 against San Francisco, 180 in a rematch win over Cincinnati, and 125 against Oakland. Having run for 295 yards against Cleveland in Week 2, Lewis embarrassed the Browns for a second time in Week 15, churning out 205 yards on 22 carries. Heading into the Week 17 finale against Pittsburgh, Lewis had 1,952 rushing yards. Forty-eight more, and he'd etch his name into an elite group.

The Ravens seemed intent on getting Lewis the mark. On their first possession, Lewis was given the ball five times, which he converted for 39 rushing yards. Only nine more remained.

After Ed Reed picked off Steelers quarterback Tommy Maddox midway through the opening period, it was Lewis' time to make history. On cue, Lewis was given the ball, with which he picked up a nine-yard gain. There it was, membership into the 2,000-yard club.

But apparently, Lewis wanted more. On the very next play, Lewis was given the ball again and ran it 25 yards into the end zone. This run moved him past Simpson and Davis and into third place for

NFL single-season rushing yards. At the 7:41 mark in the third quarter, Lewis took a handoff that he turned into an 11-yard gain. That run put him ahead of Sanders and into second all-time. Lewis finished the game with 27 carries for 114 yards and a touchdown. His season total came out to be 2,066 yards, just 39 yards shy of Dickerson's 1984 number. Lewis spent nine years with the second-best mark, until Peterson became the seventh player to reach the mark with 2,097 in 2012. (Tennessee Titans running back Chris Johnson also jumped into the 2,000-yard club with 2,006 in 2009). Lewis' 2,066 yards is clearly a franchise best, with his rookie season of 2000 coming in a distant second (1,364).

However, after a spectacular regular season, Lewis was limited to 35 yards in a 20–17 wild-card round loss to Tennessee. Despite the disappointing playoff performance, by Lewis' standards, 2003 was a year Ravens fans will never forget, all because of Jamal Lewis and his record-setting running.

63 Jarret Johnson's Iron Man Streak

Jarret Johnson was a rookie when he missed his only game as a member of the Baltimore Ravens. Drafted in the fourth round of the 2003 NFL Draft out of Alabama, Johnson quickly gained a reputation for being one of the toughest teammates in the Baltimore locker room. A severe amount of pain would be needed to keep Johnson off the field on Sundays.

Beginning with the final game of the 2003 regular season, Johnson embarked on an impressive streak that would continue another eight years in a Ravens uniform.

Johnson played in 129 consecutive games with the Ravens, a mark that still stands. His final 80 games in a row were starts. An undersized defensive tackle at first, Johnson was moved to outside linebacker where he'd excel as a run stuffer and edge setter. He could drop into coverage or rush the quarterback when called upon. Johnson's work ethic was admired by both the Brian Billick and John Harbaugh coaching staffs, to which he regularly gave everything he had in practice and in games.

The first milestone Johnson reached during the streak was when he hit 50 in a row. This game came against the Bengals in the 2007 season opener. Though the Ravens lost, Johnson had a solid game, totaling a sack and a tackle for a four-yard loss on Bengals running back Rudi Johnson.

Ten games into the 2008 season, Johnson would play in his 75th consecutive game for the Ravens. This was against the New York Giants in a 30–10 loss. Johnson finished the game with three tackles and a sack.

Johnson would play in his 100th game in Week 3 of the 2010 season. By this time, Johnson was a staple on defense and a warrior on the field.

"In 38 years of coaching, he may be the most physical, toughest football player that I've ever been around," then–defensive coordinator Greg Mattison told the *Baltimore Sun*. "And I can say that [because]…truly, I and the rest of the coaches will watch tape, and we'll say it each time: that's how a Raven plays. Jarret Johnson does it every practice, every snap, every time he is supposed to do it."

In his 100th consecutive game, against Cleveland, the Ravens defeated the Browns 24–17. Johnson tallied four tackles, two of which were solo. Johnson's 129th consecutive game was played on January 1, 2012, which was the final week of the 2011 regular season. Baltimore defeated Cincinnati 24–16 with Johnson tallying just two tackles.

However, this streak only counts regular season games. If you count postseason games, Johnson played an additional 11 games for Baltimore during that span, giving him 140 in a row.

With Johnson heading to free agency during the 2012 offseason, Baltimore was unable to keep him due to salary cap constraints. Johnson signed a four-year, $19 million contract with San Diego in what he called a family decision.

Ravens players grew fond of Johnson while he was with the Ravens' organization. Receiver Torrey Smith, a rookie in 2011, had his locker two spots down from Johnson. In just one year as teammates, Johnson made an impact on the young receiver.

"He was my guy, I miss him," Smith said the week Baltimore was preparing for Johnson's San Diego squad during the 2012 season. "I miss him being right there. But I'm happy for him. He's playing well out there, and it'll be great to see him."

"He was a no-nonsense kind of guy here," said Ray Rice during the same week. "I'm sure between the lines everything will be physical, but after the game it will be great to shake hands, take a picture with him, and let him know that we still love him."

64 Michael Oher: From *Blind Side* to Prime Time

Michael Oher's story is well known from die-hard football fans and folks who couldn't care less about sports alike. Oher's story is captivating, inspirational, and motivating, all at the same time. Oher came from a tough upbringing and defied the odds by becoming a starting NFL offensive lineman.

Oher's story was first popularized in Michael Lewis' book *The Blind Side: Evolution of a Game*. The book detailed how the left tackle position had become one of—if not the—most important position for NFL teams. Lewis wrote about Oher while he was a tackle at Ole Miss and mentioned his rough childhood and subsequent adoption into the Tuohy household.

Ravens offensive lineman Michael Oher is all smiles on the sideline during Baltimore's 34–31 victory over the San Francisco 49ers in Super Bowl XLVII.

Even before Oher was drafted into the NFL, the book had popularized Oher among sports fans across the United States.

When Hollywood got hold of the story, it took his stardom to a whole new level. Actress Sandra Bullock starred in the film *The Blind Side*, an adaptation of the book. The film was released on November 20, 2009, during Oher's rookie season with the Ravens.

Teammates of his have often stated the Hollywood portrayal of Oher has been overblown, that it doesn't depict the guy they've come to know. In an interview with BaltimoreRavens.com, former Ravens center Matt Birk said that the movie didn't show Oher as the hard-working guy he is. Birk said Oher is often among the first play-ers to arrive each day at the facility, to study the game of football, and prepare himself for each upcoming game.

"Once in a while I'll beat him into the office, and I'll be like, 'Hey, Mike, you're slipping man. I got ya today,'" Birk told the team's website. "It really bugs him. Mike busts his tail, and that's why he's so successful. It's easy to root for a guy like that."

Oher has often said the one critique he had about the film was that it showed him as someone who knew nothing about the game of football when he first started playing for Briarcrest High School in Tennessee. That couldn't have been further from the truth. Oher could play the game well from the start and always possessed a strong work ethic on the football field.

But partially due to the film, and, of course, his story in general, Oher has become an inspiration to fans everywhere. In 2010 he wrote the autobiography *I Beat the Odds: From Homelessness to The Blind Side and Beyond*, which told the story in his own words. In and out of foster care as a child, neglected and forced to repeat first and second grades, Oher didn't have the guidance children need.

But despite the setbacks, Oher worked relentlessly to reach the NFL, achieving a 3.7 grade-point average and earning a criminal justice degree at Ole Miss in the progress.

As a rookie, Oher played both left and right tackle during the 2009 season. He helped play a part in the Ravens reaching the divi-sional round of the playoffs and beating the New England Patriots with a strong running game in the wild-card round. Throughout his career, Oher has rotated back and forth on the offensive line, play-ing both tackle positions. But Oher's always done it with an open mind and with plenty of flexibility.

One of the traits the coaching staff admires the most about Oher is that he's a team player. Oher's been willing to do whatever it takes for the Baltimore Ravens to win games.

"I just like playing football. I am going to work hard at any position that I am at," Oher said.

"From the outside looking in, who knows? I know that I am going to work hard and be the best player that I can be at any position."

65 The Baltimore Coaching Tree

Over the years, the Ravens organization has been a hotbed for future head coaches in the NFL. Some have gone on to be fairly successful, others not so much.

In 1996 Eric Mangini was an offensive assistant/quality control staffer with Baltimore, in the early stages of his coaching career. After one season in Baltimore, Mangini rejoined his mentor Bill Belichick with the New York Jets, where Belichick was the defensive coordinator. Mangini would then follow Belichick again to New England, spending five seasons as the defensive backs coach. After one season as New England's defensive coordinator in 2005, Mangini was hired as the head coach of the New York Jets. Mangini was fired in 2008 due to the Jets missing the playoffs after starting the season 8–3. Mangini was subsequently hired by the Browns and spent two seasons as their head coach. After two consecutive 5–11 seasons, Mangini was fired.

On that same staff in 1996 was Jim Schwartz, a defensive assistant. After Ted Marchibroda was fired as Baltimore's head coach after the 1998 season, Schwartz took a defensive assistant job with Tennessee. After two years in that capacity, Schwartz became the Titans' defensive coordinator. Eight years later, the Detroit Lions offered him the head coaching job, which he took in 2009.

Marvin Lewis became Baltimore's defensive coordinator in 1996 and stayed with the franchise until 2001. Having coached the 2000 defense, he began generating a lot of buzz around the league for head coaching offers. After a stop with Washington in 2002 as its defensive coordinator, the Bengals came calling and offered Lewis a job. He accepted and has been there ever since.

From 1997 to 1998, Ken Whisenhunt was Baltimore's tight ends coach. After bouncing around as a tight ends coach and special teams coach, Whisenhunt became the Pittsburgh Steelers' offensive coordinator in 2004. After three years of success, the Arizona Cardinals hired him to be their head coach. Whisenhunt led Arizona to a Super Bowl appearance in 2008, in just his second year. However, by 2012 the winning ways had disappeared and Whisenhunt was fired. In 2013 Whisenhunt was hired to be San Diego's offensive coordinator.

In 1999 a trio of assistants who would later become NFL head coaches joined Brian Billick on his staff. Jack Del Rio was the linebackers coach, who would later become Carolina's defensive coordinator and Jacksonville's head coach. Del Rio's tenure in Jacksonville began in 2003 but ended in 2011 when he was let go. The following season he latched on as Denver's defensive coordinator.

From 1999 to 2004, Rex Ryan was Baltimore's defensive line coach. He was given the promotion to defensive coordinator in 2005, a position he held until Billick was fired in 2007. Ryan was also fired when Ravens owner Steve Bisciotti elected to clean house, but was rehired by new coach John Harbaugh. Ryan then received a head coaching opportunity with the New York Jets in 2009, a job he's held ever since.

Mike Smith was a defensive assistant to the defensive line in 1999. When Del Rio left to become Carolina's defensive coordinator in 2002, Smith took over his job as linebackers coach. After one year in that role, Del Rio hired Smith to join his staff in Jacksonville as the team's defensive coordinator. After five years, Smith then

Rooting for Chuck Pagano

Chuck Pagano was well-liked in the Ravens locker room during his time in Baltimore as defensive backs coach and defensive coordinator. He'd cut up with his players and treat them like his own. There was no age difference between the late-forties/early-fifties coach and his understudies. They were all the same, and that's what the Ravens players liked most about Pagano.

When Pagano took the head coaching job with the Indianapolis Colts, Ravens players were upset he was leaving, but happy that he was receiving a head coaching opportunity. It couldn't have happened to a better guy, in their minds. Then the bad news came. During Indianapolis' bye in Week 4, Pagano was diagnosed with acute promyelocytic leukemia. He couldn't battle on the football field each week for the short-term, as he took care of a much more important battle.

Ravens players joined in for the cause. Defensive end Arthur Jones shaved his head in honor of Pagano. In the wild-card round of the playoffs, Pagano got to coach against his former team. Baltimore won 24–9, but there were plenty of hugs shared between Pagano and his former players.

"He's just one of the guys," Ravens cornerback Lardarius Webb said. "It's like he's one of us, one of the teammates, not our coach. He's just a likeable guy. He always has a smile on his face. He's always joking around, having a good time, enjoying work. He was always serious about his job but was having fun. We loved that."

made his head coaching debut with the Atlanta Falcons, a team he's coached since 2008.

In 2001 Mike Nolan joined the Ravens' coaching staff as a wide receivers coach. A year later he became the defensive coordinator, a role he stayed in until 2004. After some success running Baltimore's defense, the San Francisco 49ers hired him to be their head coach. Nolan coached the Niners for four years before getting fired. After stints in Denver and Miami as a defensive coordinator, Nolan joined Mike Smith's staff in Atlanta for the same job.

Mike Singletary's first NFL job was coaching the Ravens' linebackers in 2003 and 2004. He followed that by becoming the linebackers coach with Mike Nolan at San Francisco. After the Niners fired Nolan in 2008, Singletary became the head coach after serving a brief period in an interim role. He was fired after his second full season after an 18–22 record in just over two and a half seasons.

Already with seven years of assistant head coaching experience in the NFL, the Ravens welcomed Hue Jackson on board to coach quarterbacks in 2008. He filled that role for two years before moving on to Oakland to be its offensive coordinator in 2010. A year later he was the head coach but was fired after just one season. Jackson is now the running backs coach in Cincinnati.

Chuck Pagano joined Harbaugh's staff in 2008 as a defensive backs coach. Pagano spent four years coaching the secondary before being given the opportunity to be Baltimore's defensive coordinator. Pagano served that role for the 2011 season but did too good of a job. He was noticed by Indianapolis, which offered Pagano its open head coaching position. Pagano agreed and left Baltimore to become Indianapolis' coach.

66 Michael McCrary Plays with Heart, Passion

Michael McCrary was one of those athletes who would give an arm or a leg for their team. He was like that with the Ravens when he arrived in 1997, running full speed and attacking quarterbacks and running backs at full throttle.

A defensive end, McCrary was passed over in the 1993 NFL Draft, until Seattle took him in the seventh round. McCrary was mostly a reserve until 1996, when he stepped in as a starter and totaled $13^1/_2$ sacks. When free agency opened for McCrary, he looked around and found that Baltimore was highly interested. The two parties reached an agreement, and McCrary was brought on board as another piece to the Ravens' defensive puzzle.

McCrary's motor never stopped on the football field. Undersized at defensive end, his weight varied from 260 to 280 pounds at any time of the year. But he was a workout warrior, always working on his strength. He combined that with top end speed for a defensive end, which allowed him to get by offensive linemen. He grew up participating in martial arts, which aided his all-around game, as well.

"This guy is one of the most tenacious, fiercest pass rushers in the league," Jacksonville offensive tackle Tony Boselli told the *Baltimore Sun* in 1998.

Despite the numbers he began to put up early in his career—nine sacks in 1997, $14\frac{1}{2}$ sacks in 1998, $11\frac{1}{2}$ sacks in 1999—McCrary wasn't placed in that elite category of pass rushers. He did earn Pro Bowl honors in 1998 and 1999 but still wasn't put on the same pedestal as Bruce Smith, Kevin Greene, John Randle, and the other top-tier pass rushers of that era.

"He's crazy. All-out every play. Never stops," Ogden told the *Sun* after a 1997 practice. "He's real quick, sneaky, very creative. I know he's going to make me better."

The 2000 postseason was the peak for McCrary's career. He carried a solid regular season ($6\frac{1}{2}$ sacks) into a month he'll never forget. In the wild-card round against Denver, McCrary tallied three sacks (though one came late with the game in hand) that contributed to a 21–3 win. McCrary was all over the field, wreaking havoc. He had four tackles in the contest with three of them sacks. The other tackle came after stopping running back Mike Anderson for a one-yard gain.

McCrary didn't record a sack in the divisional round of the playoffs against Tennessee, but he did tally a tackle for loss, stopping Eddie George for a two-yard loss in the second quarter. In the AFC Championship Game, McCrary opened the game by teaming up with Peter Boulware to stop running back Tyrone Wheatley on the first play. Two plays later, McCrary sacked quarterback Rich Gannon for a nine-yard loss.

In Baltimore's 34–7 win over the New York Giants to win the Super Bowl, McCrary sacked QB Kerry Collins on the Giants' first possession of the second half. In the fourth quarter, McCrary sacked Collins again and forced a fumble, though the Giants recovered. McCrary was relentless off the edge and capped a great season with a title.

Chronic knee problems hampered McCrary over the 2001 and 2002 seasons, and the Ravens released him before the 2003 season. McCrary ultimately decided to retire after a 10-year career that saw him accumulate 71 sacks (51 during his six years in Baltimore).

McCrary was the second player and fourth entry into the Ravens' Ring of Honor, getting the honor in 2004.

67 Jermaine Lewis, a Super Bowl Hero

The kick wasn't very long, and Jermaine Lewis fielded it at the 16-yard line. It gave him an opportunity to make history in an instant in a Baltimore Ravens uniform. Here Lewis was, on the biggest stage of his career. He was a part of the original draft class in 1996, selected in the fifth round, overall pick number 153. A lot of players drafted that late don't pan out or last long with an organization. But Lewis carved a niche for himself as a kickoff and punt returner and became one of the NFL's best during the years he played.

In 1997 Lewis ran back two punts for touchdowns, both in Week 15's game against Seattle. The punt returns were from 89 and 66 yards out, and then Lewis added a 29-yard receiving touchdown for one of the best games of his career. Lewis added two more punt return touchdowns in 1998, but wouldn't return a touchdown to the end zone in that capacity until the final game of the 2000 regular season. Once again, Lewis took two punts back for touchdowns, this time against the New York Jets.

To this point in Lewis' career, he'd returned six punts for touchdowns but no kickoffs to the end zone. That changed in Super Bowl XXXV. New York's Ron Dixon had just returned a kickoff 97 yards for a touchdown to cut Baltimore's lead to 17–7 late in the third quarter. It was a game all of a sudden, even though the Giants' offense was seemingly stuck in reverse throughout the game.

Lewis fielded the kick and took a bit of a high step before beginning to accelerate. Lewis saw a hole open to his right and started running that way. He got to the right sideline with Giants defenders closing in. It looked like Lewis would be forced out of bounds on the play. He took one toe tap before leaping about two yards in the air to avoid touching the white sideline. Once he touched the turf again Lewis had a clear path. Lewis ran the rest of the way into the end zone for an 84-yard kickoff return for a touchdown. It would be the only kickoff Lewis would return for a score during his nine-year NFL career.

Speaking to the *Baltimore Sun* just two days before the Ravens returned to the Super Bowl, Lewis was asked about the touchdown.

"That's the main thing you hoped for when you're playing football is to win the ultimate prize," he told the *Sun*. "That's an accomplishment I'm proud of for my kids. I want them to be proud of something. They can say my dad did this."

To this day, Lewis still holds franchise records for punt return yards (2,730), punt return touchdowns (six), number of punt returns (231), and number of kickoff returns (139).

68 Earnest Byner, the First Ravens Running Back

No, Earnest Byner isn't among the best Ravens players—or even running backs—in team history. You could easily reel off a handful of backs who, while in Baltimore, were better on the field than Byner was. But that shouldn't take away from the symbolism Byner holds for the Baltimore Ravens franchise.

When the old Browns moved to Baltimore, Byner came along with the organization. In 1996 Byner was entering his 13th NFL season, an incredible feat for a running back. Most backs are worn down at that point. It's one of the positions you don't see longevity in. But Byner stuck around, beginning his career in Cleveland, making a stop in Washington, and returning to Cleveland. While he was in Cleveland, he and the rest of his Browns teammates made the move to Baltimore when owner Art Modell made the decision to go.

Byner started eight of 16 games in 1996 and only managed 634 yards and four touchdowns. In fact, running back Bam Morris appeared in only 11 games and had a higher rushing total (737). But the two were formidable options in an offense that relied on quarterback Vinny Testaverde's arm more than the running game.

In Byner's second season with Baltimore, his numbers dipped in half, toting the ball just 84 times for 313 yards. He retired after that season after 14 years of playing football in the NFL. For his efforts as Baltimore's first running back, he was the first player inducted into the Ravens' Ring of Honor in 2001.

Drafted in the 10th round of the 1984 draft by the Browns, Byner made the most of his opportunity. After seeing time at running back in a reserve role as a rookie, Byner ran for 1,002 yards in 1985. Byner became Cleveland's go-to back for some time, consistently churning out yards for the organization.

However, he's most known for a play he'd love to forget. The play became known as "the Fumble," which helped keep the Browns out of the Super Bowl following the 1988 season. The Browns had driven down the field against the Broncos, poised to finally get over the postseason hump in the 1980s. It was second-and-5, and Byner took the handoff and broke left to what appeared to be an open field

Vested Vets End Careers in Baltimore

The Ravens have had their share of veterans end their careers in a Ravens uniform. Veterans are often attracted to end their playing days in Baltimore due to the fact it has been a consistent contender since 2000.

After 15 years in the NFL, quarterback Randall Cunningham spent his final season with Baltimore backing up Elvis Grbac in 2001. Cunningham did start two games during the season and threw for 573 yards and three touchdowns.

Deion Sanders, one of the best cornerbacks to ever play the game, spent his last two NFL seasons with Baltimore. He was primarily a backup, only starting six times in 25 games played. In his two seasons, Sanders totaled five interceptions and 10 pass deflections.

After 11 years with the Tennessee Titans franchise, quarterback Steve McNair spent his final two seasons with Baltimore. Though his 2007 season was injury-ridden, McNair guided the Ravens to a 13–3 regular season record in 2006.

Four-time Pro Bowl fullback Lorenzo Neal played the last of his 16 seasons with Baltimore in 2008. Neal started in five games and saw game action in all 16 regular season games.

Running back Ricky Williams capped off an 11-year career with Baltimore in 2011. As Ray Rice's backup, Williams carried the ball 108 times for 444 yards and two touchdowns. It was expected he'd come back for the 2012 season, but surprisingly chose retirement instead.

with the goal line ahead. Byner got closer, and closer, just two yards away from history. Broncos cornerback Jeremiah Castille was near the play and inching closer. As it looked like Byner would cross the goal line, Castille reached his hand in and stripped the ball. Byner plunged past the goal line, but the ball didn't. Denver recovered and earned a trip to the Super Bowl.

Following the fumble, Byner was distraught in the locker room, upset with his mistake. When he finally emerged to speak to the media, according to a *Cleveland Plain Dealer* story written in 2012, Modell walked up to him and embraced the solemn running back in a big hug.

There is a contingency of Ravens fans who believe Byner doesn't belong in the Ring of Honor because he wasn't one of the organization's greatest players. He ran for 8,261 yards in a 14-year career, but he only managed 947 yards and four touchdowns in two seasons with Baltimore. Then again, Byner is a link to the history Modell didn't take with him from Cleveland to Baltimore. Byner is a reminder that the Ravens' organization has its roots in Cleveland, even though Cleveland maintained the history of its football team for the expansion team in 1999.

Byner wasn't statistically one of the best to ever don a Ravens uniform. But nonetheless, he's honored among the best. He and Modell shared a special bond, dating back to those Cleveland teams of the 1980s. In Modell's mind, Byner deserved the honor.

69 Bryant McKinnie's Tumultuous Time in Baltimore

When Bryant McKinnie asserted himself as Baltimore's left tackle throughout the 2011 regular season, it was assumed he'd be back in the same role for the 2012 campaign.

But it was quite the rough road for the big, 6′8″ left tackle, used to starting each game protecting the quarterback's blind side. The Ravens signed McKinnie after reporting out of shape in Minnesota after the 2011 NFL lockout ended. He started every game in the 2011 season and bolstered a line that gave up 40 sacks in 2010.

But McKinnie's tough times started when he failed to report for the opening of training camp. It's unclear what kind of warning the organization was given, but it didn't appear to please coach John Harbaugh.

When camp opened and McKinnie wasn't present, Harbaugh was asked about it. According to coach John Harbaugh, a chiropractor had called the Ravens organization to inform it that McKinnie had injured his back and would be unable to make it to camp on time.

This certainly didn't go over well in Baltimore's front office.

McKinnie's story was this: he was running outside of his south Florida home, slipped and injured his back. His doctor advised him to rest for a few days and not fly on an airplane. This caused the five-day delay in McKinnie reporting to training camp and ultimately put him in the famed John Harbaugh doghouse.

McKinnie wasn't cleared to play right away once he reported to camp and was considered out of shape. When he eventually stepped foot on the practice field, McKinnie was relegated to second-string. He had lost his first-team left tackle status to Michael Oher, who was moved there from the right side. Ultimately, rookie Kelechi Osemele became the starting right tackle, and Ramon Harewood would up opening the season as Baltimore's starting left guard. McKinnie was only seeing snaps on Baltimore's field goal and extra-point units.

Making matters more difficult for McKinnie, during the whole process, the Ravens approached him to renegotiate his two-year contract. With Baltimore's plans to make McKinnie a backup, they wanted to reduce the salary he'd be earning. Slated to earn $3.5 million in 2012, McKinnie ultimately took a pay cut to a $2.5 million base with incentives to earn back the $1 million. Most of the incentives included how much playing time he saw, which never transpired through the course of the regular season.

Though the Ravens were confident in the five they selected for the offensive line, the unit struggled at times, especially on the road. The line never got stability at left guard, as Harewood, Bobbie Williams, and Jah Reid all started games during the season.

Midway through the year, McKinnie began assuming he'd start again, thinking the Ravens were benching him temporarily to avoid paying him the extra $1 million in incentives. With the line's issues protecting the passer, McKinnie figured his time was coming.

"If I was out there, maybe some things would be a little bit different," McKinnie said on December 19, 2012. "But there's not too much I can do."

But his time didn't come through 17 weeks. For the first time in his NFL career, McKinnie didn't start a regular season game.

Just when it was assumed McKinnie wouldn't see any meaningful snaps for the year, he got an opportunity. Reid went down with a toe injury, and initially it was assumed the Ravens would go with Bobbie Williams to replace him. But when Baltimore opened its wild-card round game against Indianapolis, McKinnie came out with the starting offensive line.

The line gave up 38 sacks during the regular season, an average of 2.4 sacks per game. In four postseason games, with McKinnie starting at left tackle, the Ravens gave up six sacks, good for an average of 1.5 sacks per game. There was no doubt that McKinnie's addition to the starting lineup had a positive impact on the Ravens' Super Bowl run.

McKinnie had plenty of ups and downs during the 2011 and 2012 seasons in Baltimore. Ultimately, he stuck it out and eventually saw playing time. His time came late, but it eventually arrived. And McKinnie was rewarded with becoming a Super Bowl champion. He then signed a two-year contract in the 2013 off-season to return to the organization. Consider McKinnie free from Harbaugh's doghouse.

70 Lardarius Webb Becomes a Shutdown Corner

The best NFL players don't always spend their collegiate careers at the biggest schools. Jerry Rice attended Mississippi Valley State. Walter Payton played ball at Jackson State. After run-ins that kicked him out of Notre Dame and Florida State, Randy Moss wound up at Marshall.

You can go on and on with these kind of players in NFL history. If you're good, teams will find you, no matter where you play college football. This was evident with Lardarius Webb, who played college football at Nicholls State, after spending his first two years with Southern Mississippi.

The Ravens drafted Webb, a safety in college, in the third round of the 2009 NFL Draft. He was an exciting prospect, having run the 40-yard dash in 4.46 seconds at the NFL Combine, which was the fastest of any player there.

He became Baltimore's primary kick returner as a rookie but suffered a torn anterior cruciate ligament (ACL) in his left knee late in the year. Though this did keep him limited performance-wise in 2010, Webb was able to show his abilities at cornerback, not safety. He picked off his first career pass against Miami and returned it 32 yards. He was still a reserve defensive back and was expected to continue in that role in 2011.

But Domonique Foxworth, Baltimore's No. 1 corner, was coming off an ACL tear during the 2010 preseason and was still not 100 percent. Chris Carr, who received a starter-worthy contract, tweaked a hamstring in training camp. Injuries pushed Webb into a starting role, one he didn't take lightly.

From the start, it appeared the Ravens had something special in Webb. He could play outside corner as well as against the slot receiver. His versatility in the back end was key, and his speed allowed him to keep up with the game's best receivers.

In the 2011 season's first four games, Webb had recorded two interceptions, one each against the Rams and Jets. He finished the regular season with five and added three more in the postseason, with two against Houston in the divisional round of the playoffs.

The Ravens knew they had something special in Webb and were determined to lock him up for years to come. The statistic-analyzing site ProFootballFocus.com gave Webb a 21.2 pass coverage rating, which was not only the best on the Ravens, but in the entire National Football League. If Webb was to be Baltimore's shutdown cornerback, the organization needed to pay him like one. According

Ravens cornerback Lardarius Webb intercepts a pass intended for St. Louis Rams wide receiver Danario Alexander (84) during a game in September 2011.

to Webb's agent, Marc Lillibridge, Webb was hoping for a $50 million payday.

"All he kept saying to me over and over was, "I need $50 million, Bridge! I'm worth $50 mil, Bridge!" Lillibridge wrote in a column for Bleacher Report. "I would play coy with him sometimes and tell him he should just be happy to be in the NFL, but kidding aside, I wanted the $50 million for him, too."

The deal was ultimately done, and Webb was now the recipient of a six-year, $50 million contract with $10 million guaranteed.

Webb was ready to continue his success in 2012 with another stellar season. But unfortunately for Webb, his season was cut short in Week 6 against Dallas. During the first quarter of a 31–29 win over the Cowboys, Webb fell to the turf and was in pain. It became clear quickly his injury was serious. A day later, it was confirmed that Webb tore the ACL in his right knee and his season was over.

Prior to the injury, Webb had one interception, a forced fumble, and fumble recovery for the season. He had also emerged as a premier run defender in the nickel defensive back spot, on a defense that struggled early in the year. Webb was forced to devote the rest of his 2012 season to rehabilitating his right knee, something he was determined to come back from.

"I'm coming off a little adversity, but it just puts a chip on my shoulder," Webb told the *Baltimore Sun* in April 2013. "It's about determination and how bad I want to get back on that field. I missed out last season and I was there for the ride, but I want to go to the Super Bowl again. The Lord won't put me through anything I can't handle. I take everything in stride."

Ray Lewis Recovers from Triceps Tear

It was bad enough the Ravens lost Lardarius Webb for the final 10 games of the 2012 regular season when he tore his right ACL against the Dallas Cowboys. But when the future Hall of Fame linebacker heard a pop in his right upper arm, matters became much worse.

Initially the team tried to downplay it. Immediately following the Dallas game, coach John Harbaugh said, "Ray has a triceps [injury], but I don't think it's really bad. We'll have to see on that."

It didn't take long to realize the severity was worse than originally thought. Rumors began to circulate. Was it partially torn? Fully torn? If so, how long would he be out for? A day later, on October 15, Harbaugh announced Lewis would likely miss the remainder of the season with a completely torn right triceps muscle. It was a devastating day for the organization, knowing it was potentially the end of Lewis' career.

Lewis didn't want to go out like that. In his mind, he couldn't possibly end his career with an injury. He wanted one more shot to go out on top, to reach the pinnacle of the NFL again. A couple of days after the injury, Lewis spoke with general manager Ozzie Newsome about leaving the window open for a late-season return.

"As soon as I had [the injury], I made a phone call to Ozzie and I told Ozzie directly…I told Ozzie, 'We need to talk, because I'm not going out like this. I'm not walking out on my boys like that,'" Lewis said.

The Ravens elected to place Lewis on the injured reserve–designated to return list, which was new for the 2012 season. This allowed each team to put one player on IR that can be eligible to return to the roster after six missed weeks. After six weeks on IR–designated to return, each NFL team has a three-week grace period to place the player back on the active roster.

Lewis was given the chance to come back, to rehab and return fresh. He told his teammates to just get the Ravens to the playoffs and he'd help lead them to the finish line.

"He let us know he's on pace to come back," Suggs said on November 9, 2012, just two days before the Ravens were set to take on the Raiders in Week 10. "If we handle business, he'll be back in a Ravens uniform this year. We have to do our part, though."

Lewis stayed behind the scenes, rehabbing the torn triceps, one of the more difficult injuries to quickly recover from. They can also be tricky. Depending on where the tear is located determines the severity.

According to BaltimoreRavens.com, one of the rehab methods Lewis was using was to hook a device to the injured triceps and send electronic simulations to the area. It's a painful process, and one even more painful when you consider Lewis would lift weights with the device still hooked up to him. Lewis wasn't giving up his fight. He wanted to return to the football field.

With the regular season winding down, Lewis began practicing with his teammates again. But he never got the go-ahead to play in a regular season game, despite the buzz that he might. The Ravens played it cautiously, electing to bring Lewis back for the postseason.

When Lewis ended his silence from the media, which began after the injury in the Cowboys game, it was on the Wednesday before the wild-card game against Indianapolis. During that press conference, Lewis announced his retirement, and hinted he'd be ready to play that Sunday. In Lewis-like fashion, he finished Baltimore's 24–9 win over Indianapolis with a team-high 13 tackles while wearing a bulky brace to protect the injured triceps. A week later in Denver, Lewis recorded 17 tackles, which was once again a team best. In the AFC Championship Game, Lewis led his unit with 14 more tackles.

But in this story of recovery came controversy. During Super Bowl Week, *Sports Illustrated* reported that Lewis had used a deer antler spray product from a company called Sports with Alternatives to Steroids (SWATS) to aid his triceps recovery. The problem with this is that deer antler spray contains the protein IGF-1, which is a banned substance in the NFL.

Critics pounced on Lewis, calling him a cheat. Some defended Lewis, explaining traces of IGF-1 can be found in plenty of legal animal products. Lewis denied ever using a banned substance when questioned about it during the Wednesday media day before the Super Bowl.

"It's so funny of a story, because I never, ever took what he says or whatever I was supposed to do," Lewis said. "And it's just sad, once again, that someone can have this much attention on a stage this big, where the dreams are really real," Lewis said. "I don't need it. My teammates don't need it. The 49ers don't need it. Nobody needs it."

Stepping In for Ray Lewis

Filling in for a legend is never easy. But in a sport like football, it's asking too much to expect someone to stay healthy all the time. So in years when Lewis was sidelined with injuries, who filled in for him?

In 2002 Lewis dislocated his shoulder and was only able to start the first five games of the season. Filling in for him was veteran linebacker Bernardo Harris. Harris finished the season with 64 tackles and two sacks.

In 2005 Lewis only started six games due to a hamstring injury that lingered throughout the year. Tommy Polley was his replacement. Polley totaled 96 tackles and four sacks.

In 2011 Lewis missed four games with a turf toe injury, and in 2012 Lewis missed 10 games with a torn triceps. A committee of linebackers filled in for him. Dannell Ellerbe, Josh Bynes, and Albert McClellan all played snaps at inside linebacker while Lewis was out during his final two NFL regular seasons.

The story was the buzz of the Super Bowl for about a day or two. By kickoff that Sunday, it was barely mentioned anymore. Lewis didn't have the statistically solid game he'd had in the previous three postseason games, but he still finished with seven tackles against a tough San Francisco offense. The Ravens prevailed 34–31 in a bizarre Super Bowl that featured offensive explosions from both Baltimore and San Francisco, as well as a 34-minute delay due to a power outage inside the Superdome.

Lewis lived up to his promise to Newsome, and Newsome was rewarded for placing him on the injured reserve–designated to return list. Lewis was able to end his career a champion. Lewis left it up to his own self to not end his career with a triceps injury. He fought through the adversity and added a second Super Bowl ring to his collection.

72 Revenge in New England

The Ravens were a dropped Lee Evans pass from possibly heading to the Super Bowl in early 2012, just after the 2011 regular season had finished. On top of that, another missed opportunity was squandered, when Billy Cundiff missed a 32-yard field goal to the left that would have sent the AFC Championship Game to overtime.

That devastating loss came against New England in Foxborough, Massachusetts, the site where the Ravens would have a chance at revenge for the right to be named 2012 AFC champions.

After being written off a week before against Denver, most national analysts were giving the Ravens little chance once again. And it's not like the reasoning was faulty. New England was a hot team finding a groove. One of the greatest NFL quarterbacks, Tom Brady, was New England's signal-caller. Wes Welker and Aaron Hernandez were two dangerous targets for Brady, and running back Stevan Ridley had a regular season in which he ran for over 1,200 yards.

But the Patriots badly missed tight end Rob Gronkowski, who broke his forearm for the second time of the season against the Texans the week before. Gronkowski was deemed the biggest matchup advantage for New England. Without Gronkowski, the Ravens' safeties wouldn't have as big of a worry in coverage.

The game itself got off to a slow start. In the first quarter alone there were a total of six punts between the two teams, with the Patriots holding a slight 3–0 lead once the first 15 minutes ticked down. But early in the second quarter, Baltimore was able to establish an offensive rhythm.

Tight end Dennis Pitta caught a pass for 17 yards, Ray Rice received one for 11 yards, and Torrey Smith was on the receiving end of a 25-yard gain. Rice was able to punch in a two-yard touchdown to cap the drive off, giving Baltimore a 7–3 lead in the second quarter.

But New England answered with a long drive of their own, running 10 plays before Welker caught a one-yard pass from Brady to put the Patriots up 10–7. The Ravens went three-and-out, and New England threatened once again.

After seven plays and two timeouts spent, Brady looked downfield, with just 26 seconds remaining in the first half. Nothing was open, so he scrambled for a three-yard gain to the Baltimore 7-yard line before sliding. But a bad blunder possibly cost New England a touchdown in this situation. Brady tried to hurry his team to the line, wasting precious time. Before he could get the snap off, Patriots coach Bill Belichick called a timeout from the sideline so he could send in the field-goal unit. Patriots kicker Stephen Gostkowski knocked in an easy 25-yard field goal to give New England a 13–7 halftime lead.

Matters could've been worse for Baltimore. Even though the offense was only able to pick up seven first-half points, the Ravens were only trailing by six points. There was plenty of time to make up ground. The halftime period also gave one leader a chance to get in the ear of another.

"We [didn't] want to have that same feeling in the locker room after the second half," left tackle Bryant McKinnie said after the game, when asked what the feeling was after the first two quarters.

Said Pitta: "We needed to get it together. We got out there and started executing and just took care of business."

That, the Ravens did.

After punts from each team opened the second half, Baltimore executed a 10-play, 87-yard drive that ended with a five-yard Pitta touchdown reception to move ahead 14–13. On the drive, Pitta also had the largest gain, a 22-yard reception that moved Baltimore to midfield.

After forcing a New England punt, the Ravens' offense got back to work once again. After running nine more plays and getting down to the New England 3-yard line, Flacco found receiver Anquan Boldin for a short completion good for a touchdown. Baltimore was now up by eight, holding a 21–13 lead with under 15 minutes remaining.

The thing that characterized those Patriots teams of the early 2000s, which were so dominant, was their ability to win in crunch time. There was always a feeling in the air that New England would come back and win. Brady will go down in history as one of the most clutch quarterbacks who ever played the game.

However, that feeling didn't exist, and the body language on the field indicated it. Baltimore's defense seized the momentum and had figured out the New England offense. Big gains became limited, and plays were made only in front of the Baltimore defense.

On a first-and-10 from the New England 39, Ravens safety Bernard Pollard popped running back Stevan Ridley with a thunderous hit, which forced a fumble that the Ravens' defensive end Arthur Jones recovered. Ridley was also knocked out of the game as a result of the hit.

Four plays later, Flacco found Boldin for another touchdown, this time from 11 yards out. Baltimore was now up 28–13 and in complete control. The closest New England would get to scoring another point was when it got to the Baltimore 19, where it was stopped and forced to turn the ball back over to the Ravens. In the fourth quarter, linebacker Dannell Ellerbe and cornerback Cary Williams both picked off Brady, with Williams' interception coming late with New England back at Baltimore's 22-yard line.

After Flacco's second kneel down, the Ravens began to celebrate. They had just exacted revenge on the team that kept them from heading to the Super Bowl a season prior. Now, it was Baltimore that became AFC champions. And it was Baltimore's turn at a try for a Super Bowl championship.

"Any other team with this win would have been unjustified," said outside linebacker Terrell Suggs. "Especially how the [2011 AFC Championship Game] ended, and who 12 [Tom Brady] is, and who their head coach is, and who their owner is. Between these two teams, you won't get another battle like this between two AFC opponents. We have the upmost respect for them."

73 Harbaugh Bowl I

Talk about the ultimate family affair. The Harbaughs, a family that lives and breathes football, were celebrating Thanksgiving, in a sense, in Baltimore. The NFL elected to pit the Ravens and 49ers against each other for a prime-time Thanksgiving game. John Harbaugh was in his fourth season as an NFL coach. His brother Jim was in his first, coaching the 49ers after a successful stint in the college ranks with Stanford.

This game on November 24, 2011, would be the first ever in NFL history between two head coaches who were brothers. It was a pinnacle of sorts for a family whose lives revolved around the sport. John and Jim's father, Jack, was a longtime football coach, which included a stop as an assistant to Bo Schembechler at the University of Michigan. Jack Harbaugh later became the head coach at Western Kentucky, where he led the Hilltoppers to a Division I-AA national championship in 2002.

The sibling head coaches story was a big deal, but quite possibly overblown throughout the week of the game. Reporters wanted to know everything possible about the Harbaugh family. The two brothers, Jim in particular, wanted to focus on the game.

"This is the first time two brothers have coached against each other. It's the first time an NFL team has traveled three time zones to play a Thursday night game since the league went to a 16-game schedule," Jim said dryly in a national conference call.

Both coaches are intense, deliberate, and pay extreme attention to detail. Otherwise, they wouldn't have made it to the NFL coaching ranks. San Francisco, which was 9–1 entering the Ravens game, finished the 2010 regular season 6–10 and had fired head coach Mike Singletary that December. Jim Harbaugh helped turn the 49ers franchise around in just one year, a job plenty of pundits expected to take longer. The 49ers players wanted to win for Jim, the coach who turned the team into winners. Though the Ravens didn't admit it at the time, the players were dying to get this win for John, to give him the upper hand in the Harbaugh sibling rivalry.

There they were on Thanksgiving, both Harbaugh brothers exchanging a pregame handshake with a cloud of cameras hovering over them to capture the family moment.

It was the time for the family to take center stage in what's become the most watched sport in the United States.

With the nation watching, the two teams ended the first quarter in a 3–3 tie. Both defenses stepped up to the challenge early, with the Ravens already getting a sack on 49ers quarterback Alex Smith.

Early in the second quarter, it looked like the 49ers were going to take a lead. Smith threw a perfect pass to Ted Ginn Jr. for a 75-yard touchdown. But it was nullified thanks to an illegal chop block from running back Frank Gore. Suddenly, momentum was taken away, and the 49ers would wind up punting the ball back to Baltimore. The first half ended with a 6–3 Baltimore lead, typical of the defensive mindsets of each football club.

The third quarter was a throwback to Jack Harbaugh's days on Bo Schembechler's staff. A lot of time rolled off the clock between plays. Each team had one possession each. The Ravens sacked Smith twice on the possession, which resulted in a 52-yard David Akers field goal.

The Ravens reached the San Francisco 8-yard line before the third quarter ended. The game was 6–6, though Baltimore looked poised to score the game's first touchdown. And on the first play in the fourth quarter, it did. Quarterback Joe Flacco found tight end Dennis Pitta for an eight-yard score, giving Baltimore a 13–6 lead.

From there, the Baltimore defense took over, led by outside linebacker Terrell Suggs. Suggs finished the game with three of Baltimore's nine sacks, in a performance that ultimately contributed to his earning 2011 NFL Defensive Player of the Year honors. Baltimore won the game 16–6, victors of the first-ever Harbaugh Bowl.

Both teams' seasons ended in their respective conference championships, so Harbaugh Bowl II had to wait. But it didn't take long, as both teams met again the following season in Super Bowl XLVII, with Baltimore winning 34–31 in a game that featured much more offense than the first one.

"Just running across the field, I felt really humble," John Harbaugh said in his postgame comments. "Really humble, just thankful. It's Thanksgiving, and we told our guys there is so much to be thankful for. God has given us a lot to be thankful for, but the main thing he gives us is each other. He gives us our relationships. Running across the field to my brother—he's my best friend, along with Mom and Dad and my wife. If you put yourself in his shoes—you don't put yourself in many other coaches' shoes, but you can put yourself in your brother's shoes—I'm really proud of him."

74 Ray Rice Runs Wild vs. Patriots

One play can set a tone in a game, especially when it's the first play from scrimmage. That happened for the Ravens in the wild-card

Ravens running back Ray Rice breaks free from a trio of Patriots defenders and rumbles for an 83-yard touchdown on the first play from scrimmage during Baltimore's wild-card playoff win over New England on January 10, 2010.

round of the 2009 postseason. Baltimore, the No. 6 seed, traveled to New England to take on a Patriots team that once again had won the AFC East.

After the opening kickoff, Baltimore took over at its own 17-yard line. At the time, the Ravens were a run-first team, so you'd think New England would be expecting a run on first down.

Linebackers were sitting back fairly far pre-snap, which would force them to take more time to fill any gaps Ravens running back Ray Rice could run through. Once the ball was snapped, quarterback Joe Flacco handed the ball off to Rice, who made a quick cut into an open hole in the middle of the offensive line. Rice ran past a group of linebackers who over-pursued the play. All he had left to beat was Patriots safety Brandon Meriweather. Rice took a quick step to the left to get by Meriweather and had the end zone in front of him. Meriweather made one last diving attempt to no avail. Rice scored an 83-yard touchdown on the first offensive play of the game.

On New England's ensuing possession, linebacker Terrell Suggs forced a fumble and recovered it, giving the Ravens the ball back. Rice carried the ball twice on Baltimore's next short drive, picking up 10 more yards. Fullback Le'Ron McClain ended up scoring a touchdown to put Baltimore up 14–0. The game was less than five minutes underway, and Rice already had three carries for 93 yards and a touchdown.

Rice added another touchdown of his own from one yard away to give Baltimore a 21–0 first quarter lead. The rout had just begun.

"One thing we said as an offense is we want to start games fast," Rice said. "I wanted to be the guy today to start fast, whether it was a five-yard run or an 83-yard run. I wanted to be the guy to say this will be a fast-tempo game. We want the other team to play catch-up to us."

In the second quarter, Rice, splitting time with Willis McGahee in the backfield, added 15 more yards to his total. On Baltimore's first possession of the third quarter, Rice was back at it, picking up a six-yard gain on the first play.

Rice later helped set up a Billy Cundiff field goal with three runs that accounted for 15 yards. After a one-play break, Rice ran for three more yards before Cundiff's 23-yard field goal put Baltimore up 27–7.

Rice ran for 18 more yards in the fourth quarter, which gave him a game total of 159 yards and two touchdowns. It was the second-best game statistically for Rice that season, as ran for 166 yards against Detroit in a 48–3 win in Week 14.

Ray Rice's Best Games

Ray Rice has had some huge moments as a Raven. He rumbled all over New England in the wild-card round of the 2009 playoffs. He picked up a miraculous fourth-and-29 play against San Diego in 2012. Here's a look at a few other of Rice's memorable moments:

- In a 48–3 blowout over Detroit in 2009, Rice ran for 166 yards on just 13 carries, scoring one touchdown. Rice averaged 12.8 yards per carry, which still remains a personal best for a single game.
- In rainy conditions, Rice took it upon himself to shoulder the load in a road game against Cleveland in 2011. Rice carried the ball 29 times for 204 yards and a touchdown.
- Rice carried the ball 31 times for 153 yards and a touchdown in a 30–24 win over New Orleans in 2010. In addition to his big rushing day, Rice caught five passes out of the backfield for 80 yards and a touchdown.

Rice blossomed into a star in 2009, his second season in the NFL. Though he had some spectacular games in 2009, and throughout his career, his playoff game against New England will forever be talked about. The Patriots had no answer for the diminutive running back out of Rutgers that January day.

75 Qadry Ismail vs. Pittsburgh in 1999

In any sport, it can be eye-popping when a player takes over and asserts his will on an opponent. The Ravens have had many of these moments. Ray Lewis and the defense in Super Bowl XXXV. Jamal Lewis did this against the Cleveland Browns in 2003, when he ran for 295 yards. Joe Flacco dominated the Rams from start to finish in a Week 3 win over St. Louis in 2011.

Of all the Baltimore receivers, no one had a better day than Qadry "the Missile" Ismail had in a December 12, 1999, game against the Pittsburgh Steelers. Winners over rival Tennessee in impressive fashion the week before, the Ravens felt they still had something to prove in Brian Billick's first year as their head coach.

Banks misfired on his first seven passes of the game, though Baltimore was able to tie Pittsburgh 7–7, thanks to a 64-yard touchdown run from Priest Holmes. But Ismail would finally catch his first pass, with Tony Banks notching his first completion, on Baltimore's fourth drive, which resulted after a punt return that was fumbled by Pittsburgh's Troy Edwards. Banks hit Ismail for 31 yards. Baltimore finished the drive with a field goal, tying the game at 10–10.

Ismail added one more catch in the first half for 15 yards, giving him two grabs for 46 yards. He had a long way to go before he'd reach his huge yardage total. Banks wasn't exactly helping in the first two quarters, completing only three of 17 passes for 55 yards.

Ismail's game began opening up early in the third quarter. On the second play of the period, Banks hit Ismail for a 21-yard gain. Three plays after, Ismail found a seam in between two Pittsburgh defensive backs. Ismail received a bump, but it was not enough to bring him down. After slightly losing his footing, "the Missile" regrouped and took off down the left sideline for a 54-yard touchdown. Just like that, Ismail had 121 yards for the day, and he wasn't done yet.

After a Pittsburgh touchdown tied the game back at 17–17, Steelers kicker Kris Brown made a mistake by kicking the ball off out of bounds, giving the Ravens the ball at their own 40. On third-and-9, Ismail ran a skinny post in between three Steelers defenders. The defensive backs were out of position for the run after the catch and Ismail made them pay by burning past the secondary up the middle of the field for a 59-yard touchdown.

Ismail had one more dagger to put in Pittsburgh's collective heart. After the defense forced the Steelers to punt, Baltimore took over at its own 12. The Ravens were able to pick up a first down, reaching the 24 after Charles Evans caught a three-yard pass on a third-and-1. On the next play, Pittsburgh's coverage busted and left Ismail wide open down the left sideline. Banks lofted a perfect touch pass to the playmaker, who took it to the end zone for a 76-yard score. The touchdown put Baltimore up 31–17. Ismail wouldn't record another catch for the rest of the game, but it wouldn't matter. The Ravens held on for a 31–24 win.

Ismail's final totals were six catches, 258 yards, and three touchdowns. His yardage total still stands as a franchise best in a single game, and it's not that close. Derrick Alexander's 198-yard performance against Pittsburgh in 1996 was vastly overshadowed with what Ismail did. More ridiculous was the fact Banks finished the day 8-of-26 for 268 yards and three touchdowns. In addition to Ismail's receptions, Banks only completed the three-yard pass to Evans and a seven-yard throw to receiver Billy Davis.

Of every NFL receiver who's recorded 250 yards or more in a single game, Ismail achieved the feat in the fewest catches, according to the Pro Football Hall of Fame.

"One of the things that has helped our passing game the last couple of weeks is that Tony [Banks] and us got together and discussed the situation," Ismail told reporters after his career day. "If we run the right routes, Tony will trust us and anticipate where we're going and put a touch on the throws. We've had some good connections, and that paid off today."

76 Home-Field Advantage in 2011

Whether its early Sunday morning or late Thursday night, the Baltimore Ravens faithful will come out in droves to support their team. The stands inside M&T Bank Stadium will be filled before kickoff, with 71,000-plus cheering their Ravens while donning the purple and black.

The Ravens are fortunate to have fans like these, who come out in droves whether the team wins or loses. The city loves football and cannot get enough of it. It's part of the reason why it's so tough for opposing teams to win in Baltimore. From 2008 to 2010, the Ravens were a combined 19–5 at home, with a 7–1 home record in the 2010 season. In 2012, ESPN ranked M&T Bank Stadium the toughest place for an NFL visiting team to play in.

The 2011 season was indicative of this. Even when teams had their best shots at pulling out a win in M&T Bank Stadium, they'd fall short. But when the Ravens were able to cap their 2011 home season 8–0, even their biggest star was a bit surprised.

"I've never been perfect at home in 16 years of football," linebacker Ray Lewis said in 2011. "And that's amazing, because as good of teams as we've had here, we've always found a way to lose one or two, here or there. But I think this year we really made our focus on taking care of home. And our team came in, and we did a great job taking care of home. And this is the result of it; being able to go 8–0, and sitting where you want to sit at the end of the day."

The home season began against Pittsburgh on September 11, 2011. One of the NFL's premier rivalries was getting a head start on the NFL's opening day. But it didn't prove to be much of a game. The Ravens walloped the Steelers 35–7 in a lopsided contest. Joe Flacco threw for three touchdowns, and Ray Rice ran for 107 yards and a touchdown.

After road games against Tennessee (a 26–13 loss) and St. Louis (a 37–7 win), the Ravens returned home to defeat the New York Jets 34–17, using three defensive TDs—a six-yard Jameel McClain fumble recovery for a score, a 26-yard Jarrett Johnson fumble return, and 73-yard Lardarius Webb pick-six—to catapult them to a win.

After a bye, Flacco threw for 305 yards in a 29–14 win over the Houston Texans. Baltimore's early home performances proved it would be one of the top teams to beat all season and extremely tough to beat in the postseason if they get home-field advantage.

But back on the road Baltimore went after beating Houston 29–14, and back home it came with a loss, a disheartening 12–7 defeat to Jacksonville, one of the NFL's worst teams in 2011. After a loss like that, it's usually best if a team can play the following one at home. The Ravens were fortunate in that regard, hosting Arizona the week after.

But that game proved more difficult than it should have been. The Cardinals were able to break out to a 24–6 halftime lead, which was only that close because Ravens kicker Billy Cundiff added a 34-yard field goal with 39 seconds left in the first half. But Baltimore buckled down and outscored Arizona 24–3 in the second half, defeating the pesky Cardinals 30–27.

"It's a tough environment to play," then–Arizona coach Ken Whisenhunt said following Arizona's loss.

The next two for Baltimore were on the road, which included a win over Pittsburgh and a loss at Seattle. After the Seahawks loss, Baltimore returned home frustrated, angry it let that one slip away. The Ravens got back on the winning track with a home win against Cincinnati, which included withstanding a late Bengals rally to hold on for a 31–24 win. A week later, John Harbaugh defeated his brother Jim's 49ers 16–6 on Thanksgiving in front of the M&T Bank Stadium crowd.

With only two home games remaining, the opportunity to win every outing at M&T Bank Stadium began to look like a reality.

"I think we have the best fans in the world," linebacker Terrell Suggs said. "We win all of our home games, and that's because it's loud and because our fans give us the energy, and we want to play well for them. So home-field advantage is key."

In Baltimore's seventh home game of the season, it got by a struggling Colts squad that hadn't won a game all season. Only one regular season home game remained, and that was against the Browns in Week 16. Defeat them, and a perfect home regular season would be reached.

The Browns put up more of a fight than they did in the season's previous meeting, a 24–10 Ravens win in Cleveland. Flacco was held to 130 yards passing in a 24–16 win. Down 17–3 at halftime, the Browns clawed their way back with 10 unanswered points. But a 51-yard Ray Rice touchdown run sealed the deal in the fourth quarter.

"Eight and O at home for the first time in the history of the franchise is a tremendous accomplishment," Harbaugh said. "And credit goes to the players, first. It goes to the coaches, but it also goes to our fans. I think over the course of time since the Ravens came to Baltimore, and for my experience here in the last four years, there's not a better stadium in the league than M&T Bank Stadium. There's not a better bunch of fans than Ravens fans, everywhere, but especially on game day in Baltimore."

77 Torrey Smith's Brother's Unexpected Death

For a lot of players, football can become a sanctuary. When times get tough in their personal lives, they can always count on a moment of solitude on the gridiron.

When Torrey Smith received a phone call at around 10:30 PM on Saturday, September 22, 2012. He was informed his brother, Tevin Chris Jones, had died in a motorcycle accident in Virginia. Jones was driving on Route 672 in Virginia before running off of the road and striking a pole. He was pronounced dead at the scene of the accident. Smith notified the coaching staff and was allowed to be with his family. It was unknown at that time if Smith would be able to play in Sunday night's game against the New England Patriots.

Smith stayed awake for the entire night and didn't fall asleep until about 6:30 AM Sunday. He said he got about an hour of sleep before waking up. At 8:36 AM, Smith took to Twitter to tell the world his little brother had passed away.

"I can't believe my little brother is gone…be thankful for your loved ones and tell them you love them…this is the hardest thing ever," Smith tweeted.

He later tweeted a picture with his little brother, writing, "I can't say a bad thing about him…proud to have him as a brother…RIP Tevin."

The two brothers were close, and Jones' untimely passing hurt Smith. He spent the day with his family, and it became unknown whether Smith would play or not. By 4:00 PM, Smith made the decision to play. He said his teammates needed him, and he didn't want to let them down.

"I never really had to deal with a death in the family, let alone my brother," Smith said. "In our family, everyone's so tight. Just like a lot of other families. It's part of life, and, due to my teammates and my family and friends, I'll be able to get over it."

When Smith arrived at M&T Bank Stadium, he texted his mother and let her know he'd suit up. Smith received a lot of support from his teammates and coaching staff before the game even began.

"I didn't see him all day until he got into the locker room," quarterback Joe Flacco said. "When I saw him, I went over and said hello, and he seemed his normal self, he really did. He seemed like he was ready to play football and ready to go out there and help us get a win. That was great; we all wanted to rally around him and go get it for him."

The Ravens started the game slow and allowed the Patriots to jump out to a 13–0 lead. Early in the second quarter, the Ravens needed a score to get back in the game and stunt New England's momentum.

Baltimore drove down to the Patriots' 25-yard line to set up a first-and-10. Flacco play-faked to Ray Rice and looked down the left sideline. Smith was in man coverage against Patriots cornerback Kyle Arrington and was able to slip past him. Flacco threw a perfect pass in his direction that Smith was able to come down with.

The M&T Bank Stadium crowd went wild with Smith's catch. Smith had fallen to the ground and began to get up. But before doing so he pointed to the sky, in memory of his fallen brother. He then posed on one knee and said a quick prayer. His teammates rushed to his side and began congratulating him for the catch. For Smith, this one was for Tevin, the younger brother who always acted as one of Smith's biggest fans.

"Obviously you play with a heavy heart, you want to play for that person," Smith said. "My mom, all my family, everyone's back at the house watching. They didn't even know I was going to play until the last minute. I texted my mom [when] I got here to the stadium. That's when I really made my decision I was going to play. So she was excited about it. She was like, 'Of course, he'd want you to play.' He'd admired me so much, which is what makes it so much, and it's just a tough situation altogether. I'm just glad I was here with my family. We got this win and look forward to going on to the next [game] Thursday."

Early in the fourth quarter, the Patriots went up 30–21 on a 20-yard field goal by Stephen Gostkowski. Baltimore needed two scores to win, and to prevent New England's high-flying offense from scoring anymore. After stalling with just under 11 minutes left to play on offense, the Baltimore defense stepped up and forced New England to punt the ball.

Flacco then led Baltimore's offense down the field with precision. Jacoby Jones caught a 21-yard pass. Smith caught a 16-yard pass. Rice took a pass and turned it into a 27-yard gain. After getting down to the New England 10-yard line, a defensive holding call gave Baltimore five more yards to set the Ravens in even better scoring position.

Flacco then took the snap and play-faked to Rice once again. But New England's pressure closed in on Flacco, who needed to take a couple of steps to his right. Smith was running toward the middle of the end zone but realized he needed to help his quarterback out. He came back to the right corner of the end zone, with Devin McCourty behind him in coverage. Flacco threw a laser, and Smith caught it, to cut into New England's lead.

"Hopefully, we gave him a little time away in his mind for him to just think about football and not that," Flacco said after the game. "I'm sure it won't last too long, but at least we gave him a little bit of time to come out and play football and have a little fun."

After giving up a couple of first downs to New England's offense, Baltimore's defense forced a punt. Flacco and the offense moved down the field quickly, with a defensive pass interference penalty putting the ball at the New England 7-yard line. Down 30–28, rookie kicker Justin Tucker barely made a game-winning kick over the right crossbar. Baltimore came away with a 31–30 win that Sunday night.

Smith appeared numb in his postgame presser, still processing the range of emotions he was going through. It was the only time he talked about his brother during the season. The memory of his passing was still fresh in his mind, and it was evident when he was asked what made Tevin a special person.

"You had to be around him," Smith said. "He's honest, he had a great heart. A lot of people say that all the time when people pass, but he truly was that person. When you see him mad, you'd always laugh because it didn't look right. So, to be around him, his big smile and his laugh, which was probably one of the most annoying laughs ever, I'm definitely going to miss him. He laughed so hard at everything, and you know, he'd do anything for you. It's a tough loss for us."

78 Ed Reed's Eight INTs in 10 Games

Prior to the 2010 season, the Ravens were dealt a serious blow when it was determined Ed Reed would have to head to the "physically unable to perform" list. This meant he would not be available in Baltimore's first six games of the season due to a nagging hip injury that required off-season surgery.

The Ravens had a tough start to the season, too. They opened on the road with the New York Jets and with a road contest at Cincinnati the week after. Games against Cleveland, Pittsburgh, and Denver in Weeks 3, 4, and 5 wouldn't be easy, not to mention Week 6 at New England.

"It's going to be challenging opening up with the schedule we have whether I'm there or not," Reed told radio station 105.7 FM (The Fan) about his impending PUP status. "It's leaning that way more than anything. Hopefully, we can weather the storm. We have great players around us to get through those games and be able to make a run."

Much to Reed's credit, the Ravens were able to weather the storm. Without Reed, arguably the game's greatest safety of all time, Baltimore was able to go 4–2, with losses to Cincinnati and New England by a combined eight points.

With a solid start to the season, Reed returned to the lineup to face the Buffalo Bills in Week 7. On the first play of the third quarter, with Buffalo up 24–20, Bills quarterback Ryan Fitzpatrick threw a pass intended for Roscoe Parrish. There was Reed, looking like his usual self, making a play to pick the ball off. This helped set up a touchdown from Joe Flacco to Anquan Boldin to put Baltimore in the lead 27–24.

Fitzpatrick tried to test the Ravens' secondary deep again on the final play of the third quarter. Looking down the right sideline for David Nelson, Fitzpatrick didn't account for Reed's ability to cover sideline to sideline. Reed picked the pass off and returned it 40 yards the other way (though Flacco turned the ball over on the next play with a lost fumble).

Baltimore would wind up winning in overtime 37–34, with Reed's interceptions aiding the cause.

The following game against Miami, after a bye week, Reed once again recorded an interception. This time it was quarterback Chad Henne looking for Brandon Marshall in the short right side of the field. Reed jumped in front of the route and ran 18 yards the other way. Baltimore would win 26–10.

Reed picked off his fourth pass in as many games two weeks later against Carolina. This time it was quarterback Brian St. Pierre lofting a deep pass against the Baltimore secondary. Reed jumped the route and set up his blockers down the left side of the field. He then cut across the field to his right and saw fellow safety Dawan Landry trailing down the right sideline. Reed then tossed the ball to Landry, who took it the remaining 23 yards into the end zone. Baltimore routed the Panthers 37–13. Reed would go the next four games without an interception, though the Ravens would still post a 3–1 record in that span.

But Reed had some opportunities in Weeks 16 and 17 against Cleveland and Cincinnati. Against the Browns, Reed was able to pick off quarterback Colt McCoy in the second quarter on a deep pass intended for receiver Mohamed Massaquoi. Reed doubled up with another interception in the fourth quarter, again on a pass McCoy intended for Massaquoi. Baltimore won the game 20–10.

Against Cincinnati in the season finale, Reed didn't waste any time adding to his interception total. On third-and-2 from the Cincinnati 28, quarterback Carson Palmer went deep looking for Andre Caldwell. But there was Reed, doing what he does best, recording his seventh interception of the season on the game's third play from scrimmage. Reed picked off Palmer a second time with 20 seconds left in the first half, with the Bengals' quarterback looking for a deep completion over the middle of the field. The Ravens would defeat Cincinnati 13–7 and finish the regular season with a 12–4 record.

Reed led the NFL that season with eight interceptions. More amazing was the fact he did it in only 10 games. It's enough to make you wonder if Reed would have had a shot at breaking former Los Angeles Rams defensive back Dick Lane's single-season record of 14 interceptions, set in 1952, if he had been available for all 16 games.

It's certainly something to ponder.

79 Ravens Win John Harbaugh's First Playoff Game

After a 5–11 season that resulted in Brian Billick's ouster, John Harbaugh turned out to be the answer to Baltimore's problems. Known around the NFL as a superb special teams coordinator, Harbaugh's name flew under the radar for the Ravens coaching gig, open for the upcoming 2008 season. Harbaugh got it, however, and hit the ground running in his first season.

Harbaugh flipped the team's fortunes around, with a rookie quarterback starting all 16 regular season games, to finish 11–5 and earn a wild-card spot in the postseason. Baltimore's opponent would be the Miami Dolphins, a pesky bunch that had just brought the Wildcat formation—where a running back lines up at quarterback—into the NFL.

Miami was an interesting matchup for the Ravens, being that in addition to the Wildcat running attack, the Ravens would have to deal with quarterback Chad Pennington, who had played mistake-free football for the majority of the season. The Ravens were known for being aggressive and forcing turnovers. Without that, Baltimore might in trouble.

The game was tied 3–3 after the first quarter, with neither team able to throw that first punch yet. It finally came for Baltimore at the 9:11 mark of the second quarter. Pennington threw a pass down the deep left sideline that was intended for receiver Ted Ginn Jr. Ravens safety Jim Leonhard read the play well and was able to pick the pass off for the game's first turnover.

Though Baltimore was unable to turn that turnover into points, it had another opportunity just minutes later. After punting the ball back to Miami, Pennington made crucial mistake No. 2—he targeted Ed Reed's area of the field. Again, Pennington was trying to hit Ginn on a deep ball. But Reed closed on the play and returned it 64 yards for a touchdown to go up 10–3. Matt Stover added a field goal before the half to give the Ravens a 13–3 lead.

Baltimore kept its stellar defensive play up in the second half, with cornerback Fabian Washington getting into the act. Pennington was picked off again on a pass going Devone Bess' way, with Washington returning it 12 yards to the Miami 39-yard line. On Miami's next offensive possession, linebacker Terrell Suggs recovered a fumble from Miami running back Patrick Cobbs, giving the Ravens the ball at Miami's 19. Four plays later, fullback Le'Ron McClain ran in an eight-yard touchdown, giving Baltimore a 20–3 lead.

The Dolphins were finally establishing a drive, with Pennington completing eight passes in a row to get Miami down to the Baltimore 15. His ninth pass went awry, however, and back into Reed's hands for an interception. With 2:04 left in the third quarter, Pennington had already tossed four picks.

"We heard all week that they don't turn the ball over," linebacker Ray Lewis said afterward. "But we force turnovers."

Pennington did throw a touchdown to Ronnie Brown in the fourth quarter to cut Baltimore's lead to 20–9 (Dan Carpenter's

John Harbaugh Highlights

Years as NFL Head Coach (all with the Ravens): 5 (2008–present)
Record: 54–26 (.675)
Playoff Appearances: 5
Playoff Record: 9–4 (.692)
Division Championships: 3
Average Wins Per Season: 10.8
10+ Win Seasons: 4
Super Bowl Record: 1–0

extra point missed). But Joe Flacco added some insurance points with a five-yard rushing touchdown with four minutes remaining in regulation. The Ravens won Harbaugh's first-ever playoff game 27–9 against a Dolphins team that uncharacteristically committed five turnovers.

Harbaugh won his first playoff game as the Ravens' head coach, and many more have followed. Since taking over coaching duties in Baltimore, Harbaugh is 9–4 in the postseason, with three AFC Championship Game appearances and a Super Bowl title.

80 92 Yards

Every young athlete dreams of a late, last-second comeback win, no matter the sport. In baseball, it's a 3-2 count with two outs in the bottom of the ninth, down three, and the bases loaded. In basketball, it's practicing the buzzer beater in the driveway, with the clock hitting triple zeroes and the ball hitting nothing but the bottom of the net. In football, it's leading your team down the field for a late score to give your team the win.

On November 6, 2011, this opportunity was given to Joe Flacco and the Ravens. Now, it wasn't like this was the first comeback opportunity for Flacco. He had already completed five previous fourth-quarter comebacks in his career. In the 2011 season alone, he led Baltimore to the largest come-from-behind win in franchise history against Arizona.

This one was different. This was against the hated Pittsburgh Steelers. Never mind that two of Flacco's five comeback wins came against Pittsburgh—those came with Dennis Dixon and Charlie Batch at quarterback, with Ben Roethlisberger not available for either game. This time, Pittsburgh was at full strength, with Roethlisberger under center. But Baltimore had pummeled Pittsburgh in the season opener, a 35–7 romp. Pittsburgh was out for revenge for the early season setback, as well as taking over as the frontrunner for the AFC North crown.

A field-goal fest early, Baltimore led 9–6 at halftime. In the third quarter, Ray Rice ran in a four-yard touchdown, giving Baltimore a 16–6 lead at Heinz Field. In the fourth quarter, however, the tide turned.

Finishing off an 11-play drive, Steelers running back Rashard Mendenhall punched in a one-yard touchdown to cut Baltimore's lead to 16–13. On Baltimore's ensuing drive, Flacco led the Ravens down to the Pittsburgh 36-yard line. But on third-and-6, outside linebacker James Harrison came around the edge, sacked Flacco, and forced a fumble. Six plays later, the Steelers took the lead 20–16, thanks to a 25-yard touchdown pass from Roethlisberger to receiver Mike Wallace.

Baltimore was unable to answer and was forced into a three-and-out on its next series. The Ravens needed a stop, and it looked like they'd be unable to get it. After picking up a first down, the Steelers faced a fourth-and-5 at Baltimore's 29. Shaun Suisham was sent on the field with hopes of lengthening the lead to seven points. However, the play clock ran out, and delay of game was called, a penalty Steelers coach Mike Tomlin later took responsibility for. It was a blunder, for sure, since the Steelers would now have a line of scrimmage at the 34-yard line. A 46-yard attempt was now a 51-yarder, and Tomlin thought the yardage difference was too much to risk. He sent in the punting unit to pin Baltimore back deep, which it did. The ball was fair caught by Lardarius Webb at the Baltimore 8-yard line, with 92 yards to go and 2:24 remaining.

After a first down incompletion, Flacco hit Anquan Boldin over the middle for a 21-yard gain, which took the game to the two-minute warning. On first-and-10, Flacco hit receiver LaQuan Williams for a 13-yard gain and hurried to the line, though his next pass fell incomplete. On second-and-10 from the Baltimore

Ravens wide receiver Torrey Smith hauls in a touchdown catch behind the Steelers' William Gay (22) and Ryan Clark (25) with just eight seconds left in the fourth quarter for a 23–20 Baltimore win on November 6, 2011, in Pittsburgh.

42, Flacco found Boldin again for a nine-yard gain and just short of a first down. The Ravens once again hurried to the line, though his pass intended for Williams was tipped and almost intercepted by Steelers linebacker Larry Foote. Fourth-and-1 was upcoming, and the Ravens were running out of time with 1:06 remaining and 58 yards to go.

But Flacco once again turned to Boldin, finding him slanting over the middle of the field. Flacco fired a pass into his reliable target, who caught it for a 10-yard gain and a first down. Flacco then found tight end Ed Dickson for a two-yard pass to his right before being pushed out of bounds, which stopped the clock for Baltimore.

The Ravens were now 37 yards away from a game-winning touchdown with 42 seconds left in the game. With Dickson going out of bounds, it figured to be a good time to test Pittsburgh deep, which is exactly what the Ravens elected to do.

The offensive line gave Flacco a solid pocket to move up in. Flacco launched a deep pass down the left side of the field. Wide open was rookie receiver Torrey Smith, all alone in the end zone. Could it be? Not quite. The ball went right through Smith's hands and fell incomplete, bringing up third-and-8. Did the Ravens just miss their chance? Almost.

Flacco, calm as ever, relayed the play to his teammates. The offensive line gave Flacco time as the Delaware product found Boldin again, this time for an 11-yard reception on an out pattern. Now there were 26 yards to go and 28 seconds to get there.

On first-and-10 from the Pittsburgh 26, Flacco overthrew receiver David Reed down the right sideline. On second-and-10, Flacco tried to hit Boldin once again over the middle, but the veteran couldn't hold on to the ball while falling to the turf.

The Ravens were running out of time, with just 14 seconds remaining. But sometimes stories have a funny way of ending. On one play a player can be a goat, someone points to as a reason for losing. On another play, that same player can become a hero. After dropping a would-be go-ahead touchdown four plays earlier, Smith would have a chance to redeem himself.

On third-and-10, Smith lined up to the far right, in man coverage with Steelers cornerback William Gay. Noticing this, Flacco lofted a fade to the back right corner of the end zone. Right before the goal line, Smith was able to bypass contact and slip behind the secondary. This time, Smith wouldn't let the ball fall through his arms. Halfway into the end zone, alone once again, and Steelers safety Ryan Clark late with help, Smith watched the ball all the way into his body, catching the go-ahead touchdown with eight seconds left on the clock.

Those 92 yards will never be forgotten in Ravens history. Whenever Flacco's playing days are over, that will certainly be a drive he remembers for a long, long time.

"This Steelers-Ravens game is a game for men," Ravens coach John Harbaugh said. "This is a game for big men. You've got to shine bright in this game if you want to win this game. And nobody shined brighter than Joe Flacco in this game."

81 First Game at M&T Bank Stadium

Though it technically wasn't M&T Bank Stadium yet, the time had finally come for the Baltimore Ravens to play in their own stadium. After all, that was one of the focal points for the Art Modell–owned franchise to move to Baltimore.

For Baltimore's first season, it played its games at Memorial Stadium. Ground broke on the new stadium shortly after the franchise moved, and it took about two years to complete. In 1998 the Ravens were ready to begin play in their new home, aptly called Ravens Stadium at Camden Yards.

The first regular season game to take place inside the new stadium was against Pittsburgh. It was a beautiful day, 73 degrees with little wind. Unfortunately for the Baltimore football team, it was a day it wished it could have back.

Though the game was tied 3–3 at halftime, the Steelers were able to jump out to a 13–3 lead in the third quarter, after Kordell Stewart rushed for a one-yard touchdown. In the fourth quarter, Stewart threw a 20-yard touchdown pass to wide receiver Charles Johnson to extend the lead to 20–3.

Baltimore was unable to find any offense that afternoon, and new starting quarterback Jim Harbaugh was taken out of the game with a chipped bone in his finger. Without Harbaugh, backup quarterback Eric Zeier entered the game and was unable to spark much on offense. Adding to the frustrations was that kicker Matt Stover, typically someone the Ravens could count on, missed three field goals. Stover did make two field goals, with his second coming in the fourth quarter from 25 yards out. With under four minutes, the Ravens did make the game interesting. Zeier completed a pass to Jermaine Lewis that went for a 64-yard touchdown to cut Pittsburgh's lead to 20–13. Baltimore did get one last crack at it to tie the game, but there were only 27 seconds left on the clock when it got the ball back. With one second left, Zeier's last pass of the game fell incomplete, giving the Steelers a 20–13 victory.

"It hurts a great deal and it hurts this football club when you put what you did in the off-season and you come up with big loss like this. It hurts," Ravens coach Ted Marchibroda said afterward. "You're not going to hold Pittsburgh forever. Our defense did a good job. We had an excellent opportunity in the first half to take advantage of the takeaways and interceptions, and we didn't do it. We didn't put anything on the board."

After the inaugural season, Baltimore's home became known as PSINet Stadium, after the company PSINet purchased the naming rights to it. In 2002, when PSINet filed for bankruptcy, the stadium

Other Uses for M&T Bank Stadium

While M&T Bank Stadium is the home of the Baltimore Ravens for eight weeks (at minimum) of each football season, the venue has plenty of other uses. For starters, it hosts other football games than Ravens ones. Every so often, Navy and Maryland will reunite their rivalry, the Crab Bowl Classic, and M&T Bank Stadium has hosted the game in 2005 and 2010. The stadium also hosts the Maryland high school football state championships.

M&T Bank Stadium has begun hosting soccer matches, with English Premier League teams Tottenham Hotspur and Liverpool playing in front of a Baltimore crowd. In 2013 the stadium hosted two quarterfinal matches in the CONCACAF Gold Cup tournament.

M&T Bank Stadium has hosted the NCAA men's lacrosse tournament in the past and will do so again in 2014. Army and Navy have agreed to play there in 2014 and 2016. It's also a frequent venue for major headlining musicians.

was changed back to Ravens Stadium temporarily. On May 6, 2003, it was renamed M&T Bank Stadium and has remained so ever since.

Plenty of memorable games that Ravens fans cherish have taken place inside the stadium located on Russell St. in downtown Baltimore. And, even though it holds a significant place in the history of the franchise, the first was not one of them. If you've never witnessed a Ravens game at M&T Bank Stadium, make this the season you see your first—it's guaranteed to be one you won't forget.

82 The Band of Baltimore

The Colts may have left town in 1984. The Baltimore Colts Marching Band that supported them did everything it could to stay together. They loved Baltimore football and everything it embodied. Just like the fans in the city, the band was heartbroken that its team had left town in the middle of the night.

Rather than fold up and quit, the band stayed together during the 12-year hiatus. They'd march for the USFL's Baltimore Stars. They'd play for the CFL's Baltimore Stallions. They'd play half-times at NFL games around the country—except Indianapolis—whenever they could get a gig. One of the earliest halftime shows they played after the Colts left was for Art Modell's Cleveland Browns.

When the Colts left town, they took the history with them, something that still gets at the older Baltimore fans. The one item they left behind was the marching band, which had been with the Colts every step of the way since the team's inception. The Colts were originally the Miami Seahawks before relocating to Baltimore in 1947 as a part of the All-America Football Conference. When Baltimore got its first football team in 1947, a volunteer marching band formed on September 7, with the intent of supporting the Colts on game days. In 1950 the Colts were one of three AAFC teams to join the NFL. However, after these Colts' lone NFL season, the organization folded, and Baltimore was without a team for two seasons.

Nevertheless, the band kept operating. It refused to quit. And it was ready to cheer the Colts on again when the NFL's Dallas Texans moved to Baltimore in 1953. This time, the Colts were in Baltimore to stay for a long time. The Baltimore Colts Marching Band created a fight song for the team, with the following lyrics:

Let's go, you Baltimore Colts
And put that ball across the line.
So drive on, you Baltimore Colts—
Go in and strike like lightning bolts.
Fight, fight, fight.
Rear up, you Colts and let's fight—
Crash through and show them your might—
For Baltimore and Maryland—
You will march on to victory.

Seven Nation Army

Borrowing a theme from Europeans at soccer matches, Ravens fans adopted the song "Seven Nation Army" as the unofficial anthem for their football team. As they do in European soccer stadiums, Ravens fans will hum along to the familiar riff made popular by the duo The White Stripes. The song was released in 2003 and began catching on in sporting venues during the 2006 World Cup, when Italy's fans often hummed the tune. When the Italians came home to celebrate their World Cup title, the fans sang the song in the streets. Since then, the trend not only caught on around Europe, but it came to the United States and is used during football games. When the Ravens win, you can often hear fans walking out of the stadium humming that distinctive melody.

So when the organization left after 31 consecutive seasons of football, the band stayed behind. When it would travel around to NFL stadiums, the band became known as Baltimore's Pro Football Musical Ambassadors. According to the ESPN *30 for 30* documentary *The Band that Wouldn't Die*, John Ziemann, the band's president, pawned his wife's wedding ring so he could get the band new equipment.

Before Baltimore received a new franchise, Ziemann and the Baltimore Colts Marching Band did their part to try and convince the Maryland state legislature to approve funding for a new stadium. The band trekked to the Maryland General Assembly in Annapolis and played the Baltimore Colts fight song on the steps of the building while the legislators were in session one night. A crowd joined, which even included Maryland governor William Donald Schaefer, who was in support of building a new football stadium to try and get an NFL franchise back in Baltimore.

Eventually, Art Modell moved the Cleveland Browns to Baltimore and renamed his team the Ravens. Interestingly enough, the Baltimore Colts Marching Band kept its name for the Ravens' first two seasons in 1996 and 1997. It didn't become Baltimore's Marching Ravens until August 8, 1998. The last time the Baltimore

Colts Marching Band performed under that name was at the grand opening of an ESPN Zone at the Baltimore Inner Harbor on July 11, 1998.

In 2010 the Ravens brought back the old Colts fight song but added new lyrics to sing on top of the original tune. They are:

Baltimore Ravens, let's go
And put that ball across the line.
So fly on with talons spread wide,
Go in and strike with Ravens pride.
Fight, fight, fight.
Ravens dark wings take to flight,
Dive in and show them your might.
For Baltimore and Maryland,
You will fly on to victory.

83 Ted Marchibroda Returns to Baltimore

Baltimore football fans were looking for a way to connect the history of the Colts to what was new with the Ravens in 1996. The Cleveland Browns were coming to town, and they were without a coach. Owner Art Modell fired Bill Belichick after five seasons, meaning he would not make the move to Baltimore.

On February 15, 1996, Modell and the Ravens turned to a familiar face to become Baltimore's new head coach. That man was Ted Marchibroda, a longtime coaching veteran who got his first head coaching gig with the Baltimore Colts in 1975. The last time Marchibroda was on the sideline in Baltimore, he wasn't doing so well. He had just completed a second consecutive 5–11 season with the Colts and was fired by owner Robert Irsay. Marchibroda was the head coach for five Colts seasons, compiling a 41–33 record. Upon leaving the Baltimore Colts, Marchibroda had stints as an offensive coordinator with the Bears, Lions, Eagles, and Bills. And, somewhat oddly, Irsay, the man who fired Marchibroda in Baltimore, rehired him to be the Indianapolis Colts' head coach in 1992.

Though Marchibroda didn't post a regular season record better than 9–7 with Indianapolis, he took the "Cardiac Colts" to the 1995 AFC Championship Game to face Pittsburgh with Jim Harbaugh as his quarterback. A last-second Hail Mary into the end zone was not converted, and the Steelers advanced to the Super Bowl.

Marchibroda decided to take the Baltimore Ravens coaching job, bringing him back to the city that gave him his NFL head coaching start. With all the drama that ensued between Baltimore and the Colts, Marchibroda can say that he coached the Colts in both cities in two different stints, as well as Baltimore's second football team.

Marchibroda's first season with the Ravens ended with a 4–12 record. His offense was able to move the ball on opponents, putting up over 30 points in four games. Quarterback Vinny Testaverde threw for 4,177 yards and 33 touchdowns, earning a Pro Bowl berth in the process. However, the problem was the defense. In the inaugural season, the Baltimore defense surrendered 24 points or more in 12 of 16 games. That kind of defensive ineptitude kept the Ravens in the loss column week after week. In three of Baltimore's four wins, the Ravens held their opponent to under 20 points. In the lone exception, Testaverde helped engineer a 13-point come-back win by completing 31 of 51 passes for 429 yards and three touchdowns.

Marchibroda's 1997 Ravens squad improved slightly, finishing the year 6–9–1. Defense was still an issue, though an up-and-coming Ray Lewis was beginning to get the town excited for the future. Marchibroda's last season was in 1998, which concluded in a 6–10 record. That was enough for Modell to decline offering

Ted Marchibroda's Highlights

Years as Ravens Head Coach: 3 (1996–1998)
Years as NFL Head Coach: 12 (1975–1979, 1992–1998)
Ravens Record: 16–31–1 (.340)
NFL Record: 87–98–1 (.470)
Ravens Playoff Appearances: 0
NFL Playoff Appearances: 4
NFL Playoff Record: 2–4 (.333)
Ravens Division Championships: 0
NFL Division Championships: 3
Average Wins Per Season (Ravens): 5.3
Average Wins Per Season (NFL): 7.25
10+ Win Seasons (Ravens): 0
10+ Win Seasons (NFL): 3
Super Bowl Record (Ravens): 0–0
Super Bowl Record (NFL): 0–0

Marchibroda a new contract after his first one expired. After the Ravens won their season finale against Detroit, Marchibroda had a feeling he would be getting the axe.

"I'm thankful for the opportunity," Marchibroda said. "I enjoy doing it, even if it doesn't always turn out the way you want."

For Marchibroda, not only was he the first to coach two separate NFL franchises in Baltimore. He also became the first coach to be fired from both NFL franchises in Baltimore.

84 1999's Building Blocks

Though the Ravens didn't reach the playoffs in Brian Billick's first season as a head coach in Baltimore, he helped lay the foundation for what was to come in 2000.

A team was being built to compete with the best in the league, though those around the NFL may not have realized it at the time. The average age of the defense was 27, indicating a perfect balance of veteran leadership and youth. Ray Lewis was becoming one of the league's best inside linebackers. Peter Boulware was wreaking havoc as an outside pass rusher.

Baltimore's 1999 season allowed it to get accustomed to Billick while figuring out how to win close games. Starting the season 1–2, the Ravens had a road trip to Atlanta to deal with. Down 13–10 in the fourth quarter, the Ravens' Rob Burnett hit Falcons running back Byron Hanspard and forced a fumble. Cornerback Kim Herring pounced on it to give Baltimore possession. Matt Stover was able to convert the turnover into three points to tie the game at 13–13. The game went to overtime, with Ravens QB Stoney Case throwing a game-winning 54-yard pass to receiver Justin Armour. That game was a clear sign of what Baltimore was building.

There were stumbles, though, just like there would be with any up-and-coming franchise. Baltimore would lose its next three games against Tennessee, Kansas City, and Buffalo. While Kansas City blew the Ravens out, the Tennessee and Buffalo losses came by a combined six points. Baltimore led Buffalo the entire way, albeit not by much. Up 10–6, Bills quarterback Doug Flutie threw a five-yard pass to Jonathan Linton with 1:35 left to win the game.

"This was a tough emotional loss," Billick said after the Bills loss. "I really don't know what to say to them after a loss like this. This is where my inexperience comes as a head coach."

But there were some bright spots in the game. The defense held an otherwise solid Bills offense to just 249 total yards. The secondary picked Flutie off three times. Again, those were signs of what was to come.

The Ravens would reel off four wins in a row down the stretch, looking like a team poised for future success. A 41–14 win over Tennessee was the peak of the season. The Ravens also had a 31–24 win over Pittsburgh during the streak. One of the more dominating performances Baltimore put in was a Week 16 game against Cincinnati, where it held the Bengals to 241 total yards and zero points.

The Ravens finished the season 8–8 after losing to New England in the season finale.

For a team that finished .500 and missed the playoffs, the defensive end-of-year statistics were staggering. The Ravens finished second in total yards allowed (263.9 per game), sixth in points (17.3), sixth in sacks (49), and ninth in interceptions (21). These numbers showed a suffocating defense that held its ground the majority of the time. Sure, there were some mental lapses. But that came with the territory of having a young team.

When those youngsters grew up just a year later, they knew what they needed to do to win. The 1999 campaign gave them a feel for the work Baltimore needed to put in to become world champions a season later.

85 Cornhole: A Budding Ravens Locker Room Tradition

Football isn't the only thing the Ravens players are passionate about inside the locker room.

Sitting in the middle of the locker are four boards, which are used to play the beanbag came cornhole. It's an easy game. Each player gets four beanbags to toss per turn. If a beanbag lands in the hole cut into the board, then it's three points. If a beanbag lands on the board, it's one point. The first to 21 points wins.

And believe it or not, the Ravens take this game, popularized in both the Midwest and Southeast of the United States, seriously. The team started playing the game when then–Ravens defensive end

Cory Redding introduced it to his teammates in 2010. It latched on quickly and has become a tool for team unity, as well. At any given time, a reserve could be playing with a multimillion-dollar-earning star. Some of the Ravens players have tried to make their in-house competition appear more official. A Ravens cornhole twitter account was created (@RavensCornhole) to update fans on any tournaments or events with the team. When rookie Justin Tucker joined the Ravens in 2012, he began creating power rankings for all the players.

One of the funniest descriptions Tucker gave in his power rankings was on Terrell Suggs.

"Undoubtedly the worst Cornholer in the building," Tucker wrote. "Displays horrible fundamentals. Sloppy delivery only leads to problems. Simon Cowell of *American Idol* and *X-Factor* has said of Sizzle's technique: 'Appalling with a capital A. Positively dreadful.'"

Unlike Suggs, Tucker became one of the better cornhole players quickly. Perhaps it's a special teams thing. Undoubtedly the best at cornhole from 2010 to 2012 was punter Sam Koch. A close second is long snapper Morgan Cox. Tucker quickly entered the consensus top 10 at the game, but it took some practice. A competitive one at the game, Tucker hates to lose, often vocally showing displeasure if he's experiencing an off day.

"He's a promising young star in the Ravens Cornhole Federation," Cox said.

Also good at the game are quarterback Joe Flacco, offensive tackle Michael Oher, and receiver Torrey Smith. Often the Ravens will hold cornhole tournaments, complete with brackets to post in the locker room. In a preseason tournament in 2012, it came down to Koch and Flacco for the championship. Koch bested Flacco 21–6 in the finals, with Cox and safety Sean Considine reaching the final four.

From the media's perspective, listening to recorded audio from an interview can be amusing. The Ravens play this game practically every day, which includes the 45-minute time frame the media is given to speak with players. Oftentimes a reporter will be chatting with someone, only to hear thud after thud in the background, from a beanbag hitting the wooden cornhole board. If there's ever a chance the Ravens can play cornhole, they'll do it. There's not a lot of free time as an NFL player.

The game has proven to be a great way for the team to get to know each other. When the Ravens traveled to New Orleans for Super Bowl XLVII in 2013, they packed up the cornhole boards along with their personal belongings. Yes, to the Ravens, cornhole is that important.

86 A Near "Mutiny"

Football is as demanding of a sport as there is. Make no mistake, each hit hurts in some fashion—some worse than others, sure. The toll it takes on the human body at the NFL level is something often underestimated by armchair quarterbacks around the country. After a game on Sunday, the soreness in an NFL player's body (one that plays the majority of a game) doesn't subside until around Thursday or Friday, and that's with limited contact throughout a week. Each player's goal is to be as healthy as possible for the upcoming game. Reinjuring yourself due to excessive contact can only complicate matters.

So when Ravens coach John Harbaugh told his team at a meeting they'd be practicing in pads on October 31, 2012, several key players erupted with displeasure, according to a highly publicized article from Mike Silver of Yahoo! Sports.

The article stated safeties Ed Reed and Bernard Pollard were among the most vocal against practicing in pads, meaning there would be heavy, physical contact that day. They became angry and

"Embrace the Grind" Shirts

If an NFL player says he enjoys training camp, he's likely lying. It's a brutal time of the year. No player enjoys practicing in the scorching heat and beating up on each other day after day. And to think, players have it easier than they used to thanks to the 2011 collective bargaining agreement, which stipulates teams can only practice once a day instead of going through the dreaded two-a-days.

Thinking with a glass-half-full approach, offensive guard Marshal Yanda gave his team some advice during the 2012 training camp period. He broke down the huddle one day and told his teammates to "embrace the grind." The phrase stuck with the team, and T-shirts were born. Yanda and others, including coach John Harbaugh, began wearing them throughout the season. After all, each season can be a grind.

tempers flared. All in all, according to Silver's story, Harbaugh let them express their complaints and concerns. One player told Silver the scene was close to "mutiny." Not helping the situation was the fact the Ravens had just lost 43–13 to Houston a week prior. It was almost seen as punishment for getting blown out.

Harbaugh listened to those in disagreement that day. In only four and a half seasons as an NFL head coach, he'd learn to let the professional players have their say. Being a dictator wouldn't aid the situation. It would only fuel the fire and possibly add resentment. Each time a critique toward Harbaugh was brought up, he admitted his fault and apologized.

"Well, I don't know about [being] secure enough or anything like that, but I think it's really important to let them be them," Harbaugh told Yahoo!'s Silver. "And to me, the more I'm able to give them leadership, the stronger that we all are together as leaders. I don't know how to put it in words, and maybe someday there'll be a way to express it, but we have such great leaders. You've got to let 'em lead, but you also have to lead 'em, you have to direct them, and someone's gotta make decisions. But, we've just got some incredibly strong men on this team. I mean, I could tell you some stories, but I'd probably rather not."

On the day a mutiny almost broke out, Harbaugh kept his cool and kept his locker room. The players appreciated him for it and continued to do their best to win games for their coach as well as the organization. There were more roadblocks in the way, including a late-season three-game losing streak that cast some doubts as to how the finality of season would play out.

But in the end, the Ravens were able to win a Super Bowl despite the madness on October 31, 2012. And a large part of the credit goes to Harbaugh allowing his players to speak their minds.

And, no, the Ravens did not practice in pads that day.

87 Join a Chapter of the Baltimore Ravens Roosts

Baltimore has a deep history of backing whichever football team is in town. First it was the Colts. When they moved to Indianapolis, along came the USFL's Stars. In the 1990s, the Stallions of the Canadian Football League came to town. Shortly after, in 1996, the Ravens came from Cleveland.

Whichever team was competing in front of the Baltimore fans, that team gained support, simply by representing the city. The love affair between Baltimore and football will never die. The city loves the sport too much.

The Council of Baltimore Ravens Roosts has given fans a chance to band together and support their team and community through various events and charities. Dating back to 1957, the organization was originally called the Council of Colts Corrals, which would engage in community activities with the Baltimore Colts in mind. The first Colt Corral began in Baltimore with other factions popping up all around the state of Maryland. The Colt Corrals decided to form a council so they could organize initiatives on a greater basis.

Interestingly enough, the Council has been rewarded with championships from each team it has supported. The Baltimore Colts won NFL championships in 1958 and 1959 and later won Super Bowl V in January 1971. The Stars won the USFL title in 1985. In 1995 the Stallions won the CFL's Grey Cup. And the Ravens have won two championships of their own, Super Bowl XXXV in January 2001 and Super Bowl XLVII in February 2013. Never did the group disband, even when there wasn't a team playing. Certainly, patience was rewarded for Baltimore to have experienced that many football championships.

When the Ravens came to town, the group had to change its name from the Council of Colts Corrals to the Council of Baltimore Ravens Roosts. There are more than 50 active Ravens Roosts throughout Maryland, Delaware, and Pennsylvania, with over 3,500 members. When they're not participating in Ravens-related events, these groups do their part to better serve the community.

Each Ravens Roost must maintain a certain status to remain in the council. One of the purposes of the group is to raise money for charitable organizations. Ravens Roost 65 in Pasadena, Maryland, awards the Dougie Jarrell Scholarship to a deserving student at Northeast High School. The scholarship is named for a young man who died in an automobile accident.

Ravens Roost 50, based in Carney, Maryland, has incorporated itself into a nonprofit organization and raises money for St. Vincent's Villa Children's Center in Timonium, Maryland, as well as the Paralyzed Veterans of America, House of Ruth, and Eastern Family Resource Center. One of the ways they raise money is by selling 400 parking spaces next to Lot O at M&T Bank Stadium.

A lot of players have become active among the Ravens Roosts, too. Former Ravens cornerback Cary Williams has participated in events with Ravens Roost 65. Running back Ray Rice has made appearances before. When a player is booked for one of these events, it usually means a lot of money will be generated for a good cause.

Kris Jones, a writer for the Baltimore Ravens fan site RussellStreet-Report.com, and member of Ravens Roost 65, said he's noticed that when new Ravens players acquired in free agency get involved, they're stunned to see such a tight-knit group working together all over the Maryland/Delaware/Pennsylvania area.

"They'll say their previous team's fans aren't like this," Jones said. "You can tell it's a special thing here."

Each summer, the Council of Ravens Roosts Convention takes place in Ocean City, Maryland. It's the biggest event for the organization, with all the various hubs spending just under a week at the beach. In 2012 the Ravens organization joined in on the fun and organized their Beach Bash to coincide with the Ravens Roosts Convention. It's becoming a huge event each year for Ravens fans to bond over.

"When you see someone in a Ravens jersey walking to the stadium, the natural reaction is to ask them to join your tailgate," Jones said. "Ravens fans are like family."

88 Ray Rice vs. Bullies

Like many professional athletes, Ray Rice had a foundation to raise money for those in need. But in his first couple of years, he didn't know where to focus his fundraising efforts. There are clearly a lot of charitable organizations in need of funding, and Rice was someone to lend a helping hand. But where?

A light bulb eventually went off in early 2012, after receiving a phone call from his mother. She told him a bully at school threw a rock at his sister, leaving a gash under her eye that required stitches.

Rice also learned that his publicist's daughter had been bullied at school, which irritated him, as well.

It was time to steer his efforts toward anti-bullying and the pain it can cause to children. But in Rice's mind, more needs to be done. He was outraged when he learned 15-year-old Grace McComas of Woodbine, Maryland, committed suicide after enduring countless amounts of abuse through social media and text messaging. He also vowed to concentrate his efforts in the memory of Philadelphia native Bailey O'Neill, a 12-year-old who died after a bully beat him so badly that he began experiencing seizures and was placed into a medically induced coma. That incident caused Rice to write an inspiring message on his personal Facebook page:

> I don't know if the kid that did this to Bailey will be punished severely enough or if he will receive the help I know he truly needs. Bullying doesn't happen for no reason...we have to figure out what the underlying cause is and treat it like the illness it is. I don't know when parents, teachers, elected officials, and administrators will sit up and take notice...and ACT. But, I DO KNOW THIS: I will NOT give up my fight. Everyday I will continue to fight AGAINST bullying and fight FOR kindness. Bailey—my little buddy, I will not let you become just another bully statistic...you are my inspiration and one more angel that will help me continue the fight for kids everywhere. You are going to help me save lives. RIP my little friend.

Rice has played a large part in Grace's Law, a bill named after McComas, which included his writing testimony for its passing. Rice wrote, "Anything we can do to prevent one more child from taking their life or suffering through the pain and anguish of bullying is the right thing to do. I believe that this law may have saved the life of Grace McComas, and it certainly will save the lives of other young men and women in the future."

The bill passed the both the Maryland House of Delegates and the Maryland State Senate.

The law was designed to criminalize acts where a person or party repeatedly targets another with insulting and threatening messages. The bill's scope is limited to this kind of speech directed toward minors.

"You know how they say, 'Sticks and stones may break your bones, but words shouldn't hurt you?'" Rice said. "Words are killing people, and it's happening over the web with cyberbullying. That's just something I couldn't believe. You know, I get it. Sometimes people tell me how terrible I am, and it doesn't affect me because I know what it's all about, but you get a vulnerable kid who takes these words to heart and feels like it's not worth living anymore. I had to say something about it. I had to."

Rice has held anti-bullying rallies around the Baltimore area since deciding this would be his philanthropic calling. According to a 2011 survey from the Centers for Disease Control and Prevention, 20 percent of students in grades 9 through 12 experienced bullying of some kind. In the 2008–2009 school year, the National Center for Education Statistics and Bureau of Justice Statistics found that 26 percent of students in grades 6 through 12 were bullied.

Rice is hoping he can help put an end to it.

"I believe social media is great, but you get people out there who take so much advantage of it, and I use it as a tool to give back positive messages," Rice said. "One thing about social media is you can get your personality out there, but it shouldn't hurt people. That's where people get it twisted."

89 Bernard Pollard, Patriots Killer

Bernard Pollard only spent two seasons in Baltimore, but he will always be remembered as the hard-hitting safety who never cared if the NFL had a problem with his style of play.

Pollard plays at a high speed, and his crushing hits have knocked players out of games. It's not that he does it on purpose. It's just how he plays. When someone has that kind of strength and power on a football field, it can sometimes lead to injuries. And somehow, throughout Pollard's career, he's injured quite a few New England Patriots players. The streak includes two games against the Patriots with Pollard in a Ravens uniform.

But first, the back story of how Pollard became known as the "Patriot Killer." When Pollard was with the Kansas City Chiefs in 2008, his team faced the Patriots in Week 1. The Patriots were fresh off of losing the Super Bowl against the Giants, yet poised to return. Then in an instant, Pollard came up the middle on a blitz early in the game. Patriots running back Sammy Morris was able to block Pollard initially, but Pollard lunged in a last ditch effort to bring Brady down. Unfortunately, Pollard's helmet connected with Tom Brady's knee, which tore the star quarterback's anterior cruciate ligament. Brady's season was over, and New England failed to reach the playoffs.

A year later Pollard was a member of the Houston Texans. In the regular season finale, Houston faced New England, with the Patriots gearing up for the postseason. Brady threw a short pass to receiver Wes Welker, who then turned up field. Pollard, in a sprint, closed in on Welker. Welker, unsure of what move to make next, tried to avoid contact with a quick cut. His left foot slipped, which caused ACL and MCL tears. Welker missed the playoffs, and New England was ousted, ironically, by the Ravens in the wild-card round.

Pollard joined the Ravens for the 2011 season and became a starter just a few games in. He became a key player midway through the year and was suddenly a leader by the postseason. An intimidating force on the football field, Pollard helped set the tone for Baltimore's defense, known historically for being rugged, tough, and determined.

Baltimore reached the AFC Championship Game and faced New England inside Gillette Stadium. Pollard couldn't injure another key Patriots player, right? Wrong.

In the third quarter of the game, Gronkowski caught a 23-yard pass with Pollard in coverage. Pollard immediately initiated contact with Gronkowski to take him to the ground. This time, Gronkowski's left ankle got caught under Pollard's right thigh. The injury caused Gronkowski to leave the game. Though he did return, he didn't appear to be the same player. New England would go on to beat Baltimore 23–20 but would lose two weeks later against the Giants in the Super Bowl. Gronkowski, still hobbled by the sprained ankle, was limited to two catches for 26 yards.

Pollard's Six Cracked Ribs

Talk about tough. Early during the 2012 season, Bernard Pollard was thought to have bruised his ribs against Philadelphia in the second week of the year. He kept playing until the pain became too much. He sat out the last three weeks of the regular season before returning for the playoffs. As it turned out, Pollard's ribs weren't bruised. They were cracked—six of them, in fact. Pollard somehow managed through the pain and played in each playoff game. Being fitted for a Super Bowl ring probably offsets any pain just a tad. "For us as football players, we know we're going to go through it," Pollard said. "At the same time, that's the name of the game. Six of them, yep. Hey, it's up to us to go out there and play, and we did."

In September 2012 Pollard was asked about the "Patriot Killer" moniker given to him. Though he won't apologize for hits that unintentionally injure players, Pollard was not a fan of that label.

"That's not me," Pollard said. "I don't laugh at anything like that because that's not my intentions. I'm not a malicious player. I look to play football hard, fast, and physical. It just so happened a lot of the injuries came against the Patriots."

Even so, there was one more time for Pollard to inflict pain on a Patriots player. It was the 2012 AFC Championship Game, and Baltimore had taken a 21–13 lead. The Patriots were driving down the field, looking to cut Baltimore's lead to one or to tie. Brady handed the ball off to running back Stevan Ridley, who started running through a slight opening.

In came Pollard, who leveled a devastating blow to Ridley. Both helmets collided and Ridley fell back in an instant. As he was falling, he fumbled the football. Baltimore recovered and was able to score a touchdown four plays later thanks to the turnover. The score helped put the game away for Baltimore.

(Author's note: A friend of mine, Jimmy O'Connell, is a lifelong Patriots fan. When the Ridley hit occurred, my phone buzzed seconds later with a new text message. It was Jimmy. The message read, "How? How is it ALWAYS Bernard Pollard?")

In an interview on ESPN's *NFL Live*, Ridley said he doesn't even remember the hit.

"Being completely honest, not much man," Ridley said on-air. "Running the football, unfortunately it's what comes with the sport that we play. It's a contact sport. He just came down and made a play, tried to make a physical tackle, and that's what he did."

It wasn't just that Pollard happened to coincidentally injure Patriots players in key games. That's an inconsequential note to who Pollard is, on the field and off. It is quite improbable for one player to have that kind of devastating impact on an opposing team when you think about it, however.

Pollard only spent two years with Baltimore and he'll be remembered fondly by fans for how he played the game—tough, gritty, and with anger. Former defensive coordinator Chuck Pagano once said the team called Pollard "the Angry Man." Pollard was released during the off-season after Baltimore won Super Bowl XLVII and signed with the Tennessee Titans.

Whether he wants the label or not, Pollard will always have the "Patriot Killer" moniker with him wherever he goes.

90 Comeback vs. the Cardinals

The Ravens walked into their locker room at M&T Bank Stadium down 18 to the Arizona Cardinals on October 30, 2011. The mood was solemn, and at first, it was quiet. Players began to speak up one by one, trying to motivate the team to come back with 30 minutes left to play.

It sure looked bleak; the offense was unable to move the ball on a banged up Cardinals team that was 1–5 entering the contest. The only reason Baltimore wasn't still down 21 was that Billy Cundiff added a late field goal in the second quarter to cut Arizona's lead to 24–6. Up until this particular day, the Ravens had never rallied from a deficit greater than 19, which happened in 2006 against Tennessee.

One by one, players spoke up in the locker room. Fullback Vonta Leach told his teammates to "play offense the way we know how to play offense." Joe Flacco reiterated the point that the Ravens were better than the first-half performance indicated. Ray Lewis said the Ravens just needed to cut out the mistakes and they'd be fine. There was still plenty of time.

This was the third consecutive lethargic half of football, following the prior week's 12–7 loss at Jacksonville, which was arguably the worse loss of the John Harbaugh era. The Ravens needed a spark, and they needed it fast.

Flacco fired things up first, hoping to gain some momentum. After receiving the ball, Flacco completed three consecutive passes, with the latter two going to tight ends Dennis Pitta and Ed Dickson for eight and 14 yards, respectively. Three plays later, the Ravens finally got the big play they needed, with Flacco hooking up with Anquan Boldin for a 37-yard gain. After a defensive pass interference penalty put the ball on the Arizona 1-yard line, Rice punched in a short touchdown to cut the Cardinals' lead to 24–13. Baltimore wouldn't move the ball down the field again until the 4:44 mark of the third quarter, as it was forced to punt on the possession in between.

On this drive, Flacco found Boldin again, this time for a 23-yard gain on second down. Later in the drive, Boldin had catches for 27 and 21 yards, doing his best to out-muscle his former team in one-on-one situations. Rice, once again, capped the drive off with a one-yard touchdown. Suddenly, it was a 24–20 ballgame with Baltimore very much in the thick of things.

Then another break happened, with Cardinals quarterback Kevin Kolb throwing an interception to linebacker Jameel McClain on the first play of the ensuing possession. Two plays and a defensive pass interference penalty later, Rice scored his third rushing touchdown of the game, this time from three yards out. Baltimore was suddenly in the lead, 27–24.

"We woke up, plain and simple," Boldin said.

Arizona was able to tie the game with a Jay Feely 45-yard field goal with under 10 minutes remaining in the game, though. Still, Baltimore went from possibly being run out of its own stadium to tied with a chance to win the game.

Both teams traded three-and-outs with each punting on the possessions that followed. Both defenses picked up the pace, not giving much ground to the offense on the other side. But it was Baltimore's final punt that became one of the top plays of the game. Punter Sam Koch was able to pin Arizona at the 1-yard line, giving it little chance to be creative offensively. The Cardinals picked up one first down but still punted back to Baltimore from their own 6-yard line, after Kolb was sacked for a nine-yard loss on a third-and-8 from the 15.

Baltimore was set up with good field position with a chance to hit a game-winning field goal, with only 52 seconds remaining on the clock. Flacco first found Pitta for a quick three-yard completion before being pushed out of bounds to move the ball to the Arizona 41-yard line. It looked like Baltimore would play it safe and see if Billy Cundiff could hit a long field goal to win.

Wrong.

On the next play, Flacco dropped back and saw Torrey Smith in man-to-man coverage to the right and outside. Flacco gave his young target a chance by putting up a perfect pass only his receiver could get. Smith hauled it in and fell to the M&T Bank Stadium turf around the 5-yard line. Just like that, Cundiff had an easy chip shot opportunity.

Rice ran for no gain and Arizona immediately called its final timeout with 36 seconds left to go. Flacco then took a knee to run the clock down, with the Ravens using a timeout with only three seconds remaining.

Baltimore trotted Cundiff onto the field for what was practically an extra point. The snap and hold were good, and Cundiff kicked the ball right through the uprights from 25 yards out. The Ravens overcame a 21-point deficit, the largest in franchise history, to defeat the Cardinals 30–27.

After the game, Lewis recalled that halftime moment when players began speaking up to take accountability. To him, that's when the comeback began.

"Everybody you heard speak were the veteran guys, offensively and defensively," Lewis said. "Coaches didn't have to say too much.

Other Big Comebacks

Baltimore has had its fair share of comebacks over the years. The largest deficit Baltimore ever overcame, as mentioned in detail, was 21 points down against Arizona in 2011. This bested a 19-point comeback against Tennessee in 2006. Here are three other important comeback wins in franchise history:

1. On November 23, 2003, the Ravens rallied from 17 down (41–24) to defeat Seattle 44–41 in overtime.
2. On September 10, 2000, the Ravens overcame a 16-point (23–7) deficit to beat Jacksonville 39–36.
3. In four other games (against the New York Jets, Cincinnati, Indianapolis, and St. Louis), the Ravens trailed by 14. They beat the Jets 20–17 in overtime (2004), the Bengals 34–31 (1999), the Colts 38–31 (1998), and the Rams 37–31 in overtime (1996).

And that's the thing that I like about this team the most; when we find ourselves in tough spots—we found ourselves in a tough spot last week. If you lose a tough one, you lose a tough one. But to come back and battle the way we did this week, and really put a complete game in the second half together; that's really hats off to our total team."

91 Chris McAlister: Baltimore's First Shutdown Corner

The Ravens needed to make the most of their four draft picks in 1999. It's rare for the Ravens to have such a low number of picks, but that was the case. Due diligence in the scouting process was needed to make the most out of the few opportunities Baltimore had to strike gold.

Brian Billick had just taken the job and needed some help on defense. The Ravens had the 10th overall pick and were hoping to

Chris McAlister drops back into pass coverage during a 26–23 victory over the Arizona Cardinals in September 2007 at M&T Bank Stadium.

land one of seven players in their elite category. Six of them that went ahead of their 10th overall selection were Kentucky quarterback Tim Couch (first overall), Oregon quarterback Akili Smith (third overall), Miami running back Edgerrin James, (fourth overall) Texas running back Ricky Williams (fifth overall), North Carolina State receiver Torry Holt (sixth overall), and Georgia cornerback Champ Bailey (seventh overall).

The three players not given this designation were Syracuse quarterback Donovan McNabb (second overall), Ohio State receiver David Boston (eighth overall), and USC linebacker Chris Claiborne (ninth overall). Baltimore lucked out by being able to land one of its coveted seven players. If the Ravens were unable to grab one of them, they would have likely traded down from the 10th pick.

The player Baltimore picked was Chris McAlister, a cornerback out of the University of Arizona. In three seasons with the Wildcats, McAlister had 18 interceptions. His size, 6'1", 210 pounds, was more than ideal, considering McAlister was timed in the 40-yard dash in the low 4.5 range.

McAlister was everything the Ravens were looking for in a rookie cornerback. He finished his rookie season a starter, picking off five passes, deflecting 16 throws, and recording 47 tackles. He followed his rookie season with an equally strong sophomore campaign, which saw McAlister pick off four additional passes en route to a Super Bowl championship.

Teams began avoiding McAlister. He became the shutdown cornerback missing from 1996 to 1999. McAlister only recorded one interception in 2001 despite starting every game. Quarterbacks didn't want to throw his way anymore. Too many passes were getting broken up or intercepted.

A couple of seasons later saw McAlister record quite possibly the most exciting play in Ravens history. It was September 30, 2002, and Baltimore was playing the Denver Broncos on *Monday Night Football*. Down 24–3, the Broncos were just trying to cut into the sizeable lead, and asked strong-legged kicker Jason Elam to attempt a 57-yard field goal on the road. No biggie if he missed, because there was only one second left before the first half ended.

Or so the Broncos thought.

Elam's kick hooked to the left as the half appeared to be coming to a close. But McAlister, who figured he'd head to the back of the end zone in case a kick fell short, was waiting. The kick did fall short, with few Broncos expecting a return. McAlister caught the ball and walked it up to the end zone line. Seeing he had some room to make a play, McAlister immediately sprinted to the left sideline. Ray Lewis leveled Denver linebacker Keith Burns, and Ed Reed, a rookie, contributed a key block on the play to free McAlister. Once he got to the sideline, no one was bringing him down. Baltimore took a 31–3 lead into the locker room and wound up winning 34–23.

In 2006 McAlister picked off six passes, returning two for touchdowns. Both were single-season highs. A knee injury slowed McAlister in his last two seasons with Baltimore. He was only able to play in 14 games, but came up with four interceptions in those games. In the 2009 off-season, the Ravens released him, much to McAlister's displeasure.

"It was a bitter divorce in Baltimore, the way I was no longer a part of the club and, for my first time in 10 years, didn't have any place to call home," McAlister said in the fall of 2009, according to an article written by ESPN's John Clayton. "The off-season took on a new life for me. There was a transition period for me to figure out exactly if I'm going to come back and play football or am I not."

McAlister ended his career with a brief stint in New Orleans, but was released that December, just months before the Saints would go on to win the Super Bowl.

92 Baltimore's Hall of Fame Fans

Jonathan Ogden might be the only longtime Ravens player inducted in the Pro Football Hall of Fame. But he's not the only one that represented the franchise in some sort of capacity inside the storied building in Canton, Ohio.

From 1999 the Pro Football Hall of Fame, in conjunction with credit card company Visa, created a Hall of Fans for those passionate about their team to be inducted into. The first year was a success to the point that they kept inducting new fans into the Hall of Fans until 2005.

The Ravens, who likely see these super fans on the Jumbotron during games, were able to send a few of their most passionate fans to Canton.

The first ever Ravens fan inducted into the Hall of Fans was Gil Sadler, one third of the Chain Gang, in 1999. The Chain Gang also included fans Scott Schmidt and Sadler's twin brother, Jerry. After every first down, the three of them would chant, "Move those chains! Move those chains! Move those chains!" These fanatics could be found in Section 146, leading a raucous Ravens crowd in cheers during home games.

In 2000 Matthew "Fan Man" Andrews earned the recognition to enter into the Hall of Fans. A longtime Colts fan who grew up in Western Pennsylvania, Andrews had super fandom in his bloodline, as his uncle, otherwise known as "Willie the Rooter," cheered on the Colts and was able to develop a relationship with the team. When the Ravens entered the NFL 12 years after the Colts left town, Andrews picked up where he left off. A year after his induction, the "Fan Man" drove to Tampa, Florida, for Super Bowl XXXV but didn't have a ticket. He ended up appearing on a special episode of MTV's *Total Request Live with Carson Daly* to match his knowledge of football with Daly's knowledge of boy bands. In the end, the "Fan Man" won two tickets to Baltimore's biggest game.

Entering the class of 2001 was Larry "Big Larry" Norwood. In 1975 Norwood became a Colts season ticket holder, until the franchise moved to Indianapolis. Norwood became huge fans of both the USFL's Stars and the CFL's Stallions when they were in

Baltimore and, of course, became a huge supporter of the NFL's Ravens. Norwood might have been the most fortunate, as he earned an all-expenses trip to Tampa for Super Bowl XXXV from Visa when he was selected. Norwood was in attendance to see the Ravens upend the Giants 34–7 in the NFL's biggest game.

Wes "Captain Dee-Fense" Henson has become a fan favorite of many Ravens fans over the years. He entered the Visa Hall of Fans in the class of 2002, due to his high energy inside M&T Bank Stadium. He's often on the Jumbotron cheering his team on and has been able to use his namesake to help local charities in Baltimore. Henson came up with his moniker when a young girl asked him at a game if he was the captain of the defense? The idea stuck and Captain Dee-Fense was born. The *Washington Post* and *Baltimore Sun* have written about Captain Dee-Fense, and he's been interviewed on NBC's *Today Show*. Captain Dee-Fense's attire resembles a Navy captain, but with spikes providing the border for his cutoff sleeves. In 2012 Captain Dee-Fense earned more fan recognition, as ESPN and StubHub created their own Hall of Fans, which encompasses all sports. Captain Dee-Fense was one of three inductees (the other two being Alabama Crimson Tide fan Emily Pitek and Vancouver Canucks super fans "the Green Men") into the inaugural class.

The class of 2003 saw Dale "Maniac" Davis represent the Ravens in the Visa Hall of Fans. Davis was always a big-time supporter of Baltimore's football teams but took it to the next level in the early 2000s. He earned the nickname "Maniac" due to his over-the-top enthusiasm on display for each Ravens game. He was assisted by the "Fan Man" to help Visa notice him as a potential inductee into the Hall of Fans. He and the "Fan Man" have teamed up to appear at events to either drive fan enthusiasm or raise money for charity.

The final class Visa put together was in 2004, with John Dongarra, also known as "Camo Man," entering the prestigious group of fans. Dargarra wears purple and black camouflage to every game, with the purpose of appearing like the team's general in the stands. The Camo Man has been active in the local sports club Birds of Prey and fully believes in the power of the 12th man on Sundays.

Visa discontinued the Hall of Fans after the class of 2004, but the Pro Football Ultimate Fan Association (PFUFA), which formed as a result of the first class of 1999, brought back the recognition of honoring the NFL's best fans. Though they don't get an all-expenses trip to the Pro Football Hall of Fame like the Visa winners got, they do get the recognition of earning a spot among their predecessors. Since the PFUFA began adding members to its group, Steve "Sports Steve" LaPlanche (2008), Cindy "Purple Dame" Pierce (2009), Rick "Poetic Justice" Bowlus (2010), Chip "Fired Up" Riley (2011), and Brian "Dee-Ciple" Donley (2012) have joined their counterparts as some of the most recognizable and enthusiastic Ravens fans there are.

93 The Early Veterans

NFL teams are often vying to get younger, faster, and stronger. But most successful groups tend to have that veteran presence to keep those younger players in check. Baltimore was no different, relying on three key players to ensure Baltimore's goals could be met.

These players were safety Rod Woodson, defensive tackle Tony Siragusa, and tight end Shannon Sharpe. Each was near the end of their careers when they arrived in Baltimore but still had plenty to give.

The first to arrive in Baltimore was Siragusa in 1997. He spent his first seven years with the Colts before signing with the Ravens. Despite some tough times that saw a lot of losses, Siragusa offered stability on the defensive front. Mainly a space eater to occupy blocks to free linebackers, Siragusa was able to notch 3$^1/_2$ sacks in 1999.

A year after Siragusa came to town, Woodson showed up, with critics claiming he was at the tail end of his career. Woodson wanted to prove the doubters wrong and show he could still play, even after 10 years with Pittsburgh and one with San Francisco.

Maybe it was by design, but the Ravens put Woodson's locker in between youngsters Peter Boulware and Ray Lewis. Both linebackers were rising stars, and perhaps they could use a veteran presence by their side.

"Nobody told me it was my job to be a mentor," Woodson told the *Baltimore Sun* in 2007. "But I knew that the young talent needed to be cultivated, to learn what it takes to be a pro both on and off the field."

Sharpe arrived in Baltimore in 2000 and stayed for just two seasons. With an offense that struggled to move the ball for long stretches, Sharpe was the playmaker needed to offset the rest of the unit's deficiencies. Even with two quarterbacks starting eight games apiece, Sharpe was able to catch 67 passes for 810 yards and five touchdowns.

During the 2000 Super Bowl season, these three players were the veteran presence inside the locker room. Sure, there was a ton of young talent on defense—Lewis, Boulware, cornerback Chris McAlister, and linebacker Jamie Sharper, to name few. But Woodson, Siragusa, and Sharpe helped solidify that veteran presence in the locker room with their leadership both on the field and off.

Though what the three veterans brought to the team was special and unique, it only lasted for the 2000 and 2001 seasons. Siragusa retired after the 2001 season. Woodson went to Oakland and played his last two seasons with the Raiders before retiring. Sharpe, who played his first 10 NFL seasons with the Broncos, went back to Denver to play two more years before retiring. All three now have jobs in broadcasting.

"In that one given year, we were arguably the best defense in NFL history," Woodson said, via the *Sun*. "The downside is that we were only together for one season."

94 Take the Polar Bear Plunge

The annual polar bear plunge at Sandy Point State Park in Annapolis is proof as to how ingrained the Ravens are in Maryland culture.

In its beginnings, the polar bear plunge, sponsored by the Maryland State Police, was to raise money for the Special Olympics within the community. Taking place each January, participants will jump into the freezing water of the Chesapeake Bay. Super plungers are those who raise $10,000 and are obligated to jump into the water once every hour in a 24-hour span.

Gradually, the event became a mini-Ravens tailgate, beginning when former Ravens defensive end Michael McCrary participated in the polar bear plunge one year. Many Ravens players have since participated. Former offensive guard Edwin Mulitalo became a recurrent participant each year. Former defensive coordinator and New York Jets head coach Rex Ryan has taken part in the polar bear plunge, as well.

Early in the polar bear plunge's history—otherwise known as Plungefest—participants could camp out and tailgate like it was a Ravens game. Now that crowds have grown considerably, those in attendance park at three locations (Navy–Marine Corps Memorial Stadium in Annapolis, Anne Arundel Community College in Arnold, and Kent Island High School in Stevensville) and are bussed to Sandy Point Beach for the event. To support the Ravens, fans are encouraged to wear what they'd typically put on for game days.

Former Ravens players Jason Brown, Quinn Sypniewski, and Adam Terry have also been past attendees, with defensive tackle Haloti Ngata and quarterback Joe Flacco taking part in recent festivities. The Ravens were unable to take part in the 2013 polar bear plunge as they were busy advancing in the playoffs en route to a Super Bowl championship.

Flacco participated in the plunge for three consecutive years, from 2009 to 2011. He was unable to attend the event in 2012, citing personal reasons. Flacco has spent a lot of time helping the Special Olympics, attending these polar bear plunges, as well as other events the organization holds in the summer.

The Ravens organization has made an event out of it, too, often sending cheerleaders and the band up to join in the festivities. Born without the Ravens in mind, the organization now has a role that fans cherish. It goes to show how football crazy Baltimore, and the state of Maryland, truly is.

95 Ravens-Titans: The First Rivalry

Long before Pittsburgh was Baltimore's primary foe, there was Tennessee. The hated Titans, the ones Ravens fans loved to spat with. Don't get it twisted, though. Ravens fans always have always hated the Steelers. Pittsburgh was an AFC Central rival with Tennessee, too. But the Ravens were in search of a marquee rival, and at the time, the Titans seemed to be the best fit.

The first two games between the two franchises came during Baltimore's first season after moving from Cleveland, though Tennessee wasn't Tennessee yet. It was still the Houston Oilers, playing their last season representing that city.

Ravens running back Jamal Lewis knocks Tennessee Titans safety Marcus Robertson out of the way on a gain in the first quarter of Baltimore's 24–23 win on November 12, 2000, in Nashville, at the height of the Ravens-Titans rivalry.

The Oilers won both games, a 29–13 decision in Houston in Week 3 and a 24–21 victory in Baltimore in the season finale. The Oilers moved to Tennessee the following season, with Baltimore returning the favor with a season sweep of its own.

It wasn't until 1999 that the rivalry began getting hot. After losing 14–11 early in the year, the Ravens wanted payback. Plus, without winning four of the last five games, this was shaping up to be the fourth consecutive losing season since arriving to Baltimore, despite the fact the players themselves understood the kind of talent present on the roster.

Tennessee had jumped out to a 5–2 advantage in games, winners of the previous three meetings. The Ravens were poised for a breakout performance. After the Titans took a 3–0 lead, quarterback Tony Banks found wide receiver Patrick Johnson for a 76-yard touchdown. Baltimore would hold a 17–14 halftime lead, which would be the closest Tennessee would get from that point.

Baltimore's Banks threw two more touchdowns, Matt Stover kicked a 27-yard field goal, and safety Rod Woodson returned a 47-yard interception for a touchdown in what became a 41–14 rout. That propelled Baltimore to a four-game winning streak before falling to New England in the season finale. Baltimore finished the year 8–8 and seemingly ready to take that next step.

The 2000 season would prove to be the pinnacle of the rivalry. Baltimore's defense went down in history as arguably the best ever assembled. However, it was Tennessee's that finished first in total defense by 9.6 yards per game. In the first meeting between the teams, this would prove evident. Baltimore's offense was struggling with Banks at quarterback. Banks threw three interceptions in a 14–6 loss at PSINet Stadium. The next time the teams played would be at Adelphia Coliseum in Nashville, which saw yet another close battle between the two teams.

Trent Dilfer had assumed the role as Baltimore's starting quarterback, and while he had plenty of limitations, he was doing a better job at limiting the mistakes Banks was making early on. In the first quarter, Dilfer found receiver Qadry Ismail for a 46-yard touchdown to put Baltimore up 7–0.

Jamal Lewis scored a touchdown, and Matt Stover kicked a 45-yard field goal in the second quarter to help give Baltimore a 17–14 halftime lead. Future Ravens Steve McNair and Derrick Mason connected on a 10-yard touchdown, and McNair also tossed a short touchdown to fullback Lorenzo Neal. After a scoreless third quarter, Titans kicker Al Del Greco kicked a 23-yard field goal to tie the game in the fourth.

Tennessee would then take the lead with a Perry Phenix interception for a touchdown with three minutes remaining in the game. But Del Greco gave the Ravens an opening by missing the extra point wide left, staking the Titans to just a six-point lead.

Running back Priest Holmes was active as a receiver on this drive, catching two passes in a row to kick start the Ravens. After an offensive pass interference penalty was called on Baltimore, Holmes took a pass for 14 yards to set up a third-and-5. Dilfer found tight end Shannon Sharpe on the next play for a 36-yard gain. Four plays later, Baltimore faced a fourth-and-2. Dilfer dropped back and targeted Ismail on the play, with the ball falling incomplete. However, a defensive pass interference flag was thrown, giving the Ravens a first down and possession at the two-yard line. It took three plays, but Dilfer was able to throw a two-yard touchdown to Patrick Johnson to tie the game. Stover hit the extra point to give Baltimore a 24–23 lead with 29 seconds left.

The game wasn't over yet, however. Chris Coleman took the ensuing kickoff 29 yards out to the Tennessee 44-yard line. McNair threw an 11-yard gain to running back Eddie George and then scrambled for 20 yards of his own. This set up a doable 43-yard attempt. Del Greco came back onto the field but missed the kick wide to the right. Baltimore walked out of Nashville winners.

That game set up the rubber match in the divisional round of the postseason. Despite possessing the ball for over 40 minutes, the Titans were only able to score 10 points. Baltimore's offense couldn't muster much of its own, continually being forced to punt. Dilfer struggled, completing just five of 16 passing attempts for 117 yards (with two of the completions going for 56 and 33 yards). In addition, the Ravens were held to just six first downs the entire game. But fourth quarter defense and special teams were the difference in the outcome. At the 12:25 mark, Del Greco lined up for a 37-yard attempt only to have it blocked by Keith Washington and returned 90 yards for a touchdown by Anthony Mitchell. Both teams traded three-and-outs with Tennessee getting another crack at tying the game. On a second-and-14, McNair threw in George's direction, but Ray Lewis jumped the pass and returned the ball 50 yards for a touchdown. This play put the game away and gave Baltimore a 24–10 win.

The 2001 season would be the last that featured Baltimore and Tennessee in the same division. After a blowout win in Week 4, Baltimore was hoping for a season sweep. However, it looked like Tennessee was going to salvage its season by taking a win away from the Ravens. With three seconds remaining at the 1-yard line, McNair hurried his team to the line, took the snap, and appeared to score a quarterback sneak that tied the game. All the Titans would need is an extra point to come away victors. However, Ravens linebacker Peter Boulware was called for encroachment, meaning the play was dead and Tennessee would have to do it over. The Titans ran the same play, but with Baltimore prepared for it. McNair also bobbled the snap for a second and was unable to score. Baltimore won 16–10.

Adding fuel to the fire after the game was a comment cornerback Chris McAlister made to a *Sports Illustrated* reporter. George finished with 71 yards on 22 carries and took a crushing hit from Ray Lewis. "Every time Eddie touched the ball after that, he just folded like a baby," McAlister said. "Check the film. He'd hit the hole and hit the ground first thing. He didn't want any part of us."

The rivalry was still fresh in 2003 when the two teams met in the wild-card round of the playoffs, even with Baltimore in the AFC North and Tennessee in the AFC South. Running back Jamal Lewis, who ran for over 2,000 yards in the regular season, was held to 35 yards on 14 carries. Kicker Gary Anderson made a 46-yard field goal with 29 seconds left to give the Titans a 20–17 win.

A regular season meeting in 2006 was perhaps the last major moment of the rivalry. Making the storyline deeper, McNair was now a Raven, and so was receiver Derrick Mason. Tennessee opened up a 26–7 lead and looked to be cruising to a win. McNair and the Ravens rallied from 19 down to win, capped with Mason catching an 11-yard game-winning touchdown from McNair with 3:39 remaining. Until a 21-point comeback win against Arizona in 2011, this was the largest deficit the organization had ever overcome.

The Ravens and Titans resumed play in 2008, but the rivalry was beginning to lose its luster. Brian Billick was no longer coaching the Ravens, and by 2011, Jeff Fisher was no longer on Tennessee's sideline. The rivalry may have been short-lived, yet it produced some great games early in Ravens history.

96 Johnny U.

When walking into M&T Bank Stadium, Ravens fans will often stop by the 13-foot statue that immortalizes Johnny Unitas. They'll shine his shoes for good luck and walk inside to cheer their Ravens on.

All of this without Unitas technically being a Raven. But that's the thing about Baltimore. It's not necessarily a Ravens or Colts thing. It's a Baltimore thing. In Baltimore football history, Unitas matters just as much with respect to the Ravens. The two entities aren't separated. They're one and the same. If Baltimore fans had it their way, what happened with the Colts would be similar to what happened to the Browns. Art Modell moved the Browns to Baltimore but allowed Cleveland to keep the name and the history. While the Colts technically own the history from their Baltimore days, Baltimore fans still claim it as their own.

This is why Johnny Unitas, quite possibly the greatest quarterback to ever play, matters with respect to the Ravens. When the Colts left for Indianapolis, Unitas, like the Baltimore fans, was devastated. The team he played 17 years for was no longer there. The ties were severed. Unitas wanted nothing to do with the Indianapolis franchise, despite the fact his No. 19 jersey was still retired.

Unitas embodied the blue-collar persona Baltimore exemplifies. He was a quiet leader, yet studious in his craft. He won three NFL championships with Baltimore, yet had to earn his place in NFL history. He was drafted by the Pittsburgh Steelers yet didn't make the roster. Not ready to give up his dream, Unitas found a place in Baltimore with the Colts. By 1958 Unitas was playing in the NFL championship, in a contest that became known as "The Greatest Game Ever Played."

Unitas played a phenomenal game, one that would rival quarterbacks of the modern passing era. Unitas completed 26 of 40 passes for 349 yards and a touchdown. With 90 seconds remaining in the game, Unitas led the Colts down the field for a game-tying field goal. In overtime, Unitas marched his team 80 yards back down the field, with fullback Alan Ameche punching in the game-winning touchdown. A nationally televised audience saw Unitas will the Colts to a 23–17 win over the Giants.

Unitas followed the 1958 championship season with another title in 1959. In a rematch against the Giants in the NFL championship game, the Colts trailed 9–7 heading into the fourth quarter. Unitas then ran in a four-yard touchdown to put the Colts up 14–9 before throwing a 12-yard TD pass to Jerry Richardson, making it 21–9. Defensive back Johnny Sample put the game away with a 42-yard interception return for a touchdown. The Colts went on to win their second consecutive championship 31–16.

Unitas won another title in 1970, when the Colts reached Super Bowl V, in Miami, to play the Dallas Cowboys. In the second quarter, Unitas threw a 75-yard touchdown pass to tight end John Mackey, which set a Super Bowl record at the time. Unitas was injured in the second quarter and ultimately knocked out of the game. But his touchdown pass helped elevate the Colts to a Super Bowl title.

Unitas, like a lot of the former Baltimore Colts, became a Ravens fan when football was brought back to Baltimore. He was often spotted at the 30-yard line on the Ravens sideline, cheering the hometown team on. In one such instance, in 1998, Unitas was standing in his usual spot when the Ravens hosted the Colts. Despite once playing for a team called the Colts, Unitas was cheering for Baltimore.

Unitas died on September 11, 2002, due to a heart attack at the age of 69. To honor Unitas, former Ravens quarterback Chris Redman wore a pair of black high top cleats in the game that followed Unitas' death, which was against the Tampa Bay Buccaneers.

"I don't have many heroes. Very plain and simply, Johnny Unitas was one of my heroes," Ravens general manager Ozzie Newsome said in 2002, after Unitas' passing. "When you think of Baltimore, you think of Johnny Unitas."

97 Battle of the Beltway

The Baltimore Ravens and Washington Redskins' stadiums are only 32 miles apart. Both teams play in the state of Maryland. Given that the Ravens are in the AFC and the Redskins are in the NFC, the two teams only play each other every four years.

Yet when they play, bragging rights are on the line. There's a certain tweener area in the state where you can find a mixture of Ravens and Redskins fans. This in the Silver Spring/Columbia area, in between the beltways that surround Washington and Baltimore. Walk around in the downtown district, and you'll see some wearing maroon and gold and others in purple and black.

From the Baltimore perspective, there is some disdain toward the Redskins, dating back to the days Jack Kent Cooke owned the organization. When the Colts moved to Indianapolis, Cooke began flirting with the idea of building a new stadium in Laurel, Maryland, which was seen by Baltimoreans as an owner trying to capitalize on converting Colts fans to Redskins fans. He eventually built a new stadium in Landover, giving the state of Maryland two locations for NFL games on any given Sunday.

There was also some concern as to whether Cooke tried to block Baltimore from getting an expansion team in 1993, which ended up going to Jacksonville. However, it should be noted that Art Modell, along with 25 other NFL owners, voted against Baltimore.

Even so, Baltimore football fans have never grown fond of the Redskins, which is a good thing for any kind of potential rivalry. When two teams are that close, they should hate each other.

"I understand how important it is any time two teams are fairly close, the fan base is usually one way or the other," Redskins coach Mike Shanahan said. "It's split a lot. You go an hour down the road, and you have all the Baltimore fans, and obviously the fans that we have here. I'd say it's always a little extra for both teams, because they have a lot of mutual friends that want one team to win or the other."

The Ravens and Redskins have only met in five regular season meetings. In the first-ever meeting in 1997, the Ravens won 20–17, with running back Bam Morris running for a career best 176 yards with a touchdown. But that wasn't necessarily what Baltimore-based reporter Joe Platania remembers about that game. In the press box at then–Jack Kent Cooke Stadium, the Redskins' flagship radio station's pregame show was piped into the press box.

"The first words out of [the broadcaster's] mouth were, 'Today, we're playing a dirty, ugly team from a dirty, ugly city,'" recalled Platania, currently a writer for the publication Press Box who's covered the Ravens since the team moved in 1996.

The two teams met again in Week 7 of the 2000 season. Baltimore was in the middle of its four-game offensive slump when it didn't score a touchdown, losing a 10–3 defensive struggle.

The Ravens would win the next two times against Washington, in 2004 (17–10) and 2008 (24–10). Washington would reverse the trend with a win in 2012, with rookie quarterback Robert Griffin III fighting through a knee injury sustained when defensive tackle Haloti Ngata's helmet crashed into it. Backup quarterback Kirk Cousins had to finish the game for Griffin, and it was Cousins who threw the touchdown to receiver Pierre Garcon to set up his game-tying two-point conversion to send the game to overtime. The Redskins won with a Kai Forbath 34-yard field goal.

Are these teams on the level of Ravens-Steelers or Redskins-Cowboys? Not a chance. Are they even considered rivals from a franchise standpoint? Probably not. But the proximity of the two teams has made for some interesting discussions every time these two teams are slated to play. With the Redskins suddenly improving under Shanahan and Griffin, it's not out of the question to see these two teams playing for a title. How would the Beltway react then?

"I always said it would be kind of crazy if we ever had a Ravens-Redskins Super Bowl," said Ravens running back Ray Rice.

98 Baltimore-Jacksonville in 2000: The Turning Point

The Ravens finished the 1999 season on a high note, winning four of their last five games and looking fairly strong on defense in the process. Ravens fans were beginning to think that kind of finish to an 8–8 season could lead to bigger things in 2000.

Week 1 saw the Ravens defeat the Steelers 16–0 in impressive fashion defensively. But there was still some doubt as to whether this team was ready to take off. Baltimore had never beaten Jacksonville, losing all eight of the previous meetings. From a franchise standpoint, this was a must-win game. The Ravens couldn't let an AFC Central foe continue to beat up on them.

Early in the contest, Jacksonville did what it was used to doing against Baltimore. Jaguars quarterback Mark Brunell drove down to Baltimore's 17 to set up a field goal to take an early 3–0 lead. After a three-and-out from Baltimore, Brunell drove back down the field before launching a 45-yard touchdown to receiver Jimmy Smith. The Ravens offense stayed stagnant, giving the ball back to Jacksonville after a second consecutive three-and-out.

Four plays and a 19-yard defensive pass interference play later, Brunell found Smith for a long score again, this time from 43 yards out. It was only the first quarter, and the Ravens were trailing 17–0 to their divisional nemesis. Would this be a ninth consecutive loss to the Jaguars?

"How many fans looked at that score and said, 'Here we go again?'" Ravens coach Brian Billick said postgame. "And I can't blame them. But our guys were not going to allow that to happen."

The Ravens had to wait until the second quarter to put their first points on the board. After punting the ball away to Jacksonville at the end of the first, Jaguars running back Chris Howard fumbled after defensive end Rob Burnett tackled him after a one-yard gain. A play later, Ravens quarterback Tony Banks found receiver Travis Taylor for a 14-yard touchdown. However, the Jaguars would add two field goals to their points total and head into halftime with a 23–7 lead.

Banks went to work in the second half, however. On his first play from scrimmage in the third quarter, Banks completed a pass to Taylor for 40 yards. Three plays later, Banks linked up with Taylor again for a 23-yard touchdown. Banks completed a two-point conversion to Ben Coates to cut Jacksonville's lead to 23–15. But Mike Hollis would add another three points on Jacksonville's next possession to lengthen the lead to 26–15. But as it was, Jacksonville began settling for field goals while Baltimore began adding touchdowns

Ravens vs. the Rest of the NFL

Thanks to a sizable lead in the all-time series with Cleveland, the Ravens have a favorable record against AFC North opponents, going 55–41 against them since 1996. As expected, of the AFC North teams, the Steelers have been the most problematic for Baltimore, holding a four-game advantage in the series.

The team Baltimore has the best winning percentage against is the Dallas Cowboys, having never lost in four meetings.

Baltimore's had the biggest issues with New England, going 1–6 (.143) against the Patriots all-time in the regular season (but 2–1 against them in the playoffs).

Opponent	W	L	T	Pct.
Arizona Cardinals	4	1		.800
Atlanta Falcons	2	2		.500
Buffalo Bills	3	2		.600
Carolina Panthers	1	3		.250
Chicago Bears	2	2		.500
Cincinnati Bengals	19	15		.559
Cleveland Browns	21	7		.750
Dallas Cowboys	4	0		1.000
Denver Broncos	5	4		.556
Detroit Lions	2	1		.667
Green Bay Packers	1	3		.250
Houston Texans	5	1		.833
Indianapolis Colts	3	7		.300
Jacksonville Jaguars	7	10		.412
Kansas City Chiefs	3	3		.500
Miami Dolphins	3	5		.375
Minnesota Vikings	2	2		.500
New England Patriots	1	6		.143
New Orleans Saints	4	1		.800
New York Giants	3	1		.750
New York Jets	7	1		.875
Oakland Raiders	6	1		.857
Philadelphia Eagles	1	2	1	.375
Pittsburgh Steelers	15	19		.441

Opponent	W	L	T	Pct.
San Diego Chargers	5	4		.556
San Francisco 49ers	3	1		.750
Seattle Seahawks	2	2		.500
St. Louis Rams	3	2		.600
Tampa Bay Buccaneers	2	2		.500
Tennessee Titans	8	9		.471
Washington Redskins	3	2		.600
Totals	*150*	*121*	*1*	*.553*

to cut into the lead. Banks led another successful drive down the field, this time hitting running back Obafemi Ayanbadejo for a five-yard touchdown. The score became 26–22 after the Ravens were forced to settle for an extra point due to tight end Shannon Sharpe drawing an offensive pass interference penalty on a two-point try he otherwise converted.

In the fourth quarter, up 26–22, Jacksonville coughed up the ball again. This time it was Stacey Mack fumbling the ball away, with Jamie Sharper forcing the football loose as well as recovering it at the Jacksonville 12-yard line. A couple of plays later, Banks threw a 12-yard touchdown pass to receiver Jermaine Lewis, giving Baltimore its first lead of the game at 29–26.

Baltimore's defense forced another turnover on Jacksonville's next possession, with Kim Herring picking off Brunell at the Baltimore 35. He returned it to the Jacksonville 30, giving Baltimore's offense a chance to actually add to the lead. That it did, though Baltimore had to settle for a Matt Stover 44-yard field goal. The Ravens were now up six and sitting pretty, with the defense flying all over the football field making plays.

Jacksonville wouldn't go away, however. Hollis converted a 48-yard field-goal try to cut Baltimore's lead to 32–29 and was able to force a Baltimore punt. Brunell once again hooked up with

Jimmy Smith for a deep play, this time from 40 yards out. The Jaguars took the lead to Baltimore's disbelief.

Plenty of time remained on the clock, 1:55 to be exact. Banks would need one more drive to add to his already remarkable day. In his first four passes, Banks completed two to Billy Davis for gains of 19 and 15 yards. At the Jacksonville 41, Banks completed a pass to Ayanbadejo for 12 yards before hurrying to spike the ball with 48 seconds left.

On the next play, Banks would find his tight end, Sharpe, for a 29-yard touchdown. Just 41 seconds remained, and Banks had just converted a career-best fifth touchdown in a single game. Not enough time was left, and Baltimore escaped with a 39–36 win.

In a losing effort, Brunell threw for 386 yards and three touchdowns against a defense that dominated the majority of its opponents during the 2000 season. Jimmy Smith had a career day, as well, catching 15 passes for 291 yards and three touchdowns.

But it was Banks who stole the headlines with his 262 yards and five touchdowns, as he willed his team from a 16-point halftime deficit. The win gave Baltimore a 2–0 start and sole possession of the AFC Central for the first time in franchise history. The notion that 2000 would be Baltimore's year was affirmed in this game and proved as the season moved along.

"It was like we won the Super Bowl," Banks said after the win over Jacksonville.

Little did he know, at the time, that he'd be a part of that, too.

99 The 2002 Season: Brian Billick's Best Coaching Job?

After winning Super Bowl XLVII, general manager Ozzie Newsome was asked if the Ravens would look to restructure most of the veteran contracts to keep them around, much like the organization did after winning Super Bowl XXXV. "We will not repeat what we did in 2001, because we are trying to build where we can win Super Bowls more than just one more time," he said, in a tone that would show he learned from a previous mistake.

At the time, the move was made to hold a Super Bowl team together. But as Newsome and the front office learned, you can't count on the same players year in and year out, especially when they age. By 2002 safety Rod Woodson and tight end Shannon Sharpe were no longer in Baltimore. Defensive tackle Tony Siragusa had retired. The Ravens were unable to bring back free agent defensive tackle Sam Adams. Rob Burnett was no longer there. It was a made-over team in 2002, which ultimately cost them a lot of games.

The Ravens jumped out to a slow start, losing their first two games to Carolina and Tampa Bay with the offense scoring a combined seven points. It's possible the best thing that ever happened to the Ravens was having a bye in Week 3, because the first two games were that horrendous.

The Ravens, playing on Monday night in Week 4, put forth a much better showing, defeating Denver 34–23. That game featured cornerback Chris McAlister returning a missed field goal 107 yards for a touchdown just before halftime. This gave Baltimore a 31–3 halftime lead.

After seven weeks of the NFL season, the Ravens were at 3–3 and very much in consideration for reaching the playoffs. However, Baltimore sat at 4–6 after a 26–7 loss to Miami, which put the season in a bleak spot. Pittsburgh was rolling, and Baltimore would need to earn a wild-card berth to get to the postseason.

Baltimore would win its next two games against Tennessee and Cincinnati to get back to .500. After dropping a 37–25 decision to New Orleans the following week, quarterback Jeff Blake led Baltimore to a 23–19 win over the Houston Texans, keeping the Ravens' playoff hopes alive.

This put the Ravens at 7–7, with a meeting against Cleveland the following week. A win, and the postseason was that much closer to being a reality. Down 7–3, Blake converted a touchdown pass to receiver Travis Taylor to put Baltimore up 10–7. Matt Stover added a field goal in the third quarter to pad the lead to 13–7, but that was all Baltimore's offense would score. The rest of the game was dictated by defense until Cleveland's last drive of the game. With 38 seconds left in the game, Browns quarterback Tim Couch connected with tight end Mark Campbell for a one-yard touchdown, which gave Cleveland a 14–13 win. Baltimore was still mathematically alive. But it was not likely to happen, and the Ravens players knew it. Still, they were proud of what they were able to accomplish based on what was predicted to start the season.

"It was a great opportunity to prove something to a lot of people, and we were so close," Blake told reporters after the Cleveland loss. "To lose like that is tough."

Pittsburgh, the last team remaining on the schedule, was up next, and they had a potential first-round bye to play for. At 9–5–1, the Steelers needed either Oakland or Tennessee to lose, and to beat Baltimore. If that scenario happened, then Pittsburgh would earn a bye in the first round. Baltimore was up 31–26 late, but Steelers quarterback Tommy Maddox found receiver Antwaan Randle-El for an eight-yard touchdown, with the ensuing two-point try converted. Pittsburgh held on to a 34–31 win, though were still forced to play in the wild-card round as Tennessee and Oakland both won.

Baltimore finished 7–9, yet the season wasn't deemed a failure by any stretch of the imagination. Based on the roster turnover from the prior season, the Ravens weren't given much of a chance to be in the playoff hunt down the stretch. They were able to accomplish that and make all 16 games count.

"With everything that happened, and losing the first two games the way they did, the 2002 season was probably Brian Billick's best coaching job," said Luke Jones, the Ravens beat writer and radio show producer at WNST (1570-AM).

100 Anthony Wright to Marcus Robinson

No one could have predicted during the 2003 season that receiver Marcus Robinson would set a record that would stand through the 2012 season.

Up until Baltimore's Week 12 game against the Seattle Seahawks, Robinson hadn't recorded a game with more than 14 yards, which came in the season opener against Pittsburgh. The week before, in Week 11, saw Robinson catch multiple passes for the first time during the season: a grand total of two.

What transpired against the Seahawks baffled Ravens fans—in a good way, of course.

The Ravens were 5–5 entering the game, looking for more consistency on offense. Quarterback Anthony Wright was starting his second game of the season with Kyle Boller sidelined with a quadriceps injury. After experiencing a 9–6 loss to Miami the previous week, Wright was hoping for a much better performance against Seattle.

Baltimore started slow and trailed 17–3 at halftime, with Wright completing just three of nine passes for 37 yards. It wasn't exactly the first half he was hoping for, to say the least. Wright knew that if Baltimore was going to win, the game would come down to him and how well he could get the ball to his receivers.

On the third play from scrimmage in the third quarter, Wright connected with Travis Taylor for a 43-yard gain. After two runs, Wright then found Robinson, a 6'3", 215-pound target, for a 13-yard touchdown. It was Robinson's first touchdown of the season, and first since December 1, 2002, when he was with the Chicago Bears. Not only that, it was a tough grab to make. Robinson won a highly contested jump ball to record the touchdown.

Robinson hadn't been used much in the run-heavy Ravens offense, so it was assumed that touchdown, to cut Seattle's lead to 17–10, was a shot in the dark when it happened.

Not quite.

The Seahawks were able to add 10 more points to their lead to go up 27–10. At risk of the game getting out of hand, Wright turned to Robinson again. This time, it came on a skinny post to Robinson, who then bounced off a Seattle defender. Robinson then turned the jets and scooted to a 50-yard touchdown.

But just like that, Seahawks quarterback Matt Hasselbeck threw an 80-yard touchdown pass to receiver Darrell Jackson to give Seattle a 17-point lead again. Still in the third quarter, the Ravens needed to score, and they needed to do so fast. After three runs and an incomplete pass, Wright once again found Robinson for a touchdown, this time on a 25-yard fade route, with Robinson timing his jump perfectly to out-leap the defensive back.

"It was one of those games that it was just fun to be in," Robinson said in an interview with the *Baltimore Sun* in 2011. "In the second half, it seemed like we just kept trading scores. No sooner did the offense come off the field, sit down and take a drink, than it was time to go back out."

Every time Baltimore had an answer, Seattle would up the ante. On the second play of the fourth quarter, Hasselbeck completed a five-yard touchdown pass to receiver Bobby Engram that put the Seahawks up 41–24. It would be tough to rally from 17 down in the fourth quarter, no matter how great the offense was playing.

After two stalled Baltimore offensive possessions, it was time for another phase to help out. Ed Reed lined up on the punt block team and became a free runner on a fourth-and-8 with 6:54 remaining. Reed blocked the punt and ran it in for a touchdown, to

Ravens wide receiver Marcus Robinson makes a nine-yard touchdown reception in front of Seattle Seahawks cornerback Marcus Trufant in the fourth quarter of the Ravens' 44–41 overtime win on November 23, 2003, in Baltimore.

cut Seattle's lead to 41–31. On Seattle's next possession, it was the defense that stepped up. Threatening to score again, Seattle running back Mack Strong took a carry and ran for about three yards before meeting Ray Lewis. Lewis jarred the ball loose and recovered it, giving the Ravens offense hope.

Wright and Robinson certainly weren't about to miss the opportunity presented to them. After scoring three touchdowns on the right side of the end zone, Wright lofted a high-arcing pass toward the left goal line. There was Robinson yet again, wide open to make the catch from nine yards out. Seattle defenders rallied to get there but arrived late. Just over a minute remained in the game, so Baltimore attempted an onside kick but was unable to recover.

The Ravens used timeouts after first and third downs in hopes of getting the ball back. The third timeout came with 44 seconds left, with fourth-and-1 upcoming. Seattle had the ball at the Baltimore 33-yard line, so it figured that if it went for it and converted, the game would be over. If not, Baltimore still had a long way to go to try and tie the game. Hasselbeck tried to sneak the ball for a yard but came up short. Baltimore had a chance.

After looking Robinson's way on first down, Wright turned to him again. This time, Robinson drew a 44-yard pass interference penalty that put the ball at the Seattle 23. Jamal Lewis ran for a six-yard gain before Wright spiked the ball. Matt Stover then kicked a game-tying 40-yard field goal as time expired to send the game to overtime.

Robinson didn't catch a pass in overtime, but Lewis and the running game were able to set Stover up for a game-winner from 42 yards away. Baltimore rallied in unforeseen fashion to defeat Seattle 44–41. Robinson finished the game with seven catches, 131 yards, and four touchdowns—the first four of his season.

"It was looking very, very dim," Wright said afterward. "But we just let it all hang out. Everything came together. It's unbelievable, for us to be down as much as were and to come back."

Sources

Newspapers
> *Baltimore Sun*
> *New York Times*
> *Philadelphia Inquirer*
> *Tucson Citizen*
> *USA Today*

Wire Services
> Associated Press
> UPI

Magazines
> *Sports Illustrated*

Books
> *Pro Football's Most Passionate Fans: Profiles of Fans Honored at the Pro Football Hall of Fame with the Visa Hall of Fans Award* (Compiled by Harvey Aronson)

Websites
> ESPN.com
> CBSSports.com
> Pro-football-reference.com
> NFL Game Statistics & Information System
> Yahoo! Sports
> Press Box Online
> ProFootballTalk.com
> FoxSports.com
> BaltimoreRavens.com

WNST.net
NFL.com
FoxSports.com/Scout.com
Pro Football's Ultimate Fan Association (PFUFA.org)